D1136203

INDIA BY RAIL

Other Bradt rail guides

Australia and New Zealand by Rail   Colin Taylor
Eastern Europe by Rail   Rob Dodson
Greece by Rail (with major ferry routes)   Zane Katsikis
Russia by Rail (with Belarus and Ukraine)   Athol Yates
Spain and Portugal by Rail   Norman Renouf
Sri Lanka by Rail   Royston Ellis
Switzerland by Rail   Anthony Lambert

INDIA
BY RAIL

3rd edition

Royston Ellis

with contributions by Samit Roychoudhury

Bradt Publications, UK
The Globe Pequot Press Inc, USA

First published in 1989 by Bradt Publications.
Third edition published in 1997 by Bradt Publications,
41 Nortoft Road, Chalfont St Peter, Bucks, SL9 0LA, England.
Published in the USA by the Globe Pequot Press, 6 Business Park Road,
PO Box 833, Old Saybrook, CT 06475-0833

British Library Cataloguing in Publication Data
A catalogue record for this book is available from the British Library
ISBN 1 898323 49 6

Library of Congress Cataloging-in-Publication Data
Ellis, Royston
    India by rail / Royston Ellis. – 3rd ed.
        p.   cm.
    Includes index.
    ISBN 1-898323-49-6
    1. India–Guidebooks.   2. Railroad travel–India–Guidebooks.
    I. Title.
DS406.E46   1997
915.404'52–dc21   96-46443
                                                                    CIP

Cover photographs
Front: Palace of the Winds, Jaipur (Peter Baker)
Back: *Palace on Wheels* and attendants (Gemunu Amarasinghe)
Colour photographs Gemunu Amarasinghe (GA); Peter Baker (PB)
Maps *Inside covers*: Steve Munns *Others*: Hans van Well

Typeset by Acorn Bookwork, Salisbury, Wiltshire
Printed in Spain by Grafo SA

AUTHOR

Royston Ellis, born in England, left school age 16, determined to be a writer. He quickly won fame as a poet in the 1960s performing "rocketry" (rock 'n' roll poetry) on stage and television with musicians who later became known as The Beatles, Led Zeppelin and Cliff Richard's Shadows. He wrote novels and pop star biographies before leaving England permanently, aged 20, for a life of travel.

Under pen names he has written many bestselling novels, including *The Bondmaster* by Richard Tresillian. He is the author of *Sri Lanka By Rail, Guide to Mauritius* and *Guide to Maldives*, all published by Bradt Publications, and regularly contributes travel features to British and Asian newspapers and magazines. He was a consultant for the National Geographic television special on the Railways of India, and is an honorary member of the Institute of Rail Transport (India). A Life Fellow of the Royal Commonwealth Society, he often lectures on cruise liners about Indian Ocean countries.

Royston Ellis first visited India in 1963, and he has had a home in the Indian subcontinent since 1980. He has travelled extensively the length and breadth of India by train, including several trips in 1995 and 1996 to update this, the third edition in English of *India by Rail*.

DEDICATION

For V Keshav Raj – an officer and a gentleman – whose friendship and encouragement helped me complete over 35,000km of train rides to research the first edition, and for Gemunu Amarasinghe who accompanied me on some great trips.

ACKNOWLEDGEMENTS

Even after more than 100,000km of train rides during at least 30 visits to India, I still find travelling by train fascinating and, usually, enjoyable. When things have gone wrong, it is surprising how willing complete strangers are to offer help. To those people whose names I never knew, I am indebted for their kindness which made India such an enriching experience.

Many of the friends I made when I was writing the first and second editions have remained steadfast supporters despite my constant nagging over the years for information and assistance. The list is headed by the redoubtable Dr S Dandapani. If it were not for his avuncular advice and expertise, myself and thousands of others from around the world would not have discovered the delights of travelling smoothly in India by train.

I am grateful, too, to Ranjit Mathur, now retired after being Member, Traffic, Railway Board, who opened every possible door during my first series of journeys, and continues to take an interest in each new edition, whether in French, German or English, of this book. To Mr N M Balasubrahmanyam, Executive Director, Institute of Rail Transport, my thanks for advice over the years and for winkling out the latest statistics for this edition.

A passionate interest in his country's railways led student Samit Roychoudhury, now a freelance designer, to send me tips for the second edition. He has now become a colleague and earns a byline in appreciation for his tireless research and contributions to this edition.

I acknowledge with gratitude the help in various ways from friends in India and Sri Lanka, especially Keshav Raj, A P Muthuramalingam, Amit Choudhury, Gemunu Amarasinghe and, as always, Neel Jayantha. I am also grateful to the Oberoi Group of Hotels for the understanding hospitality whenever I needed a rest from the railways.

Royston Ellis
1997

CONTENTS

Chapter One	Discovering India by Rail	1

Chapter Two   **Planning the Trip**   **11**
Preliminaries 11, Tourist Offices 12, Timetables 14, Itineraries 15, Health 22, Safety 23, Money 24, Red Tape 26, Solo and Group Travel 28, In India 31

Chapter Three   **Ticket to Ride**   **41**
Fares 48, The Indrail Pass 51, Reservations 60

Chapter Four   **Class Distinction**   **75**
Class Structure and Accommodation 76, Track and Trains 91

Chapter Five   **On The Move**   **97**
Sleeping 102, Security 106, Meals on Wheels 107, Other Services and Facilities 112

Chapter Six   **Trains Past and Present**   **121**
Steam in India 127, Suburban Services 131

Chapter Seven   **Where to Stay**   **133**
Retiring Rooms 133, Railway Hotels 138, City Hotels 139, Hotel Reservations 140

Chapter Eight   **The Journey Begins**   **143**
Delhi 143, Bombay 151, Calcutta 159, Madras 167, Trivandrum 171, Tiruchchirappalli 173

Chapter Nine   **Around India by Rail**   **177**
Destinations 177, Itineraries 180

Chapter Ten   **Some Popular Rail Destinations**   **185**
Agra 185, Ahmedabad 187, Allahabad 188, Alleppey 189, Ambala Cantt 190, Amritsar 190, Aurangabad 190, Bangalore 190, Berhampur 192, Bhubaneswar 192, Cannanore 193, Chandigarh 193, Chittaurgarh 194, Cochin (Kochi) 194, Coimbatore 195, Dehra Dun 195, Ernakulam Jn 196, Ernakulam Town 196, Erode 196, Gaya 196, Gorakhpur 197, Haridwar 198, Hyderabad 198, Jaipur 198, Jaisalmer 200, Jammu Tawi 201, Jamnagar 201, Jhansi 201, Jodhpur 202, Kanniya Kumari 203, Karjat 203, Kottayam 204, Lonavla 204, Lucknow 205, Madgaon (Goa) 206, Madurai 206, Mahe 207, Malda Town 207, Mangalore 208,

Matheran 209, Miraj 209, Mughal Sarai 210,
Mysore 210, Nagpur 212, Neral 212, Patna 213,
Pondicherry 213, Pune 214, Puri 214, Quilon 215,
Rajkot 215, Rameswaram 215, Ranchi 216, Salem
217, Secunderabad 217, Shimla 218,
Udagamandalam 219, Udaipur 219, Varanasi 220,
Vasco da Gama (Goa) 221

Chapter Eleven   **Great Trips**   **225**
Shatabdi Express 225, *Palace on Wheels* 228, *Royal
Orient Express* 230, *Rajdhani Express* 232, *Pandyan
Express* 234, Darjeeling Toy Train 235, Matheran
Hill Railway 236, Nilagiri Mountain Railway 237,
Kalka Shimla Railway 240, Butterfield's Indian
Railway Tour 241

Chapter Twelve   **Super Trains**   **243**

Chapter Thirteen   **Help**   **247**

Chapter Fourteen   **Endpiece**   **249**
The Last Word 250

Language   **254**
Glossary   **254**
Further Reading   **256**

Index   **258**

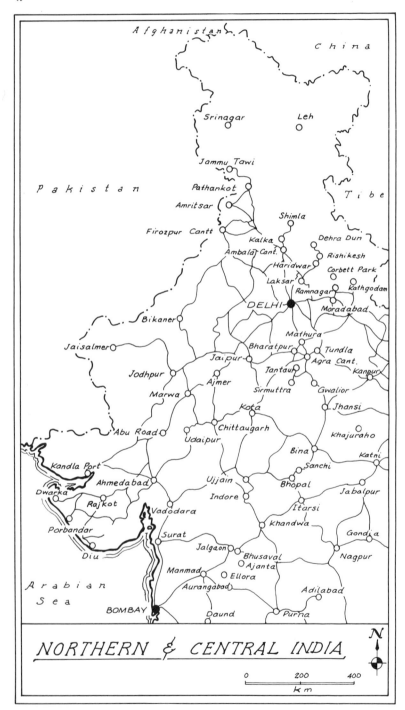

NORTHERN & CENTRAL INDIA

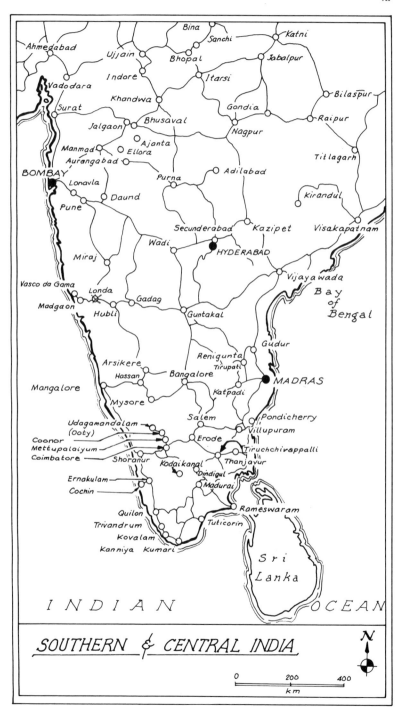

SOUTHERN & CENTRAL INDIA

N

0   200   400
km

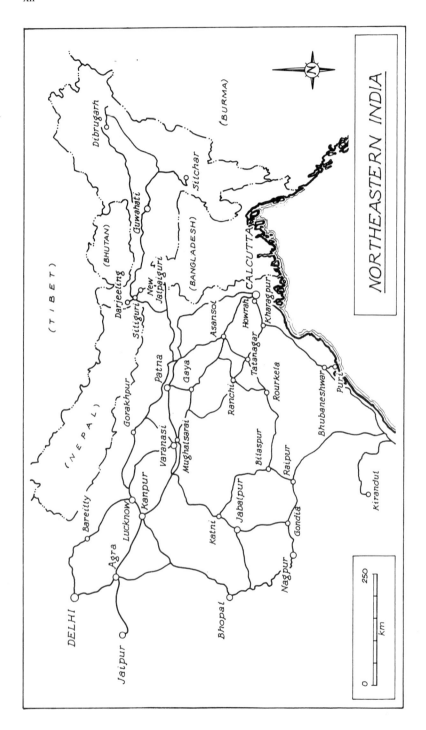

NORTHEASTERN INDIA

Chapter One

Discovering India by Rail

Whether you are a first time visitor to India, or an experienced traveller there, you'll find the best way to know India is to travel her length and breadth by train. It's an adventure that will teach you a lot about yourself as well as about India, and it's no hardship since trains in India are efficient, fast, frequent and fun.

Fly in a group or tour by coach and you'll be safely isolated from prolonged contact with India. Travel by local bus and you'll certainly see more than a tourist would, but you'll be uncomfortable and will end up hating the country simply because you feel awful.

Only train travel provides a comfortable berth for you to sleep on, meals at your seat, on-board toilets (even with a shower in first class), travelling companions as diverse as the whole of India, and an aisle along which you can walk to stretch your legs or to meet new people. All that while travelling a network so extensive it has direct trains linking stations over 3,000km apart.

The facilities are not just for the first class passenger; all classes have bunks and bearer (waiter) service of meals, snacks and soft or hot drinks to your seat. On top of that, train travel is so inexpensive that you can travel in luxury in air-conditioned 1st class at less than £3 for 100km.

When you travel by train you are taking part in contemporary Indian culture. It is a learning experience as well as a means of getting from, say, Madras to Bangalore. Indian fellow travellers will be kind and tolerant, talking to you if you wish, or respecting your need for solitude if you make it plain you want to be left alone. Put yourself in the right frame of mind, a positive one, and you will get far more out of discovering Indian by rail than a cheap train ride.

The beauty of all this is that there has never been a better time to travel in India by train. Within the past five years or so, rail travel has been transformed until it has become an experience which foreigners, as well as Indians, find convenient and pleasurable.

The word is out in railwayland to help foreign tourists. It's easy to understand why. They bring foreign currency which the country, and Indian Railways, needs. Tourism generates at least 10% of

India's foreign currency earnings without exporting any of the country's valuable material resources. In 1995 and 1996 over two million tourists visited India.

In recent years the British have topped the list of foreign visitors: about 80% of the Indrail Passes sold each year are bought by Britons. The International Tourist Bureau (ITB) at New Delhi station handled over 76,400 rail bookings by foreign tourists in 1987, its first year of operation. In 1996 it averaged 400 passengers a day.

Improved services

It's not just because Indian Railways wants foreign tourists that services have improved. Computers have revolutionised the reservations process, benefiting every rail traveller. Meals and drinks are served more hygienically in covered foil casseroles and disposable cups. And for the foreign tourist there is a quota of seats reserved in many trains, while some stations have special counters for Indrail Pass holders, so a foreigner need not join the general queue to make reservations.

Actually, not all of India's 7,000 stations pamper foreign tourists as a matter of course. Many of the stations I visited are off the tourist track where some officials might be bemused by a foreigner's demands; others, though, will be exceptionally helpful to foreign tourists. You'll discover, as I did, that by following the system and procedures set out in this guide, travel problems will be few.

Facilities for foreigners

First, a word of explanation for my use of the term "foreign tourist". A foreign passport holder who visits India for business or leisure is termed a "foreign tourist" by Indian Railways, as opposed to an Indian who is touring by rail. I share the dismay of those who don't like to be called "tourists", especially as we are clearly a different breed from the average "package tourist". But that's the way it is!

Foreign tourists, through the special quota, can make advance reservations for berths on busy trains when an Indian might only be wait-listed. "Foreigners are our guests", an official said when I queried the reason for giving foreigners priority over nationals. The real reason might be commercial: foreign currency makes foreigners valuable. I mention this to salve the conscience of sensitive travellers who have qualms about being treated to special privileges. Of course, if you want to join a long line and try to make your reservation from the general quota, and travel in the cheapest 2nd class accommodation, you can. But, remember, you are thereby depriving an Indian, who can only afford the cheapest ticket, of a place in that queue and on that train. By using the facilities developed for foreigners (such as priority bookings and travel in upper class carriages) the traveller is not only contributing much-needed foreign exchange but easing the pressure for the ordinary Indian rail passenger as well.

Don't worry about missing anything through making your reservation from the foreign tourist quota, or through the station superintendent's influence, you will still see (and smell and feel) the real India. You can't escape it when travelling by train.

Names

There is a trend by politicos in India to change names, hence Bombay has become Mumbai and Trivandrum the totally

---

NAME CHANGES

Samit Roychoudhury

Recently Indian administrations have begun to change names, be it cities, towns, roads, areas or institutions. This appears to be a reaction to the British (and also French and Portuguese) influence during the considerable period that this country was under their rule (during which time most of what we know as modern India was formed).

Even if the names were not actually of foreign origin, they would often be anglicised versions of the original local term. After independence, and especially since the recent rise of Hindutva (the concept of Hindu nationalism), combined with nationalist feelings, local governments have resorted to name-changing sprees to gain popularity.

Probably the most critical name change has been that of Bombay; India's most cosmopolitan, most Westernised commercial capital has been renamed Mumbai. This has affected other names as well. Bombay Victoria Terminus Station, built by the British, has officially become Mumbai Chhatrapati Shivaji Terminus. (It is named after the great Maratha warrior and statesman of yesteryear.)

BEST was formerly the Bombay Electric Supply & Transport, which runs the best public transport service in the country. It has become Brihanmumbai Electric Supply & Transport, which goes to show that, cosmetic changes apart, the company still aspires to be the BEST.

Many other name changes have taken place. Cochin has become Kochi, while Trivandrum is now Thiruvananthapuram. Ooty (actually Ootacamund) has long been officially known as Udagamandalam. Cannanore is now Kannur. Alleppey is Alapuzha and Calicut is Kozhikode, while Quilon has become Kollam. Madras has been renamed Chennai and there are attempts to change Ahmedabad to Karnavati and Patna to Pataliputra.

Strangest of all is the changing of the name of Mhow, which was actually an acronym for Military Headquarters of War, to Mau.

Other places have seen changes in the spellings, even if not in the actual names. Simla has become Shimla, while Gauhati is now Guwahati and Poona is, of course, Pune.

MUMBAI

In a letter to *The Economist* from Mumbai, Ashok Chowgule wrote: "The city was (and is) always referred to as Mumbai in the local language, Marathi ... In Hindi and Urdu and many other Indian languages, this country is always referred to as Hindustan, and not India. Ships which ply the Arabic Gulf had to have the name of the country of registration painted on their sides. On one side it is written 'India' in the same Roman script, and the other 'Hindustan' in Arabic."

---

unpronounceable Thiruvananthapuram. While respecting the politicians' right to rename towns as they wish, I have kept to the familiar names for easier understanding. For those anxious to be politically correct, details of new names appears on page 3.

Spelling

Many stations and trains names have two or more ways of spelling them in English, such as Hardwar/Haridwar, Nilgiri/Nilagiri, and Shimla/Simla. I have tried to use the spelling which appears in the zonal timetables although sometimes even those sources are not consistent.

Home on the rails

You can confidently make your home for a few days on the train, or simply take a train for a short trip, such as on India's "bullet train", the *Shatabdi Express* which takes only 115 minutes for the 199km run from New Delhi to Agra. The *Shatabdi Express* is a symbol of the changes taking place in Indian Railways. The best train to Agra used to take 50 minutes longer in non air-conditioned discomfort. The new train is all air-conditioned, with a pantry in each coach and meals included in the fare (see *Chapter Eleven*).

However, because of the distance between important stations, most train journeys in India involve overnight travel. An advantage in travelling overnight is that it saves time and the cost of hotel accommodation. Some tourists plan their itineraries around overnight trains, making the train their home. They arrive by train at a station in the morning, check their bags into the left-luggage cloakroom and dash off to see the sights, returning in the evening for an overnight train to the next destination on their list. If your time and funds are limited, that's probably the best way but, despite the improved comfort of train travel (many of the old 2nd class carriages have been replaced with air-conditioned dormitories on wheels with bunks in three tiers), it does require stamina and a certain kind of personality to spend endless nights on a train. Additionally if there is a daylight alternative, you might like to take it so you can see India's scenery instead of sleeping through it.

Station amenities

As always with Indian Railways, there is a solution to every difficulty. A long journey can be broken at stations en route for a shower (most stations have them either in bathrooms attached to waiting rooms or in a separate building) or for a motionless night on terra firma at a railway retiring room.

Retiring rooms are one of Indian Railways' best kept secrets which few foreigners bother to discover since sometimes they are a bit grubby. They are guest rooms with attached bathrooms, available at stations for rent by ticket (and Indrail Pass) holders for any period of 24 hours. They are generally secure bases from which to explore a town, or to recover from several nights on the rails. The station restaurants are close by and sometimes room service is provided.

Retiring rooms are usually the cheapest or the best value in town. If you only need a bed and don't worry about privacy, some stations also have dormitories, with lockers, showers and toilets (see *Chapter Seven*).

Other facilities available depend on a station's importance. Some major ones have loud closed-circuit television (CCTV) showing US panel games, wrestling and Hindi movies chopped up between live station announcements but these have – mercifully – been reduced. There could also be a chemist and curio shops, a book kiosk with US and UK best-selling paperbacks, a fruit stall, and drinking water either from coolers or dispensed by formidable ladies with ladles. All stations will have food and tea vendors, and waiting rooms.

Password

If you have several train journeys in mind or simply want to avoid hassles, it can be more economical, and certainly much easier, to travel on an Indrail Pass, an IRP (see *Chapter Three*). There are now short-period passes, for a single journey lasting an afternoon or a day, which can be purchased before you get to India, but the IRP really is the only ticket worth having.

Rail facts

Indian Railways is actually the largest railway system on earth under a single management. The state-owned railway network in Russia employs more workers (two million) and has more track (127,000km) but Indian Railways run more services and carry more passengers.

Origin	1853 with 34km of track, Bombay/Thane
Network	62,660 route km; 108,513 track km

Services	7,800 passenger services operated daily
Passengers	11 million every day
Stations	7,056
Locomotives	6,911 (as at March 31, 1996), composed of: Broad gauge (BG): 3,388 diesel; 2,402 electric Metre gauge (MG): 177 steam; 731 diesel; 20 electric Narrow gauge (NG): 26 steam; 167 diesel
Rolling stock	30,060 conventional passenger coaches, 3,618 EMU coaches and 5,536 other passenger coaches
Running track:	BG: 1.67m wide, most of the mainline trunk routes: 78,694km MG: 1.00m wide, mostly as feeder lines: 25,545km NG: 0.762m or 0.610m wide, on limited sections of difficult terrain: 4,274km
Overall average speed, including halts	Express/Mail trains: 46.7km/h (BG), 36.8km/h (MG) Passenger trains: 30.7km/h (BG), 27.5km/h (MG)
Bridges	118,000
Level crossings	40,847
Regular employees	1,602,000 plus 69,000 casual workers
Retiring rooms	At 420 stations
Catering	Available at 3,152 stations and on 118 pairs of trains

(Except where stated, statistics supplied by Indian Railways, as at March 31 1995.)

Railway set up

The railways are run by the Ministry of Railways headed by a minister who presents his own budget in parliament. The ministry operates through the Railway Board. At board level there are six members, including the chairman who functions as the managing director. The members represent different disciplines: engineering, mechanical, traffic, electrical, finance and staff, with the chairman looking after one portfolio. At Rail Bhavan (building), the headquarters of the board in New Delhi, a plethora of units and directorates function to pump information to the zones and to monitor their performance.

At zonal level, a general manager heads a small empire in each of the regional railways. Various managers and divisional heads serve under him including a host of chief superintendents controlling operations, commercial functions, freight, passenger traffic, catering, passenger reservations, safety and rolling stock. Belt-tightening is underway in the railways and it won't be long after you start your journey that you'll see ways Indian Railways could save money and make the service more efficient and convenient too. Suggestions to the general manager, not to me (see *Complaints, Chapter Five*).

In an article on the demise of steam published in *The Times* (November 4, 1995), Christopher Thomas commented, "Indian Railways, outrageously overstaffed, is a hidden social welfare system, providing its people with meagre but liveable salaries, free schools and hospitals, pensions and cheap houses. A railwayman is safe from poverty: even the International Monetary Fund was told to mind its own business when it proposed cutting the railway workforce by half."

The bureaucracy that runs the railways has evolved over nearly a century and a half, so pruning it is very complicated. The organisation devised by the British has been embroidered with manic genius by Indian Railways and this vast, inexplicable system actually works, despite such impediments as the man who holds a post for which he is obviously not competent (you'll meet him too).

According to the Railway Board's yearbook, "The economic, agricultural and industrial development of India is inextricably interwoven with Indian Railways' development and fortunes."

Railwayland in India is really a country within a country. It has its own electricity service, telephone system, hospitals, colleges, bureaucracy. It is so self-sufficient it stands apart from the normal life of India, yet without the railways there would be no normal life.

The Railway Board in 1992 ordered a 10% cut in basic administration costs, not just on the frills but with the shears snipping at posts as well. It was part of the global trim happening in all areas of India. Then plans were announced in the Railway Budget of July 1996 to tamper with the bureaucracy that had been in place for years, not to reduce but to create more railway zones. Instead of nine railways there will be 15, such as the East Coast Railway zone, with headquarters at Bhubaneswar, which will be carved out of the existing South Eastern Railway.

The existing regional railways and their headquarters are:

1   **Central Railway** Victoria Terminus, Bombay
3   **Eastern Railway** 17, Netaji Subhas Road, Calcutta
4   **Northern Railway** Baroda House, New Delhi
5   **North Eastern Railway** Gorakhpur
5   (sharing the number) **Northeast Frontier** Maligaon, Guwahati
6   **Southern Railway** Park Town, Madras
7   **South Central Railway** Rail Nilayam, Secunderabad
8   **South Eastern Railway** 11, Garden Reach Road, Calcutta
9   **Western Railway** Churchgate, Bombay

(Where any of the numbers above appear in timetables as the first digit of a four digit train number, the number indicates which of the regional railways operates the train.)

The new zones are to be headquartered at Allahabad, Bangalore, Bhubaneswar, Hazipur, Jabalpur and Jaipur.

Steam and special trains

Since the first edition of this book was published in 1989, the number of steam locomotives has dwindled from 4,427 to just 203 by March 31, 1996. This ruthless elimination of steam locomotives seems to have been carried out with a vengeance that ignored their potential as income earners for special trains.

There are no more broad gauge steam engines left in India, not even one to haul the prestigious train that caters for the nostalgic tourist: the *Palace on Wheels*. If you want to enjoy a ride by broad gauge stream train you have to make your way to Sri Lanka where the steam-hauled *Viceroy Special* makes special trips between Colombo and Kandy.

Details of where the 203 steam locomotives remain in India are given in *Chapter Six*.

It is still possible to ride the rack-and-pinion steam train to Coonoor (on the way to Ooty, now known as Udagamandalam) from Mettupalaiyam on the Nilagiri Mountain Railway. However, visit soon as this is bound to be replaced by a diesel engine as soon as they can design one capable of making the ascent.

The toy train to Darjeeling still plies occasionally for steam-smitten tourists. Another fascinating trip is by the 1920s lorry-like rail car from Kalka to Shimla.

Rail travel in luxury, but with decor supposed to inspire memories of the days of Maharajas, is provided by the *Palace on Wheels* and the *Royal Orient* trains. The *Royal Orient* does actually start and end its journey, out of and into Delhi Cantt station, being hauled by a metre gauge steam loco, the venerable *Desert Queen*.

The thrill of rail travel is different now. There is the excitement of the diesel or electric traction-hauled *Rajdhani* or *Shatabdi* Expresses which represent Indian Railways at its best. There are interesting journeys to be made, too, on the commuter specials like the *Deccan Queen* and the double-deckers from Bombay, and even on the newly opened Calcutta metro. Or you can travel in your own private coach on special tours (see *Chapter Eleven*).

Give it a try

"On arrival in India my initial reaction was to get the next flight home but after 24 days I grew to like it and was very sorry to leave," wrote Pauline Harford of Poole, Dorset when she sent in some tips. "We had a 21-day Indrail Pass, everything went without

Requisition for reservation – form

उ.रे./N.R.

सी.एम. 25?? ???? (हं.)
C.R. 25? (NR)

आरक्षण/खारिज/वापसी/आगे की यात्रा हेतु अनुरोध पत्र
REQUISITION FOR RESERVATION/CANCELLATION/RETURN OR ONWARD JOURNEY

जिस स्टेशन से Station from............... जिस स्थान को To..............
यात्रा की तिथि Date of journey................... ट्रेन नं. Train No............
श्रेणी Class.......................... बर्थ/सीट Berth/Seat..............

क्रम सं. S No	नाम Name in Block letters	स्त्री/पु. Sex	आयु Age	कर्मचारी द्वारा भरा जायेगा To be filled in by the staff
1.				टिकट नं.············· Ticket No./PNR No.
2.				कोच नं.············· Coach No.
3.				बर्थ/सीट नं.········· Berth/Seat No.
4.				प्रतीक्षा सूची नं.······ Wait list No.
5.				ह.ई. आर. सी.········· Sig. of E.R.C.
6.				

आवेदक का नाम Name of the applicant.............................
आवेदक के हस्ताक्षर Signature of applicant..........................
तारीख Date............................

विशेष अनुरोध
Special Request

(i) कूपा/केबिन/निचली शायिका/
मध्यवर्ती शायिका/ऊपरी शायिका
Coupe/Cabin/Lower Berth/
Middle Berth/Upper Berth

(ii) धूम्रपान निषेधयान
Non Smoker Coach

(iii) पसन्द का भोजन (शाकाहारी/मांसाहारी)
Choice of Meals (Veg./N Veg.)

पसन्द के लिए खाने में ✓ निशान लगायें।
✓ in the block to show your choice.

पूरा पता Address in full ....
....

टेलीफोन Telephone........ .... समय Time.........

(क.सु.उ./प ???)

a hitch ... and that is saying something as we're absolute novices in our mid 50s."

Another reader, actually writing during a temporary stay in an English prison, recalled his trip from Delhi to Agra and Varanasi and back to Delhi (a popular rail journey for the independent traveller) and said: "I think all Brits should ... spend six months in India. It might just make them appreciate the things in life that one would normally take for granted."

But Thomas B Morgan, a solicitor in Canada, wrote to me of his second visit to India, "We used barely half of the validity of our 60-day Indrail pass before we escaped the Indian Railway system and fled the country."

Of course there are some danger spots for foreign tourists in India, particularly Kashmir, so commonsense – and even advice from your own country's foreign ministry – should guide your decision whether to risk visiting certain areas.

Don't be surprised if you feel exasperated at the way things are done, not only on the railways but everywhere in India. Often misunderstandings might be your fault – not theirs – since there are so many viewpoints to life and work. While you might benefit from there being more signs in English and people of competence at railway stations explaining what to do, you'll soon discover that a smile and a polite approach will keep your temper under control and lead to unexpected, pleasant adventures.

To anyone who asks me whether they should travel in India by rail – is it really fun? – I say yes, give it a try at least for a journey or two around a region. Of course, it's not like home ... but isn't that one of the reasons for going away?

Chapter Two

Planning the Trip

PRELIMINARIES

Advance planning is essential to get the most out of travelling by train in India. Foreigners who expect a train service run the way it is at home will be annoyed to find they can't buy a ticket to travel overnight at a moment's notice. Reservations have to be made on certain day-time trains and on all overnight trains. It is to your advantage to do so as far in advance as possible.

When planning the trip, set aside at least one day after your arrival in India to make reservations. At the gateway cities of New Delhi, Bombay, Calcutta and Madras, there are special bureaux as well as counters at the airports, dealing with foreign rail tourist bookings. When you buy an Indrail Pass outside India, reservations can be done at the same time but you will need to confirm them on arrival (see *Chapter Three*).

Maps

The first requirement for planning your trip is a map of India on which to locate the places you want to visit. Maps of India are available from good bookshops and, in England, from Stanfords, 12/14 Long Acre, London WC2E 9LP, tel: 0171 836 1321. In the USA, try The Complete Traveler at 199 Madison Avenue, New York, NY 10016, tel: (212) 685 9007, or Forsyth Travel Library Inc, PO Box 2975, 9154 West 57 St, Shawnee Mission, Ks 66201-1357, tel: (913) 384 3440.

Free maps and lots of city and state information, as well as a leaflet about rail travel, are available from the Government of India tourist offices.

Recommended by Rob Dodson, a rail traveller I met at Delhi's Rail Yatri Niwas (Railway Inn) in 1992, is a plastic-bound 64-page folder of maps which contains city plans as well as maps of individual states and lists of selected attractions. Although it's actually a road atlas, railway lines are also shown. I bought my copy of *TT Maps' Road Atlas of India* at Howrah Station for Rs30 in 1992. Publishers are TT Maps & Publications Ltd, 328, GST Road, Chrompete, Madras 600 044. They are also the producers of an excellent *Map Guide To India*, a folder which was issued free by the Government of India Tourist Office for the 1991 Visit India Year. Copies still turn up and, since it has an insert of rail routes showing the different regional zones, it is a boon to rail travellers. Samit Roychoudhury recommends the new Lonely Planet *India (and Bangladesh) Travel Atlas*. "There are some mistakes and the maps could have better legends but it is well printed and has lots of detail."

On your map, mark the places you want to visit so you can choose the most convenient airport. The typical first-time visitor to India usually wants to visit Agra and Rajasthan and possibly Varanasi with a wide trip to Nepal, in which case Delhi is the gateway city. As the rail booking facilities at the International Tourist Bureau (ITB) at New Delhi station are the best in India, it's the ideal place for starting any rail journey.

TOURIST OFFICES

In India

Agra 191 The Mall, Agra 282001, Uttar Pradesh; tel: 363377/363959

Aurangabad Krishna Vilas, Station Road, Aurangabad 431 005, Maharashtra; tel: 31217

Bangalore KFC Building, 48 Church Street, Bangalore 560 001, Karnataka; tel: 5585417

Bhubaneswar B-21, B J B Nagar, Bhubaneswar 751 014, Orissa; tel: (0674) 432203

Bombay 123 M Karve Road, Opp. Churchgate, Bombay 400 020, Maharashtra; tel: 2032932, 2033144, 2033145m, 2036054; telex: 011 82922; fax: 91 22 2014496

Calcutta 'Embassy', 4 Shakespeare Sarani, Calcutta 700 071, West Bengal; tel: 2421402, 2421475, 2425813; telex: 021 8176; fax: (033) 242 3521

Guwahati B K Kakati Road, Ulubari, Guwahati 781 007, Assam; tel: 547407

Hyderabad 3 6 369/A 30, Sandozi Building, 2nd Floor, 26 Himayat Nagar, Hyderabad 500 029, Andhra Pradesh; tel: 660037

Imphal Old Lambulane, Jail Road, Imphal 795 001, Manipur; tel: 21131

Jaipur State Hotel, Khasa Kothi, Jaipur 302 001, Rajasthan; Tel: 372200

Khajuraho Near Western Group of Temples, Khajuraho 471 606, Madhya Pradesh; tel: 2047, 2048

Kochi (Cochin) Willingdon Island, Kochi 682 009, Kerala; tel: 6683521 (R) 666218; telex: 0885 6847

Madras 154 Anna Salai, Madras 600 002, Tamil Nadu; tel: 8269685, 869695; telex: 041 7359; fax: 044 8266893

Naharlagun Sector 'C', Naharlagun 791110, Arunachal Pradesh; tel: 328

New Delhi 88 Janpath, new Dellhi 110001; tel: 3320005, 3320008, 3320109, 3320266, 3320342; *Domestic Airport Information Counter* tel: 3295296; *International Airport Information Counter* tel: 3291171

Panaji (Goa) Communidade Building, Church Square, Panaji 403001, Goa; tel: 43412

Patna Sudama Palace, Kakarbagh Road, Patna 800020, Bihar; tel: 345776

Port Blair VIP Road, Junglighat, PO Port Blair 744 103, Andaman & Nicobar Islands; tel: 21006

Shillong Tirot Singh Syiem Road, Police Bazar, Shillong 793 001, Meghalaya; tel: 224532

Thiruvananthapuram Airport, Thiruvananthapuram, Kerala; tel: 451498

Varanasi 15B, The Mall, Varanasi 221002, Uttar Pradesh; tel: 43744

Overseas

Australia Level 1, 17 Castlereagh Street, Sydney, New South Wales 2000; tel: 0232 1600/17961, 0233 7579; fax: 02 2233003

Bahrain PO Box 11294, Villa No 5, Gudaibiya, Manama; tel: 715713; fax: 715527

Canada 60 Bloor Street (West), Suite 1003, Toronto, Ontario M4 W3 B8; tel: 416 962 3787, 416 962 3788; fax: 416 962 6279

France 13 Boulevard Haussmann 75009 Paris; tel: 45 23 30 45; fax: 45 23 33 45

Germany Baseler St. 48, 60329, Frankfurt, AM-main 1; tel: 069 235423, 235424; fax: 069 234724

Italy 9 Via-Albricci, Milan 20122; tel: 804952, 8053506; fax: 72021681

Japan Pearl Building, 9–18 Ginza, 7 Chome, Chuo-Ku, Tokyo 104; tel: 33 571 5062/3, 33 571 5197; fax: 33 571 5235

Malaysia Wisma HLA, Lot 203, 2nd Floor, Jalan Raja Chulan, 50200 Kuala Lumpur; tel: 2425285; fax: 00 603 2425301

Netherlands Rokin 9–15, 1012 KK Amsterdam; tel: 020 6208991; fax: 120 6383059

Singapore 20, Kramat Lane, 01-01A United House, Singapoe 0922; tel: 235 3800; fax: 235 8677.

Spain c/o Embassy of India, Avenida PIO XII 30-32, Madrid 28016; tel: 3457339, 3457340; fax: 4577996, 3457340; telex: 22604 EOME

Sweden   Sveavagen 9–11, 1st Floor, S-III 57, Stockholm 11157; tel: 215081/ 101187; fax: 210186

Switzerland   1–3 Rue De Chantepoulet, 1201 Geneva; tel: 022 7321813/ 1677; fax: 22 7315660; telex: 412727

Thailand   3rd Floor, Kentucky Fried Chicken Building, 62/5 Thaniya Road (SIL OM) Bangkok 10500; tel: 2352585, 2356670; fax: 2352585, 2368411

UAE   Post Box 12856, NASA Building, AL Maktoum Road, Deira, Dubai; tel: 274848, 236870; fax: 274013

UK   7 Cork Street, London W1X 2AB; tel: 01233 211999 (brochures), 0171 437 3677 (enquiries), 0891 444 5444 (visas); fax: 71 494 1048

USA   3550 Wilshire Boulevard, Room 204, Los Angeles, California 90010; tel: 213 477 3824, 380 8855; fax: 00 1 213 380 6111

30 Rockefeller Plaza, Suite 15, North Mezzanine, New York, NY 10112; tel: 212 586 4901, 4902, 4903, 4904; fax: 00 1 212 582 3274; telex; 9102508316

TIMETABLES

A rail timetable is useful so you can see how long it takes to travel between cities, but if you don't have one, measure the distance on the map between the major cities you want to visit. For every 50km, allow one hour of train time. For example, the distance between Delhi and Jammu Tawi (the station for Kashmir) is about 550km which means a journey of 11 hours. The fastest journey time between those cities is actually 10hr 45min (or 9hr 24min by the recently introduced *Rajdhani Express*). Other trains take from 14 to 15 hours.

The best timetable readily available outside India is the *Thomas Cook Overseas Timetable* which contains 30 pages devoted to India and shows, in easy to understand format, the times of all important trains and the classes available. There is also a route map which is useful for planning the trip since most rail lines are shown. The timetable is published six times a year and is available from the Timetable Publishing Office, Thomas Cook Ltd, Thorpe Wood, Peterborough PE3 6PU, England, tel: 01733 502568.

Indian Railways publish a timetable called *Trains at a Glance* (*TAG*) in July every year (although it doesn't usually appear until October); it is available outside India through the general sales agents (GSAs) for the Indrail Pass (see *Chapter Three*). In India it costs Rs15. It contains most of the train times and information a visitor will need and has a map. It has a station index although it does not give the page number of every reference to each station. Also, there is no indication of what classes of accommodation are available on each train, nor all the stops the train makes. There are a few new publications published independently in India that reproduce the information given in

Trains at a Glance.

More detailed timetables which include all the halts made by slow passenger trains are published annually by each of the nine railway zones, covering the services operated by each zone. They are available only in India, at main station bookstalls within their zone. These timetables cost Rs15 each and contain lots of extra information as well as a regional map.

Although they all follow the same format, the timetable published by South Central Railway has the clearest layout and plenty of additional information, including an extra map with a timetable key. A list of "aphorisms" included has a number 13, "Diarrhoea – answer is sugar-salt solution". The timetable of Northeast Frontier railway carries a box saying simply, "Not before twenty – never after thirty, two are plenty". It also gives the sound advice, "Less luggage, more comfort", and the warning that "Pelting of stones towards the train is a punishable offence".

There is a publication that combines all the zone timetables in one thick volume, with an index showing every station. Called *Newman's Indian Bradshaw*, it is published monthly and costs Rs50. It is sometimes difficult to obtain in India, although its cover lists 80 stations, including Howrah and Sealdah in Calcutta, Delhi (but not New Delhi) and Bombay (VT but not Central), where it can be bought. An overseas agent for this excellent if crudely printed volume is Wm Dawson & Sons Ltd, Cannon House, Folkestone, Kent, England.

Midnight is indicated as 2400 for train arrivals, and 0000 for departures.

ITINERARIES

How long?

The ideal length of holiday in India is at least three weeks, but with careful planning you can see a lot by train in just one week. I've suggested some itineraries in *Chapter Nine*. A three-week visit allows sufficient time to recover from the flight, get used to the heat, the clamour and the food, and to feel at ease. And you'll be able to see enough different parts of India in three weeks to whet your appetite for further visits when you can concentrate on the areas you most enjoyed. If you have time for a longer visit, use it to discover the south or east as well as the north and west, and allow time to relax away from the railways for a while.

Planning the itinerary

It is a common mistake to try to include too much in an itinerary planned in the comfort of an armchair at home. It is difficult to imagine the distances involved, or the effect on a newcomer to India of a lot of train travelling. For instance, from Delhi to Madras is

2,194km (1,361 miles), the equivalent of travelling from London to Edinburgh four times. You'll feel the strain whatever class you travel in (although you'll feel worse after two nights in 2nd class than two nights in 1st AC class) simply because the rhythm of train travel is bound to disturb your system. Allow time in your itinerary not just for the train journey but for extras such as delays and waiting time, and also for recovery, relaxation, a chance to see the sights, and to let things happen.

Unfortunately, the sheer volume of traffic makes delays almost inevitable. Many routes are single track only so a train has to wait on a double track section for any oncoming trains. This is known as "crossing" and explains why a train stops in the middle of nowhere. The late running of one train extends to the train behind it and can affect the train coming towards it too.

If you are on a train that seems bound to arrive late, don't worry about missing the connection since that could be late as well. Also, because of "cushion time" in rail schedules, as much as an hour's delay could have been allowed for. This gives an opportunity for the train to make up time on the last lap of its journey and arrive on schedule.

Just in case, allow at least three hours to make connections unless there are plenty of alternative trains should you actually miss the one you want. Stations in India are always interesting places to wait; if you tire of watching the other passengers you could have a meal, a shower or take a walk into town. If you have to hang around a station during the night, check into a retiring room and sleep; the attendant will wake you on request (see *Chapter Seven*). If you do miss a connecting train, you'll have lost your onward reservation and that will take time to sort out. Better to expect a missed connection and allow an overnight stop anyway.

As well as train delays, there are likely to be unexpected frustrations when you do arrive at your destination, such as a local holiday or a strike, or it could even be something nice that makes you want to stay longer. Build plenty of "cushion time" into your own itinerary with days of nothing planned so that you have some spare days if you need them.

Plan your route to save on time. Once you've left your originating city, it makes sense not to return there unless you have to. Avoid backtracking; trains in India go across country too, not just via Delhi or the main cities. For instance, you can go from Agra to Lucknow without having to change at Delhi.

If timetables bore you, work out basically where you want to go and leave it to the Indrail Pass GSA (see next chapter) or, in India, the rail tourist guide at one of the Foreign Tourist Bureaux, to suggest an itinerary. They will know the main trains but you may have to curb their enthusiasm to book you on trains leaving or arriving at impossible times.

Avoid trains that bring you to your destination late at night, especially if you've never been there before. Also trains leaving before 0600 should be resisted. Not only does that mean early rising but the passengers already on the train will be sleeping, which will make settling in difficult.

The ideal departure time is about 1000, with 1800 the latest for overnight journeys so you have time to size up the other occupants of the compartment before bedding down for the night. Lower berths, incidentally, are only supposed to be occupied as berths from 2100 to 0600. They are used as seats for all occupants during the day.

Not all trains have 1st or AC class, although all do have 2nd class of some sort. Some trains over certain routes are better than others over the same route; it's worth finding out which are faster, more convenient and have 1st AC.

Most important trains run daily but there are some superfast long-distance expresses which run only on certain days of the week. You will need to study the timetables carefully, and all the little notes too, to find the best trains. I've listed some of them in *Chapter Twelve*.

When to go

The most popular time for rail tourists is November to February, which is the peak of the usual tourist season of September to March. April, May and June should be avoided, not because the weather is unbearably hot (which it is), but because that's the domestic tourist season and when schools and colleges have their vacations. All India takes to the tracks then to visit relatives, attend weddings, go home, make a pilgrimage or simply to ride a train because everyone else is doing it. Eighty-five per cent of Indians on holiday travel by rail. The trains are packed, impulse reservations are impossible to get, and it's hell on wheels. If you must travel then, make your reservations as far in advance as possible.

July and August is the monsoon season and a favourite time for foreigners to take the train to Jammu Tawi on the way to Kashmir, or to head for Shimla. If you can only visit India during April to August, plan on staying in the cooler hill areas and make sure you have train and hotel reservations secured.

Although in July and August you'll be drenched with perspiration in Delhi (humidity can reach 90%), in December and January the capital can be cold. If you're starting a trip from Delhi, the spring (February and March) and autumn (October and November) are best.

How to go

The four international airports of Delhi, Bombay, Calcutta and Madras are accessible by frequent direct flights from Europe and Asia. Air India have direct flights from New York and Toronto as well as from London, Paris, Frankfurt, Geneva and Rome, and from Africa and the Middle and Far East.

Flights to Delhi from London take nine hours nonstop and up to 15 hours via other points. Return fares range from £2,631 1st class and £1,503 business class down to £600 for a special economy class fare. The same fares apply for Bombay; Calcutta and Madras are a few pounds more. There are cheaper fares available. For instance, Trailfinders Travel Centre at 46/48 Earls Court Road, London W8 6EJ, England, tel: 0171 938 3366, offers a complete service for the independent traveller, and no membership is required. They have return fares to Delhi by many airlines from £330 to £550 depending on the season, and can also offer great discounts on top hotels. They have an immunisation centre, a travel insurance service and a library for their clients, as well as a travel bookshop. Reduced rate tickets can be bought by cash or credit card and issued on the spot.

The travel organisation WEXAS International (45 Brompton Road, London SW3 1DE, England, tel: 0171 589 3315) quotes the following round-trip fares from London to its members (annual membership is approximately £30).

	Delhi	Bombay	Calcutta	Madras
First class	£1,166	£1,443	£1,664	£1,664
Business class	£877	£944	£1,220	£1,220
Economy excursion	£394	£394	£477	£433

Student and independent travellers can make their arrangements through STA. Their main office is at Priory House, 6 Wrights Lane, London W8 6TA, tel: 0171 361 6262. They have 120 branches worldwide. US travellers should phone (212) 627 3111. Their fares are competitive with the best and their staff are experienced travellers.

A novel way of flying to India is to go to Goa or Trivandrum. Goa Way (UK) Ltd, 14 Hills Place, London W1R 1AE, tel: 0171 439 4939, sell a special flight/rail package throughout the season (October to April) from Gatwick to Goa and Trivandrum. Since Goa and Trivandrum are much more pleasant airports to arrive at than any of the "big four", this seems an attractive deal.

Access to Trivandrum is also possible from Colombo, Sri Lanka, by Air Lanka (recommended) and Indian Airlines, as are the airports of Tiruchchirappalli (not as efficient as Trivandrum), Bombay and Madras. Sea travel by ferry from Sri Lanka to Rameswaram has been suspended for many years. Travel overland from Nepal is possible by linking up with a rail connection to Gorakhpur or Patna where onward reservations can be made. When I travelled in July (in 1996), I was surprised how easy it was to get reservations, another advantage of going by train in the "off-season".

If you arrive at Trivandrum, Goa or Tiruchchirappalli, or

overland from Nepal, allow at least a day to make rail reservations since there are no special Foreign Tourist Bureaux to plan itineraries at these stations. When buying a rail ticket in Nepal, make it for the short journey to the first major station in India where you can buy an onward ticket. Otherwise you can get ripped off, paying more for the ticket in Nepal than you would in India and not getting the reservations you think you've got (see *Chapter Ten, Gorakhpur*).

Where to go

In addition to the cities of Delhi (the top favourite), Bombay, Calcutta and Madras, the most popular destinations for foreign rail travellers are:

Agra (Taj Mahal)ℐ
Aurangabad (for Ellora caves)
Bangalore (a Raj resort)
Bhubaneswar (Temple City)
Goa (via Vasco de Gama station)
Gorakhpur (for Nepal)
Jaipur (Pink City)✗
Jaisalmer (desert fort)
Jalgaon (for the caves at Ajanta)
Jammu Tawi (for bus to Kashmir)
Jhansi (for Khajuraho carvings)
Jodhpur (for Rajasthan)
Madurai (Tamil culture)
New Jalpaiguri (for Darjeeling)
Ooty (Udagamandalam, for hill railway and resort)
Puri (for Konark sun temple and sea)✷
Quilon (for Kerala backwaters)
Shimla (hill resort)
Varanasi (Benares, ancient holy city)

Other places worth visiting are Udaipur, the Venice of India; Mysore, for its charm and sandalwood; Cochin (via Ernakulam), for its maritime heritage, and the Land's End of India, Kanniya Kumari, with its sun and moon rising over three seas.

In a list supplied by Indian Railways, the following stations are also given as popular destinations for foreign tourists, but for some stations it might be the outcome of wishful thinking not actually supported by crowds of enthusiastic foreign visitors; Bijapur (for Golgumbaz Dome), Chittaurgarh (Rajasthan), Gwalior (fort), Raxaul (access to Katmandu), Sawai Madhopur (wildlife and Ranthambhor fortress), Tiruchchirappalli (historic holy city), Trivandrum (for Kovalam beaches), Haridwar (for Rishikesh), Hospet (for Hampi and Thungabhadra Dam), Hyderabad/ Secunderabad, Indore (Mandu fort), Jabalpur (Kanha National

Park), Lonavla (for Karla and Bhaja caves), Madgaon (for Goa) and Madurai (for temple and ancient Pandyan capital).

What to take

As little as possible. Even a flight bag weighing only 5kg can be a strain to carry in extreme heat. You really do not need half the things you feel you should take. Anyway, if you do find you've left something behind, you can usually buy a replacement in India.

By reducing your belongings to the minimum essentials, you can probably pack everything in a bag small enough to carry on the plane with you. A duffle bag is good because its flexible shape allows it to be stuffed away or used as a pillow, but be careful of storing valuables in it since it can be ripped open. If you will be trekking or hiking, a backpack is best. It should have an internal frame as an external one can break easily and sticks into people and things. Keep it as light as possible.

Rob Dodson says a good quality sleeping bag weighing about 2kg will easily fit into a backpack and its own bag stuffed with clothes will also serve as a pillow (indispensable where bedrolls are not available). Good Western camping equipment and clothes are greatly valued in India as imported goods are restricted, so you could sell it before leaving.

A small suitcase, made of a lightweight, durable shell, gives you mobility, stores neatly under a train seat and is more secure because it can be locked. If you take a lot of luggage, it could be worthwhile storing it while you are travelling by train, and buying a cheap case in India (at less than £10/$15) to take only what you need on your rail trip.

Books are usually the heaviest and bulkiest item in a traveller's luggage. Fortunately, you won't need many. Railway bookstalls (Wheelers in the north and Higginbothams in the south) are excellent, with a vast range of popular and classical paperbacks in English. If you need to keep in touch with the world, a miniature portable radio that receives BBC World Service is useful. Some travellers are inseparable from their Walkmans; it seems a shame to block your ears to India like that.

Prepare yourself for train travel in the same way that you would for a long-haul flight. Take an eyeshade and earplugs so you can sleep if the compartment light is on and people are talking late into the night.

For sleeping on trains, a cotton sleeping bag liner from the YHA can be useful, with a blanket bought in India instead of taking a sleeping bag. Ashley Butterfield points out that cotton sheet sleeping bags can easily be made up in India. Bedrolls are supplied in some classes and can be hired in others. If you intend visiting chilly hill stations, then a sweater and even a jacket, scarf and woolly hat could be needed.

Whatever clothes you take should be lightweight and quick drying. Cotton underwear (as long as it's loose) is the best, with a spare set for when you're washing the dirty ones. Shirts with lots of deep pockets with buttons or zips are a good idea. A cotton money belt is favoured by experienced travellers and is especially useful for keeping valuables close to your body when you're asleep. But make sure it's secure around your waist when you use the train loo.

Safari-type shirts can be made up in 24 hours from jazzy cotton material for about £3 each. A tailor will be willing to copy your favourite garments, so you need not take spares but have them made there.

The light cotton shirts and pyjama-like trousers worn by Indian travellers are ideal for male and female foreigners and can be bought cheaply. A *lungi*, a floor-length piece of cloth wrapped around the waist, is good for nightwear or for hiding under when you're changing clothes in a crowded carriage.

Most garments sold in Europe for wear in the tropics are a disappointment, either too hot or too fashionable to be practical. Instead of buying expensive, designer tropical wear, save your money and buy cool clothes made from cotton when you are in India.

A pair of sandals is essential for wearing in trains, especially in toilets. Cheap plastic ones (from Rs25) can be bought at street markets. These, and a stout pair of walking shoes or good trainers, will be sufficient footwear. Socks should be cotton. On trains, keep your shoes in your luggage, never under the seat as, during the night or when you are away from your seat, they might seem to walk off by themselves.

A small pocket torch is necessary for night travel, plus a padlock or two, and a pocket knife for peeling fruit. You may like an air-filled pillow, and this can be bought at main stations for about £2.00/$3.00. Buy a cotton pillow case from the same place to save irritation from the rough rubber of the pillow. The neck support pillows marketed worldwide have synthetic material covers and cause too much sweating in the heat. They're expensive, too, compared with full size pillows in India.

Take a plastic container for your special toiletries. Toothpaste and soap can be purchased everywhere but imported eau de colognes are expensive. You will need toilet paper; although it can be bought in India, it's in small rolls and you will have to hunt for it. A large plastic bag is always useful, especially when you take a shower on a train (see *Chapter Five*).

You will need a small towel, although bath towels are provided in railway retiring rooms, for drying your hands when you wash them before and after eating a meal with your fingers. No handtowel, or paper, is provided in train toilets but the bedroll you can rent at night does have a handtowel in it. A handkerchief will do in an emergency although it will soon smell of curry unless you wash it out frequently. Wet wipes or similar could help then, but that is an extra refinement you could do without.

An essential item is a water bottle and you can buy them at most stations. Outdoor equipment shops in Europe, and the USA sell tougher ones designed for hikers. These are ideal. Carry a crown bottle opener too or, more versatile, a Swiss Army knife, for opening soft drinks and beer bottles. But if you only have hand baggage when you fly, remember the knife might be removed by airport security, so it might be better to buy a cheap bottle-opener/ penknife when you are in India.

It is worthwhile taking your full quota of liquor into India since imported spirits are expensive. Take film as well, more than you think you'll need. (Pack it in a plastic bag for hand-searching by airport security instead of letting it go through those X-ray machines.) You can buy notebooks and pens in India. Buy your own cup in India into which enough tea or coffee can be poured by station vendors. You pay according to the measure. The tea is delicious, milky and with cinnamon or ginger flavour.

HEALTH

I was advised to take all sorts of medical preparations but I threw out most of the ointment and pills soon after arrival when I discovered I could buy them locally: medicines are extremely cheap in India. However, take your favourite headache and diarrhoea remedies and any prescription medicines you need, anti-malaria pills and water purifying tablets (available from Boots). Sometimes brand name medicines available in India are out of date but there are pharmacies everywhere. Because of the dust, you'll probably need throat sweets.

Unless a visitor arrives in India from a yellow fever area, no vaccinations are required for entry. However, they are recommended.

Cholera

If you are going from India to a country that imposes restrictions on arrivals from India because of cholera, then you need to have an inoculation and a certificate to prove it. In any case, a cholera jab is a good thing to have before you go. It is effective for six months.

Yellow fever

Do not arrive in India without a certificate of vaccination against yellow fever within six months of departing from a declared yellow fever area, such as Kenya, or by an aircraft that's transited such areas; you'll find yourself isolated in quarantine for six days. The vaccination is effective for ten years.

Malaria

There is a risk of malaria throughout the year, so be prepared. The British Airways medical service advises Paludrin (no prescription); two tablets a day starting one day before arrival. Nivoquine (no prescription) should also be taken; two tablets weekly, starting one week before travel. The tablets should also be taken for four weeks after leaving India. In the UK, advice on malaria precautions is available by taped message on telephone number 0171 636 7921.

Diarrhoea

Non-prescription remedies are limited in variety in the UK, but don't worry, you can easily buy prescription pills (such as Lomotil) to stabilise yourself from station pharmacies in India. Take Imodium with you, just in case. The Indian Railways' medical service is excellent so, if you are suffering, a railway doctor could fix you up. Since water is a cause of gippy tummy, carry purifying tablets (iodine) to use in it if there is absolutely nothing else to drink. A water filter is even more effective, and may be purchased from MASTA (Medical Advisory Services for Travellers Abroad), Keppel St, London WC1E 7HT, tel: 0171 631 4408. MASTA can also sell you a Concise Health Brief containing up to date medical information for India.

SAFETY

Keep your passport with you (in a deep, zippered pocket, or body belt) all the time, not just for security but to show whenever it's asked for by officials.

Do not display large amounts of money. Keep enough for the day's expenses in your wallet or purse and hide the rest somewhere else. Resist all temptation to exchange foreign currency other than with licensed dealers. It's illegal and you stand a very good chance of being ripped off.

Leave your most valued possessions at home; they could get lost or stolen. Leave your address book and Filofax behind too, and only bring copies of the addresses and information you need. Keep a record of your credit card and passport numbers at home together with a photocopy of your airline ticket and insurance policy in case of emergency.

A padlock is essential, either for locking your luggage to the chain provided under the seats of newer carriages, or to lock the retiring room, locker or compartment door when you're absent. A combination padlock removes the risk of losing the key. There is a combination padlock with a metre of steel wire (it's called the "Travellers Lock Away") that is ideal for securing luggage to a carriage fixture when you're sleeping or leave it unattended.

A small combination padlock is useful for locking the zipper to the ring of canvas holdalls to deter snatch thieves. Since many left luggage offices will only accept locked luggage, a chain and a padlock (you can buy both at most major stations) are useful for trussing up a backpack.

Keep travellers cheques, money and tickets close to you. When sleeping on trains, have them on your body somewhere (in the pocket of your pants or stuffed in your body belt but not under the pillow). To carry passports, tickets, etc, Sara Keen made a variety of different sized, unattached pockets, in soft but hardwearing cotton fabric. They were kept closed with Velcro. These attached to the inside of the elastic waist of trousers with snap-lock nappy pins, enabling a comfortable sleep, with everything safe. Keep the numbers of anything important in a separate place so if you do lose anything you have the details. Insure to cover loss of possessions as well as for accident and illness.

Sooner or later when you tell people you are planning to travel in India by train, someone will ask "Are you sure it's safe?" It is, as long as you are sensible. Train travel itself has generally a good standard of safety, especially when the volume of passengers travelling every day is taken into consideration. For security while on a train see *Chapter Five*.

MONEY

Take your money in US dollar or pound sterling travellers cheques. Many travellers find the changing process is time-consuming at city banks. The solution is to change money at the airport on arrival, or at the cashier's desk of major hotels. (You don't necessarily have to stay there but would need to be using one of their public rooms such as the coffee shop.)

You can also use travellers cheques to buy rail tickets at the ITB in New Delhi and the Foreign Tourist Bureaux elsewhere and receive the change in rupees (see *Chapter Three*). Tickets and reservations from the foreign tourist quota have to be paid in foreign currency or travellers cheques anyway. Credit cards can be used in hotels and shops but not for buying rail tickets unless they are local cards.

If you don't have an onward or return air ticket, make certain you have access to enough funds to leave India when you want to. Better to bring the money in some form (travellers cheques, credit cards) since having funds sent from overseas can take ages. Don't expect your consul to send you home if you get destitute.

The usual safeguard of being able to cash a home country personal cheque guaranteed by a banker's card (at your consul) or credit card, when you need money in an emergency, cannot be relied on in India because of exchange controls. If you do run out of money, you may have to borrow from friends or check into a good hotel and sign the bills until funds arrive from home.

Currency

The currency of India is the rupee (Rs) and there are a 100 paise (P) to one rupee. Coins are in denominations of 5, 10, 25, 50 paise and 1, 2, and 5 rupees. There are 1, 2, 5, 10, 20, 50, 100 and 500 rupee notes. The small denomination notes are generally in a bad state.

Finding change isn't the problem it used to be. However, save coins and low denomination notes to pay the correct amount to platform vendors; the train could pull out before you get your change.

What will it cost?

It depends on you. If you intend to buy your air ticket to leave India and your rail tickets while there, then allow sufficient for those in your budgeting. The cost of Indrail Passes and train tickets are in the next chapter.

While you are on a train, expenses are easy to control: just meals, drinks (no alcohol), reading matter and a bedroll for the night. Expenses increase when you get off the train, although if you stay in station retiring rooms and eat in railway restaurants these will still be low.

Getting to and from what you've come to see, the cost of souvenirs, medicines, laundry, beers, nights in hotels and occasional extravagance will demand a larger budget.

The cost of a day on a train and a night at a railway station could work out as follows:

Standard budget meals		Economy budget meals	
Non-veg breakfast	Rs 12.00	Vegetarian breakfast	Rs 10.00
Special NV lunch	35.00	Vegetarian lunch	16.00
Standard NV dinner	18.00	Standard NV dinner	18.00
Snacks/fruit	25.00	Snacks/fruit	15.00
Drinks		**Drinks**	
Tea/soft drinks		Tea (and water)	20.00
Mineral water	35.00		
Reading			
News magazines	20.00		
Night		**Night**	
Bed (twin-bedded		Dormitory bed	25.00
room)	75.00		
	Rs 220.00		Rs 104.00
(Approximately £4.20/US$6.30)		(£2.00/$3.00)	

Thanks to the devaluation of the rupee, the cost in pounds

sterling or US dollars is actually less than it was when the first edition of this book was published in 1989. But if you go off the rails, expect your expenses to be much higher. Allow plenty for those nights in luxury hotels – for when you want pampering – as their rates are in line with inflation, and not much lower than in the West.

RED TAPE
Visa
Citizens of all countries, including the Commonwealth, require visas to enter India. A multiple entry visa will be needed if you intend to visit Nepal or Sri Lanka from India and then return home via India. If you plan to go to Nepal you'll need a visa for that country (The Royal Nepalese Embassy is in Barakhamba Road, New Delhi 110 001; tel: 3329969). No visa is required for entry into Sri Lanka. Incidentally, a multiple entry visa is not valid for re-entry if you actually return to your home country, or go on further than neighbouring countries, and then try to use it to get back into India.

A tourist visa can be extended up to six months in total by applying to the Foreigners' Registration offices in New Delhi, Bombay, Calcutta or Madras. There are also entry visas and transit visas, but the tourist visa is the one rail travellers on holiday need.

An application form, obtainable from travel agents, tourist offices or the Indian High Commission or Embassy, requires personal particulars including father's/husband's name. Three passport-size photographs have to be submitted with the completed form. Personal applications are usually approved for the next working day while postal applications take two to three weeks.

Indian Embassies and High Commissions overseas
Australia High Commission of India, 3–5 Moonah Place, Yarralumla, Canberra, ACT 2600; tel 616 2733774/2733999; fax: 616 2 2733328

Belgium Embassy of India, 217 Chaussée de Vleurgat, 1050, Brussels; tel: 322 6409802, 6409140; fax: 322 6489638

Canada High Commission of India, 10 Springfield Road, Ottawa, Ontario K1M 1C9; tel: 1 613 744751/52/53; fax: 1 613 7440913

France Embassy of India, 15 Rue Alfred Dehodenoq, 75016 Paris; tel; 33 1 40507070; fax: 33 1 40500996

Germany Embassy of India, Adenauerallee 262-264, 53113 Bonn I & II; tel 49 228 54050; fax: 49 228 5405153/54

Italy Embassy of India, Via XX Settembre 5, 00187, Rome; tel: 39 6 4884642–45; fax: 39 6 4819539

Netherlands Embassy of India, Buitenrustweg-2, 2517 KD, The Hague; tel: 31 70 3469771; fax: 31 70 3617072

New Zealand High Commission of India, 180 Molesworth Street, PO Box 4045, Wellington; tel; 64 4 4736390, 4736391; fax: 64 4 4990665

South Africa High Commission of India, Suite 208, Infotech Building 1090, Arcadia Street, PO Box 40216, Arcadia 0007; tel: 27 12 3425392/97; fax: 27 12 3411571/600

Switzerland Embassy of India, Effingerstrasse 45, CH-3008, Berne; tel: 41 31 3823111; fax: 41 31 3822687

UK High Commission of India, India House, Aldwych, London WC2B 4NA; tel: 44 171 836 8484; fax: 44 171 836 4331

USA Embassy of India, 2107 Massachusetts Avenue NW, Washington DC 20008; tel: 1 202 9397000; fax: 1 202 9397027

Photographs

Permits are required to photograph locomotives, trains and loco sheds; some railway stations exhibit notices saying photography is banned. If you are planning extensive and serious photography, make sure you have one before you go so you can ward off the rare official who may want to hinder you. Apply to your nearest Indian High Commission or Embassy at least 90 days in advance to make sure of getting the necessary piece of paper. On the other hand, for casual photography (as long as no notice is displayed specifically prohibiting it) you can snap away without a permit.

Arrival

On the flight to India you will be given a card to fill in for immigration. A classic misprint on this seems to be asking for the name of your father's husband. Fill the card in accurately and be prepared for a long wait at the Immigration desk since your passport and the card will be scrutinised by two sets of officials in different offices.

There are red and green channels in customs but you'll be stopped even in the green channel. Importation of personal jewellery, camera, tape recorder, binoculars, transistor radio, professional equipment, etc, is permitted duty free provided all items are taken out with you when you leave.

200 cigarettes or 50 cigars or 250g of tobacco and alcoholic liquor up to 0.95 litres (you'll have to drink some of it if you have a full litre bottle) are permitted duty free. The interrogation can be either searching or casual; don't try to be clever.

There is no restriction on the amount of foreign currency that may be taken into India. However, more than US$1,000, or its equivalent, should be declared on a currency declaration form. This helps if you want to take it out again. No Indian currency may be taken in.

You can change travellers cheques and cash at the airport exchange counters (open 24 hours a day). Keep the receipt of the transaction since you will need this when you try to pay a hotel bill in rupees, to prove you bought rupees with foreign currency. Don't change all your foreign currency as you might need it to buy rail tickets (see *Chapter Three*). Your exchange receipts will be needed if you want to exchange rupees back to foreign currency.

Departure

By the time you leave India, you will be used to queuing, but make sure you joining the right queue when checking in for your flight; you might have to queue to pay the embarkation tax first. The foreign travel tax, as it's called, is Rs150 for passengers departing for Sri Lanka, Nepal, Maldives, Pakistan, Afghanistan, Bangladesh, Bhutan and Burma. Departure for other overseas destinations costs Rs300 in tax, payable in rupees.

Exit permits are not required by holders of tourist visas who have not stayed longer than their original visa allowed them. If you have extended your visa and hold a registration certificate, you will have to obtain, before departure, exit endorsements from the registration office of the district in which you registered. There are other hassles too, like income tax. Better to leave India before your time is up – Sri Lanka makes a welcome break – and then start again.

You will be given a departure card to fill in before joining the long wait at Immigration. Duty-free goods such as cameras brought into India may have to be produced to customs; be prepared for questions. There will be several security searches before you eventually board the plane.

SOLO AND GROUP TRAVEL

The success of a decision to go alone, with friends or in a group ultimately depends on your own personality. Whatever you decide, you'll see the same India but your experience will be more intense if you're alone. You'll probably be adopted by friendly fellow passengers but it can be lonely too. If you travel with a companion, you'll have someone with whom to share everything, the bad as well as the good, and also the luggage-minding duties.

It's only natural to want to travel with a companion in a country as extraordinary as India. However, the pairs of travellers I've met never seemed to be enjoying themselves as much as I was. They sat together, played cards, talked, ate and slept as an exclusive group of two, making no effort to speak to their fellow passengers unless to demand some information.

While there are obvious advantages in travelling with a friend, there are snags which only become apparent once you're on the train. If you don't know your companion very well, little quirks of behaviour could ruin your own enjoyment of the trip. Trains are not the place for the honeymoon stage of any relationship. Also, when travelling with companions, you may have to defer to their wishes, and thus miss sights and experiences. My personal choice is to travel alone. As a solo traveller, you will feel more at ease, especially at night, in an air-conditioned two-tier coach or 1st class than in a claustrophobic 72-berth 2nd class carriage.

Children

Couples whom I met travelling with children seemed happy enough. Most Western children adore rail travel and can spend hours train spotting or wandering around stations. Obviously, very young children will be a problem because of the extra care and attention they need. It is not always possible for families to be accommodated in the same sleeping compartments at night, so parents may have to make a special request to the conductor to see that their daughter is assigned a berth with at least one of them, and not separately.

Women travellers

Women travellers, alone or in pairs, face the usual problems, often through Western insensitivity to Indian mores; modest dress and behaviour can help prevent misunderstandings. There is safety in numbers so women may feel more secure in a fourth-berth cabin than in a two-berth coupé. In a carriage with 45 or 71 other passengers, there would be no privacy for outright assault and other passengers would intervene at overt unpleasantness. The story about a foreign woman being raped on the roof of a moving train has become part of the rail travellers folklore. The moral is to keep off the roof!

Some trains have a separate, unreserved coach for female passengers, usually part of, or next to, the guard's brake van. This coach has SYLR painted on it, meaning Second Class Ladies' Luggage Room coach. On trains involving a night journey, government railway police will be posted to travel in the coach. In some 2nd class reserved carriages there is a cabin for 'Ladies Only' in which boys under 12 are also allowed, as are the boyfriends and husbands of occupants during daylight hours. These compartments, although with upholstered seats/berths, are uncomfortable for long-distance travel as they get stuffy, crowded and noisy.

Best for a woman alone is a berth in the 46-berth 2nd class air-conditioned two-tier dormitory coach (2nd AC) since these have two attendants on duty, lots of fellow passengers to protect a lone woman, and some have a "ladies only" loo. Because a berth in them is more expensive (actually higher than in 1st class), they appeal to a different kind of passenger. An English woman I met travelling alone said she always requested the upper bunk when making her reservation as she felt safer up there than in a lower one where people might be tempted to sit.

You will find as a woman sharing a cabin solely with Indian women that conversation is difficult, unless you speak Hindi or they are very Westernised. "Indian women," wrote one British woman traveller to me, "are so gentle and graceful, but difficult to make contact with."

The same correspondent travelled alone overnight in 2nd class on several occasions. "I chose the top bunk, although I had to crawl into it. It was OK until the early morning when on one trip I awoke to find a man sitting on the end of the bunk. He refused to move and I couldn't do anything about it as it was after 6am. I certainly felt invaded." (Berths are supposed to be for sitting from 0600 to 2100.)

She continues, "I noticed how, when I did travel with a male friend, I was almost disregarded by many men – after six weeks on my own, it was amusing and gave me a break from the endless, tedious questions. I would certainly recommend any solo woman traveller to go to *southern* India – she will be an object of curiosity and good-humoured questioning, but there is far less hassle and hard sell than in the north."

There are separate ladies' only waiting rooms at most stations. My friend writes, "There is an excellent 'ladies' waiting room' at Agra, very clean and quiet, where I managed to have a shower. Where they exist they can be a lovely respite from the chaos of platform life." Some stations have separate counters (and thus special queues) for ladies to buy rail tickets or to make reservations, but these are not found everywhere.

SPECIAL FACILITIES

In the 1996/97 railways budget, special facilities for the disabled were announced. It is planned to reserve one seat near the door in every second class compartment for disabled and handicapped passengers.

Another innovation is an executive chair car with audio channels for independent use and common video facilities. It is "to provide recreation to passengers," according to Indian Railways.

A coach with this video/audio system has been attached to the Western Railway's *Shatabdi Express*. A report says that "some problems have been experienced during this trial which are being sorted out". It adds, "On successful completion of the trials, it is proposed to introduce this system progressively in superfast trains".

Thanks for the warning.

Disabled travellers

Disabled travellers should be warned that the steps into and out of carriages (especially on to low platforms) are so steep that even for able-bodied passengers they can be hazardous. Wheelchairs are available at some stations for the (temporarily?) disabled with plenty of willing assistance from porters (for a tip) and from railway staff in an emergency. Rail travel for a disabled foreigner alone would be very difficult.

Group travel

The major long-haul tour operators, through their high street retailers, offer package holidays in India which include some rail travel. For the novice, this is a hassle-free way of sampling an Indian train but it is likely to be much more expensive than travelling independently. There are also specialist travel agents who arrange tours for dedicated rail enthusiasts, among them, Dorridge Travel Service Ltd, 7 Station Approach, Dorridge, Solihull, West Midlands, B93 8JA, England, tel: 01564 776252. Some of Dorridge's tours are escorted by the renowned rail photographer, Hugh Ballantyne. One couple, Jane and Ashley Butterfield, charter their own carriage and have it attached to different trains for groups to tour India (see *Chapter Eleven*). If you fancy going with a specialist agency, do check on their guarantees before parting with cash.

IN INDIA
Public holidays

Festivals, dry days, special events ... there seems to be no end to disruption to normal life, and the traveller will often arrive in a

---

HOLIDAY SPECIALS

In the holiday seasons of April to July and November to January it is often impossible to secure reservations, on the general quota in the better trains on trunk routes, unless bookings are made on the day they open. There are also regional variations which can create an excessive passenger demand because of local holidays and religious festivals.

To cater for the holiday demand, the various zonal railways run holiday specials to popular destinations. Details of them are available at stations and through newspapers. It is sometimes possible to get tickets on those extra trains.

Although many of these holiday specials are comprised of surplus carriages of dubious comfort, and run on slow flexible schedules, some are run on the lines of crack expresses, and may not be worse than their regular counterparts. (SR)

strange town when everything is closed. Further inconvenience comes from strikes, parades and demonstrations.

However carefully you plan, you will probably arrive somewhere when it's a local dry day. If it is and you are desperate for a drink, an experienced bicycle- or auto-rickshaw taxi driver should know a place where you can buy a bottle.

I tried it once. It wasn't a religious holiday but some sort of strike. We found the wine shop heavily shuttered. The rickshaw driver took my money, looked up and down the road, then banged on the shutters. A panel at the bottom of the door opened at pavement level and a hand shot out for the money. The panel closed only to open seconds later and the hand emerged holding a bottle of chilled beer.

National public holidays are January 26, Republic Day; August 15, Independence Day; October 2, Mahatma Gandhi's birthday; December 25, Christmas Day.

Time

Indian Standard Time is 5½ hours ahead of GMT, 4½ hours behind Australian Eastern Time and 9½ hours ahead of Eastern Standard Time in the USA. It's the same time in Nepal, but Sri Lanka is half an hour ahead. The Maldives is half an hour behind.

Train times are listed on the 24-hour clock in timetables and at most stations, although you will occasionally see notices referring to 12.00am, meaning 12 noon. In timetables, midnight is shown as 2400 hours for arrivals and 0000 hours for departures.

Business hours

Hours of business vary from region to region. Banks are generally open Monday to Friday from 1000 to 1400 hours, and 1000 to 1200 on Saturdays. Post offices operate from 1000 to 1700, Monday to Friday, and on Saturday mornings. Offices function from 0930 to 1700 and some Saturdays. Shops generally open from 0930 to 1800, except Sundays.

Reservation offices at stations have their own habits but those that are computerised open 0800 to 2000. Avoid the period between 1230 and 1400 as clerks will disappear for lunch at some stage, regardless of the people queuing for tickets.

Important stations are open 24 hours a day with ordinary tickets on sale, but some booking offices close 30 minutes before the departure of a train. The station superintendent's office is usually open 1000 to 1800; his duties are undertaken by his deputy outside those hours.

Electricity

Voltage in most places is 220 volts AC, 50 cycles, with some areas also having DC supplies. Check the voltage before using electrical appliances. Socket sizes vary, they're usually round pin.

Station retiring rooms are nearly all dimly lit so, if you intend reading in bed, your own 100 watt light bulb would help. Rooms with air-conditioning units often have huge boxes like disco equipment as part of their control system. Some retiring rooms have electrically heated hot water in their showers.

Taxis

The different kind of taxis available when you arrive at a station can be bewildering. Cars in the style of fifties saloons with yellow tops serve as standard taxis, sometimes with a meter which for tourists often does not work. Auto-rickshaws (known as "autos") – three wheeler vehicles with plastic canopies – are ubiquitous and generally very cheap. In some states they are metered; some even have stereo speakers and cassette players.

You'll find bicycle rickshaws, too, where the terrain is flat. A rare find nowadays is a rickshaw pulled by manpower, but these are plentiful around Calcutta's Howrah station (which also boasts river ferry access and tram transport, and India's only underground metro (see *Chapter Eight*.) Tongas (horse-drawn two-wheelers) and victorias (horse-drawn carriages) can also be hired. Always negotiate the price before boarding any kind of taxi. Being a foreigner, you'll be overcharged but you can at least be prepared for the fare by agreeing it before the start of the journey instead of getting a shock at the end of it.

One infuriating aspect of a rail journey is the wait at the destination station for a cab. In places like Calcutta's Howrah station, this can extend for two hours. Some people are tempted to take the offer of the out-of-turn taxi drivers who are willing to take a passenger, especially a foreigner, immediately if he is prepared to pay more. Remember these are illegal, as well as being unethical, and often dangerous. I was once told halfway through the busy Howrah Bridge to pay Rs250 for a Rs30 journey or, otherwise, get out. Negotiate first.

Drinking water

All stations have water for drinking at several points along the platform, either from standpipes, cold water dispensers or from water carts. This is drawn from the local supply so its potability is the same as that of the water drunk by the area's residents. A visitor will not have the immunity of locals so if you intend to drink it, collect it in a water bottle and dissolve a purifying tablet in it or filter it first. Like most travellers I never drink tap water, nor do I have ice in my drinks. Almost every tourist you see in India bears a bottle of mineral water in one hand. The best known water is called Bisleri, costing from Rs13 upwards for a litre bottle. To my mind the best water of all (perhaps it's the French connection) is called – and is from – Pondicherry.

The problem with some bottled mineral waters, according to

Chris, a student who had been in India for three weeks when I met him on the *Tamil Nadu Express*, is that although they have sealed caps, these can be removed without breaking the seal. This means that an empty, used water bottle could be filled with ordinary tap water and resealed and sold by unscrupulous or uncomprehending vendors. You'll soon know if you've got a dud by the taste.

Chris always slashed his empty, plastic bottles with a knife to prevent their re-use. I cut mine neatly in half, using the bottom half as a plastic cup, ideal for drinking duty-free scotch and soda when I don't trust the glasses in station retiring rooms.

You will find bottled mineral water on sale at main stations and others frequented by foreigners, although Indian travellers generally prefer sweet drinks as thirst quenchers. Bottled mineral water is available for sale on some trains; on *Rajdhani Expresses*, it is provided free in 1st AC class and plastic sachets of water are included with meals in other classes and on some other trains.

Alcohol

"English wine shops" are to be found close to stations; they don't sell English or any kind of wine, only Indian-made spirits and beer. Alcohol is not sold at any station or on any train, except on tourist specials like the *Palace on Wheels.*

Officially, drinking alcohol is illegal on trains, which only encourages passengers to fill their thermos flasks with whisky and ice instead of tea. A willing bearer (steward) will see that beer is provided with meals: he adds the code words "Bottle of Tomato Sauce" to your meal order. (But don't count on it. Having got used to those code words, I winked at a bearer taking my lunch order and asked for a bottle of tomato sauce. To my surprise, that's exactly what I got.) Sometimes an amenable bearer might produce a cold beer when the train stops long enough at a station with a wine shop close by.

The names, and strength, of Indian beers are amazing, with the most blatant being HE MAN 9,000, Bullet, Knock Out and Cannon 10,000. A popular lighter beer is Kingfisher. According to a catering inspector at the Rail Yatri Niwas in Howrah, the main choice of foreigners in beers is Black Label, produced by Kalyani Brewers. Its label describes it as "a masterpiece of the brewer's art, slow brewed for the connoisseur. Champagne carbonation." Look out – and enjoy – beers bearing labels that warn "Liquor ruins country, family and life".

At Balharshah station I was puzzled to hear a vendor calling out "Officer *chai* (or so I thought) as he walked along the platform. *Chai* is the Indian word for tea. It was only when the vendor reached into his pocket and produced a flask, that I realized what "officer's chai" really is: not tea, but whisky, actually named Officer's Choice.

Indian wine is not up to much, with the notable exception of Indian "champagne" and a new white wine, quite dry, called Riviera. Champagne India Ltd, with technical help from Piper-Heidsieck, produce a splendid sparkling wine called Marquise de Pompadour by the *méthode champénoise* from grapes grown near Bombay in Maharashtra state. It is the equivalent of a good French sparkling wine but you'll have to hunt hard for it because it has become very popular with the cognescenti, and for export. Many international brands of liquor are now available in ordinary bars, as are their Indian equivalents.

Smoking

Smoking on trains without the consent of fellow passengers is a punishable offence. It is not allowed in air-conditioned sleeper carriages, nor on local/suburban trains. Very few carriages are exclusively designated "non smoking" but you will find one 2nd class 3-tier non-smoking coach on the following trains: *Marwar Superfast Express, Grand Trunk Express, Kalka Mail, Paschim Express* and the *Kashi Vishwanath Express.*

Food

Meals cooked in railway kitchens will be prepared from fresh ingredients since supplies are bought daily to meet the huge demand. Kitchens are run by the railway zone catering division or by licencees and there is an army of catering inspectors and plenty of guidelines on standards to ensure quality.

There are usually two restaurants at stations: the vegetarian, abbreviated in conversation to "veg" (V) and non-vegetarian, referred to as "non-veg" (NV). Sometimes they will be the same restaurant with a door at one end for V and NV door at the other; usually they will have separate kitchens, but not always. Prices are standardised throughout the railway zone, and clearly displayed.

The meals served on trains are according to a limited standardised menu. Usually they are prepared at a base kitchen and put on to the train for serving at meal times to your seat. Simple items such as breakfast and snacks will be prepared in the pantry car, if there is one.

In railway catering one sometimes means two. For instance "one fried egg" is actually two eggs fried, and "one boiled egg" is two eggs boiled. Boiled eggs are hard boiled but if you ask for *hard* boiled eggs you are likely to get soft boiled ones since it is believed you are asking for *half* boiled.

You will be asked if you want a veg or non-veg meal when ordering lunch or dinner. Although a vegetarian meal has vegetables with the rice and lentils, a non-veg meal actually has no vegetables at all, with curried eggs as a substitute. To get a balanced meal I order a veg meal and a special non-veg one (chicken curry). Actually, the food is pretty dreadful and it takes a hardened stomach, or a very hungry one, to relish what's on offer. There are usually plenty of biscuit and fruit salesmen on station platforms to keep you provided with snacks. Chocolate is good for keeping the spirits up.

On most trains, meals are served in foil casseroles, with individual items wrapped in polythene bags. Some trains still use the chrome *thali* plates with compartments for different sauces around the rice. Drinks are served in disposable plastic cups although the disposable, clay teacups of old are still sometimes used by platform vendors. Some plastic cups bear the slogan "Please deform after use".

Tipping

Railway employees do not expect to be tipped. However, a bearer (the railway name for a waiter or steward) will look after a passenger extra well if there is the likelihood of a tip. Since the bearer rides the train for its entire journey, your welfare will be in his hands throughout a long trip, so it will suit you both to establish a friendly relationship from the outset.

If you haven't been paying after each meal, the bill for all meals, tea, soft drinks, etc, will be presented just before you reach your destination, so you can tip then if you want to: 10% or more up to Rs20, according to how much extra the bearer's done for you.

At the end of the journey, on prestigious trains like the *Rajdhani Express*, a bearer will present you with a tray of seeds on which is some money. He expects you to take a pinch of the seeds (for chewing as a digestif) and leave him some money as a tip. Whether you do is up to you. I usually don't as I prefer to tip at my discretion, not at a steward's insistence.

The attendant who brings the bedroll might hover for a tip, especially if he actually makes up the bed. It's not necessary. Sometimes you'll encounter an urchin who sweeps out the carriage and comes for a tip afterwards. That's really the coach attendant's job and the urchin shouldn't be on the train anyway. The Government of India tourist brochure says "Don't encourage beggars by giving them money".

Porters, who are supposed to carry your bag for Rs7 or so for a head load of 40kg, depending on the station rates, will always want a tip and probably more than you're prepared to give them. I was once feeling generous and gave a Rs10 tip on top of the standard fee and was astonished when the porter demanded more for carrying my bags to the retiring room. I threw him out.

In hotels and restaurants a service charge is sometimes added but tip if you feel it's worth it. Retiring room attendants only deserve a tip if they have looked after you, your luggage and the room properly. But it's not essential.

Communications

Many stations have post offices within their premises or close by. For an extra fee, letters can be posted on some trains for delivery at the train's destination. Letters can be sent to passengers at railway stations and will be deposited in a glass-fronted cabinet outside the office of the station superintendent (SS) for collection, but the system is not reliable since anyone can remove the letter.

Telegrams can be sent from Railway Licensed Telegraph Offices to passengers travelling by train in any class. The name of the station where the train stops (it must be for at least ten minutes) and the number or name of the train should be included in the address. Inland telegrams can be sent from stations. The rates are low.

It is possible to telephone from major stations, either locally or long distance. Sometimes the telephones are run by attendants who are handicapped, with their booth being sponsored by the local Rotary or Lions Club.

You will often run into unexpected difficulties in communicating with railway catering staff, especially if you ask for something that they think is odd. Getting a tea bag and a flask of hot water (which is standard issue on the *Shatabdi Express*) to make your own tea is sometimes hard to explain, even to a college-trained and English-speaking catering inspector.

I have a theory that this failure of communication stems from a preconceived notion of what you want, instead of actually listening to the request, or perhaps it is through a nervous desire to please

NEW TECHNOLOGY

Some important stations have telephone numbers with recorded announcements of train departure times, etc. Even seat availability can be determined by telephone.

After the introduction of the interactive voice response system for reservation enquiry, Eastern Railway announced another great service: the position availability enquiry. I tried it out.

On dialling, I was asked to dial a zero, and then asked to dial the train number, then the date in a four-digit format (1708 for August 17), followed by the class code where 1 is for sleeper, 2 for 2AC, 3 for 3AC and 9 for others. When I dialled 9 I was prompted once more to enter in the class by further subdividing into 1AC, first, AC chair and executive chair class, etc.

I was then given the availability position for the requested date. If confirmed bookings were not available, the voice would give the earliest available date too. Then it asked if I wanted to try for some other date or class, and finally bid me goodbye. Very classy, very helpful.

Unfortunately, when I tried again two days after the introduction of the service, the phone remained unanswered. (SR)

which results in the reverse of what you request, in case you change your mind.

Enquiries

Do not rely on the staff at the enquiry office to give you the correct times of trains, especially if your English is heavily accented, since they might not understand your question properly. Anyway, they will be preoccupied with all the Indian travellers shouting at them. Train arrival and departure times are given on noticeboards in all stations. If you are uncertain, ask a responsible looking official face to face – you'll probably be delighted at the help you'll receive.

Telephone enquiries

For general travel enquiries, the major stations have computerised answering with prompting to achieve the desired answer. In Delhi, for instance, after dialling 1330 for a reservation enquiry (with answers in English) you should hear a voice saying "Please dial zero". After doing so, there is a beep. You then dial 1 for arrival/departure and 2 for reservation status. On being prompted, you dial the train number for the arrival/departure information and the key number on the computerised reservation coupon (see next chapter) and you will find out if you have a confirmed reservation or not. If you're lucky.

The railway enquiry telephone numbers are not standardised throughout the railways and they also seem to change quite often. The hotel where you are staying, or a wayside, attendant-operated telephone kiosk, should have up-to-date numbers.

Enquiry	Delhi	Bombay	Calcutta	Madras
General	3313535	4933535	Howrah: 2203535 Sealdah: 3503535	
(Recorded)	131	(CR)134 (WR)131	131	
Reservation	1330	(CR)135 (WR)306	135	132
Arrival		4937575	2203535	
	North 1331	(CR)136		
	East 1332	(WR)132		567575
	West 1333			133(BG)
	South 1334			134(MG)
Departure	North 1336	(CR)137		
	East 1337			
	West 1338			
	South 1335			

Foreign embassies in India

Canada 7/8 Shantipath, Chanakyapuri, New Delhi 110021; tel: 6876560

UK Shantipath, Chanakyapuri, New Delhi 110021; tel: 6872161

USA Shantipath, Chanakyapuri, New Delhi 110021; tel: 600651/6113033

Other embassy details may be found in local telephone directories.

Language

Signs at stations are supposed to be in three languages: Hindi, English and the state language. Some stations have signs hanging above a platform and as you walk down its length they all seem to be in Hindi. Turn around and walk back and they are all in English, since the signs are double sided.

English is understood throughout India and you will get involved in some deep discussion in English with fellow passengers. The station superintendents speak English as do other senior station staff. In the south, English will be more readily understood among ordinary people than in the north. If you are stuck, someone will usually be around who can help translate. See also *Language*, page 254.

Chapter Three

Ticket to Ride

"What I can't understand," said the tall Dutchman who boarded the train at Bhubaneswar and sat opposite me, "is how to buy a ticket to travel by train."

The Dutchman was a professor in his forties, passionately interested in medieval temples which is what had drawn him to Bhubaneswar. He explained the reason for his question.

"I have a ticket but I don't understand how I got it. I came to the station yesterday and told a clerk I wanted to travel on this train. I filled in the form he gave me then he told me to join a queue.

"I waited an hour but when I was almost at the counter, the clerk said he was going to lunch. I was very angry and left my form there and went to lunch too. When I returned, I'd lost my place in the queue so I went up to another window where no one was queuing. The clerk looked at me, took my money and gave me a ticket."

The Dutch professor looked bemused. "How did it happen? How did the second clerk know where I wanted to go? He didn't ask me."

The professor's experience illustrates the good and the bad of the ticket-buying process. He was frustrated by queuing at a counter that closed just as he was about to reach it, so he lost his temper and made a fuss.

Being tall and fair he was easily recognisable so when he returned, even though he went to another ticket window, the clerk knew what he wanted and helped him.

There is a policy in Indian Railways to help foreign tourists to make their reservations. However, most foreigners would rather join a queue and wait their turn than demand special treatment because they are foreigners.

Indian tourists who feel themselves to be important will not hesitate to ask the chief reservation supervisor (CRS) or the station superintendent (SS) for help if they need it. On Indian Railways, foreigners are regarded as important and are actually expected to approach officials for help. However awkward you may feel, if you want to reserve without hassles, take advantage of this.

Where to buy a ticket

Unless you have an Indrail Pass (see page 51) you will need to buy a ticket for the journey. This means a visit to the railway station. The first rule is not to join any queue until you are absolutely certain it is the right one, and don't join it near closing time.

If in doubt, start at the enquiry counter. Alternatively, a polite request to the chief reservation supervisor (CRS) for help can work wonders, so don't be shy to approach him. Tickets should only be purchased from station counters or from official sources. There are touts at the major stations who will take advantage of a foreigner's confusion (or frustration) to offer tickets on trains that are fully booked, or even cut-price tickets. Avoid them since trouble and complications are bound to result. These touts are not always immediately recognisable. Many railway officials dress in white.

TOUTS

In *Rail News*, a bi-weekly newsletter edited by a veteran campaigner for better railways, C B L Bhatnagar, president of the Indian Railway Passengers' Conference Association, the following comment appeared in May, 1995.

"Oh what a relief! God bless the kind tout who arranged the reservation for me at the 11th hour.

"Got a telegram from Delhi that I must appear in a court there the next day. Intending to travel by the Paschim Express, I reached Bombay Railway station at 9am and joined a long queue. With the help of an obliging stranger I broke the queue and pushed my requisition slip through the window at the counter. I was told that no accommodation was available and that there were 149 people ahead of me on the Waiting List.

"Dismayed and dejected I looked hither and thither when I was accosted by the kind stranger who had pushed me in the front of the queue. The stranger asked me to give him the requisition slip to enable him to find out if he could help me.

"He sauntered away and after some time returned, gave back the slip to me and casually told me that if I could pay Rs150 in addition to the rail fare the accommodation could be arranged. I was in a difficult and helpless position and I had reluctantly to accept his offer. I paid him the money and after a few minutes he brought a computerised ticket with confirmed reservation, handed it over to me and told me not to worry and go to the train standing on the platform and occupy the accommodation ear-marked on the ticket.

"I had my doubts but I could do nothing. I was pleasantly surprised when the conductor guided me to my berth in the coach. I blessed the stranger from the bottom of my heart.

"I realise he was a tout. I do not know how touts operate and what is their arrangement with the railway staff and the railway police constables, but in view of the difficulties faced by railway passengers, these touts are the saviours."

When I was approached at New Delhi station by a gentleman in white shirt and trousers who asked if I was looking for the ITB (International Tourist Bureau), I assumed he was an official. I was busy at the time and didn't stop to talk. Later I saw him with two foreigners in the ITB offering to change money for them. He was not a railway employee at all and quickly left when the ITB supervisor questioned him.

Rail travellers' service agents have been appointed in some areas to purchase tickets and secure reservations on behalf of passengers. They are authorised to charge a fee of not more than Rs15 for upper class bookings and Rs8 for other classes.

An Australian couple told me they always use travel agents in India for their ticket purchase, usually paying about Rs20 for the reservation as the travel agent's fee. Since it saves time, they considered it worth it.

Trains at a Glance (TAG) states that tickets can be purchased at "Railway Booking Agencies or through Railway Tourist Agent".

Single journey ticket

At most stations, the ticket purchasing and reservations procedure has been combined (see *Making a reservation*, page 61). Tickets to travel without a reserved seat or in 2nd class non-reserved carriages can be purchased from the booking office window labelled for the class you intend to travel, usually up to the time the train departs. The booking counters will normally be found in the station lobby, not with the counters issuing journey-cum-reservation tickets.

A passenger who has no reservation and who buys a ticket and boards the train and finds a seat may still have to pay a reservation fee if that seat is normally subject to a reservation charge. This can be the only way of getting a seat on some trains if the unreservable seats, usually in a 2nd class carriage at the end of the train, are all occupied to overflowing.

A passenger who intends to travel in the unreserved 2nd class coach of a superfast train must purchase a supplementary charge ticket (for Rs5) before boarding the train. Otherwise there is a penalty payable on the train as well as the supplementary charge.

It is possible at some stations to buy an unreserved single journey 2nd class ticket a day in advance of travelling, to save queuing on the actual day of travel. The day of travel will be endorsed on the ticket, which will only be valid until midnight on that day.

Tickets not issued by computer are cardboard and coloured according to class:

White	AC 1st class
Green	1st class (mail, express or ordinary) and AC sleeper (2 tier) class
Orange	AC chair car

Drab   2nd class (mail or express)
Yellow   2nd class (ordinary)

Where printed tickets are not available, you will be issued with a coupon on which the ticket details are entered by hand.

Platform tickets

In theory, only people holding tickets are allowed on station platforms. Platform tickets are obtainable from a separate ticket window. They cost Rs2.00 and are valid for two hours.

If you are trying to buy a ticket at the last minute and can't get one in time because the queue at the window is too long, buy a platform ticket instead. Before boarding the train, present the platform ticket to the guard. He will issue a guard's certificate and charge you the full fare for the journey. A passenger trying to travel on a platform ticket without the guard's certificate will be treated as a ticketless traveller. Since the Indrail Pass is a ticket, holders do not need a platform ticket.

Ticketless travel

The penalties for travelling without a ticket are high and can include jail. Some stations have a magistrate's court within their premises for dealing with ticketless travellers and other offenders.

Travelling without a ticket is almost a tradition in India, originating during the British days when passengers did it to harm an alien ruler. After partition it was done to express a grievance against the government. The motive now, unless part of an organised protest, is simply to cheat the railways.

In the north of India especially, ticketless passengers add to the problem of overcrowding in the cheaper carriages where checks aren't so rigorous. Another problem in northern areas are those passengers who don't recognise that some carriages are for those who have paid more for the privilege of an upper class seat. They want to sit there too, regardless of what class of travel they have actually paid for. If a passenger with a 2nd class ticket is caught in a 1st class seat, not only must the full 1st class fare be paid but a penalty too. However, it is possible for a 2nd class ticket holder to upgrade to 1st class by paying the difference in fares. Permission must be obtained from the guard before the passenger occupies the higher class of seat.

Ticketless travel is most prevalent in the states of Bihar and Uttar Pradesh where thousands gatecrash on to overcrowded trains daily. If the train isn't stopping where they want to get off, they have been known to pull the emergency brake cord. Ticketless travel is increasing, especially on slow country passenger trains where there are seldom any checks.

Ticket inspection

A passenger must have a ticket, even if it is only a platform ticket with a guard's certificate. Travelling ticket examiners (TTEs) check tickets, even on trains that don't have a vestibule. TTEs are sometimes in plain clothes but carry identification to show when requested. On long distance trains, few passengers are ticketless except for those hitching a lift between rural stops.

Tickets are sometimes inspected at the entrance to platforms and they will be collected at the exits after a journey. Tickets are required by people wanting to use the waiting and retiring rooms, to prove that they are genuine passengers.

Lost tickets and refunds

If you buy a ticket and lose it, there is no chance of a refund, although you can get a duplicate ticket, issued at the discretion of the railways, if it was for reserved travel and can thus be traced through the system. However, there are charges to pay. For a journey under 500km, an additional 25% of the total fare is levied. If the lost ticket was for a journey of more than 500km, then 10% of the fare is charged. The minimum that will be charged is the equivalent of 25% of the 500km ticket.

Lost tickets for trains like the *Rajdhani* and *Shatabdi* Expresses, which have an all inclusive fare structure, are replaced on payment of 25% of the total fare, irrespective of distance.

Refunds are possible on unused tickets without reservations only if presented up to three hours after the departure of the train. A fee of Rs10 is deducted as clerkage from the full refund.

Tickets with reservations which are unused can be presented up to a certain time but a lot depends on the circumstances of your missing the train (such as being delayed in getting to the station due to a landslide or flight cancellation, proof of which must be supplied), and much is left to the discretion of the stationmaster.

Cancellation of reserved tickets before departure attracts penalties according to the following formula:

• Application for refund more than one day in advance, excluding the date of the journey:

AC 1st class	Rs50
1st class/AC sleeper	Rs30
AC chair car	Rs30
Sleeper class	Rs20
2nd class	Rs10

• Application one day in advance and up to four hours before the scheduled departure of the train:
Forfeit of 25% of the fare, subject to the minimum charges appearing above.

• Application within four hours before the scheduled departure, or within three hours for journeys of up to 200km, or within six hours for journeys of 200–500km, and within 12 hours for journeys of more than 500km, and after the actual departure of the train:
Refund of only 50%, subject to a minimum deduction of the amounts listed above.

Travel restrictions

Some trains have restrictions on carrying passengers over short distances. These are usually the major expresses and they will not carry passengers making journeys of less than 160km and in some cases not less than 600km, according to the train. Indrail Pass holders escape these restrictions. The small print of the timetables reveals other restrictions too. For instance, passengers are not allowed to carry milk in cans or bottles on the 1352 Bhusaval passenger train between Kalyan and Bombay.

Breaking the journey

If you hold a ticket for a single journey of more than 500km, you can break the journey en route, providing the first break is made after you have travelled at least 500km from the starting station. With a ticket for a journey of up to 1,000km you can break the journey only once. For a journey of over 1,000km, a second break of journey is allowed. The period of break of journey must not exceed two days, excluding day of arrival and departure. You would not be allowed to break the journey over a suburban section. If you have to change trains on a through-ticket journey, it is treated as a journey break only if you stay at the connecting station for more than 24 hours. The ticket should be endorsed by the stationmaster (SM) where the break occurs, with the station code, the date and the SM's initials. Foreign tourists travelling on an Indrail Pass can break their journey anywhere en route without the distance restriction.

If you decide to extend your journey beyond your destination, the TTE (travelling ticket examiner) can authorise it, but only before you reach your original destination.

Fare extras: superfast trains

There is a supplement payable for travel on certain superfast expresses and mail trains. A list of the trains appears in *Chapter Twelve*. The supplements are paid at the time of reservation/ticket purchase and are the same for children and adults. Indrail Pass holders pay nothing extra. The rates are:

AC 1st class	Rs25
AC 2 tier sleeper	Rs15
AC 3 tier sleeper	Rs15
AC chair car	Rs15
1st class	Rs15
Sleeper class	Rs10
2nd class (sitting)	Rs5

Sleeper charge

The surcharge for sleeper accommodation was abolished with the introduction of the "sleeper class" of accommodation; all fares for reserved berths in all classes now include the cost of the sleeper berth.

FARES

Carrying passengers is not lucrative for Indian Railways, according to a DRM who told me that it is a public, not a profitable, service. He seemed to regard passengers as a necessary evil. The carrying of freight was his main interest since that is profit generating and actually subsidises the passenger services. Attempts to raise fares are resisted by the travelling public who consider they pay enough already. However, fares now rise a little in the railway budgets, with a raise in the 1996 railway budget of 10% on upper class fares for mail and express journeys over 200km, and 5% on sleeper class fares. At the lower end of the scale, fares are cheap; at the upper end – for Indians – they are not. The top fare on the *Rajdhani Express* in Ac 1st class for the 1,384km overnight ride from New Delhi to Bombay Central is more than ten times the lowest fare by mail or express train in Sleeper class on the same route.

Throughout the Indian Railways network, fares are calculated on a fixed price per kilometre from station of origin to destination, according to the class travelled. The timetables show the kilometres between stations so it is possible to work out the approximate cost by reference to the fare table produced in the zonal timetables and in TAG. Examples of standard fares between stations cannot be quoted with complete accuracy because every fare depends on the route taken. For instance, there are four different routes between

Passenger fares table (in rupees)

	Distance in km					
	1	100	500	1,000	2,000	5,000
Mail/Express						
AC 1st class	176	329	1,048	1,713	2,878	6,255
AC 2 tier sleeper	132	238	612	970	1,537	2,873
AC 3 tier sleeper	72	107	344	525	852	1,764
1st class	72	139	464	756	1,259	2,731
AC chair car	72	85	275	420	681	1,411
Sleeper class	62	62	135	219	309	529
2nd class (sitting)	10	27	102	166	235	402
Ordinary trains						
1st class	22	126	421	687	1,144	2,482
Sleeper class	33	33	67	95	140	270
2nd class	2	14	50	72	106	205
Extra charges not included						

Delhi and Calcutta and three between Delhi and Jammu Tawi, all with different fares. In addition, there are various supplements according to the train actually travelled on, as well as reservation fees.

The minimum cost of travel by train is Rs2.00 which buys up to 10km of train ride in ordinary 2nd class. The most expensive minimum cost is Rs176 which will give 25km of air-conditioned 1st class travel. A sample of fares from 1 to 5,000km appears on page 48, in Indian rupees.

Discounts

Even though 2nd class fares are low for foreigners they can represent an obstacle to rail travel for low income or no-income Indians. Concessions are made to certain groups with reductions up to 75% on fares. The list of groups includes sportsmen, professional entertaining parties, students up to 25 years old on study and vacation trips, articled clerks, research scholars, blind or deaf and dumb people, TB, cancer and leprosy sufferers, the orthopaedically handicapped, nurses and midwives, and war and police widows.

Free rail travel is given to MPs and former MPs, to nearly 100,000 freedom fighters, as well as to serving – and former – railway employees and their families. No wonder the trains are crowded!

The only discount for foreigners is the Indrail Pass. However, foreign students under 25 who are resident in India (and therefore not eligible for the Indrail Pass) can qualify for a 50% reduction on fares for approved journeys, such as to attend a government-organised seminar, to visit places of historical or other importance, or to go home during vacations.

Children between five and 12 years of age travel at half fare but are subject to the same minimum fares as for an adult. Children age five and under travel free.

Kilometre distance

As with air fares, the price per kilometre drops the further a passenger travels so it makes sense to buy a ticket to the furthest point on your journey and take advantage of the rules about allowing a break in the journey on the way. To help arrive at an estimate of what it might cost, the following is a list of the kilometre distance between selected stations. However, different distances may be used in fare construction and there are also the various supplements.

New Delhi to	Madras Central	2,188km
	Howrah (Calcutta)	1,441
	Bombay Central (with WR)	1,384
	Bombay VT (via Bhusaval)	1,538

	Trivandrum	3,054km
	Agra Cantt	199
	Bangalore City	2,491
	Jammu Tawi	589
	Patna	992
Howrah to	Bombay VT	1,968
	Jammu Tawi	1,967
	Madras Central	1,662
Bombay VT	Madras Central	1,279

The following table shows the fares between selected pairs of stations as at July 1996:

Station	AC 1st class	AC 2 tier	1st class mail/exp	AC 3 tier	AC chair car	Sleeper class mail/exp
Mumbain–Pune	489	333	217	172	137	62
Delhi–Chandigarh	636	417	283	223	178	82
Delhi–Jaipur	733	466	324	247	197	98
Madras–Bangalore	809	506	359	270	216	104
Mumbai–Ahmedabad	1,048	612	464	344	275	135
Delhi–Jammu Tawi	1,202	720	528	389	311	153
Delhi–Shimla	1,202	720	528	389	311	153
Delhi–Bhopal	1,379	823	604	438	350	177
Madras–Trivandrum	1,602	924	704	494	395	209
Delhi–Patna	1,753	1,037	768	548	438	225
Mumbai–Bangalore	1,999	1,147	876	614	491	247
Delhi–Mumbai	2,202	1,239	965	672	537	263
Delhi–Howrah	2,258	1,262	995	687	549	270
Mumbai–Varanasi	2,316	1,281	1,014	702	561	272
Howrah–Madras	2,519	1,389	1,095	752	601	287
Delhi–Secunderabad	2,540	1,405	1,116	764	611	287
Delhi–Bhubaneshwar	2,727	1,474	1,192	810	648	304
Madras–Ahmedabad	2,767	1,494	1,213	823	658	304
Mumbai–Jammu Tawi	2,841	1,525	1,243	844	675	309
Delhi–Guwahati	2,878	1,537	1,259	852	681	309
Delhi–Madras	3,104	1,626	1,359	915	732	324
Delhi–Vasco da Gama	3,104	1,626	1,359	915	732	324
Delhi–Bangalore	3,403	1,744	1,488	997	797	346
Delhi–Trivandrum	4,120	2,027	1,800	1,189	951	396

Adjusted fares

The fares to many destinations are posted on the walls of station booking halls. They are the basic fares without the addition of any supplements.

On some routes, the fare per kilometre is adjusted in order, according to one official source, "to avoid losses as the cost of construction and maintenance on certain sections is considerably heavy". These routes provide spectacular journeys which are often undertaken by tourists. They are listed below.

Railway	Chargeable distance
Neral–Matheran	63km
Khandwa–Hingoli	Distance plus $33\frac{1}{3}$ %
Ambala–Kalka	Distance × $1\frac{1}{3}$
Kalka–Shimla	Distance × 3
Pathankot–Jogindernagar	Distance × $1\frac{1}{2}$
Mettupalaiyam–Wellington	Distance × $2\frac{3}{4}$
Wellington–Udagmandalam	Distance × 2
Kottavalasa–Kirandul	Distance × $1\frac{1}{2}$
Fatehpur Shekhawati–Churu	Distance × 2
Udaipur–Himatnagar	Distance × $1\frac{1}{3}$

THE INDRAIL PASS (IRP)

If you intend making more than two trips by train, consider buying an Indrail Pass: it may not always save you money but there are other advantages, mainly of convenience. Some of them, compared with the purchase of several single journey tickets, are listed below.

The Indrail Pass can be bought in India or abroad from general sales agents (GSAs). The cost is calculated in US dollars and payment in foreign currency is based on the dollar price. Passes purchased in India must be paid for in dollars or pounds sterling; credit cards are not accepted.

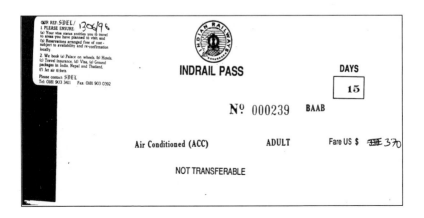

Ticket comparisons

Indrail Pass	Single journey tickets
Unlimited kilometres	Distance restriction
Network freedom	Travel restricted
Separate ticket purchase not required	Ticket must be purchased for every journey
All reservations can be made at the same time	Separate reservations must be made for every journey
Reservations can be made by mail through home country GSA	Reservations must be made at stations in person
Reservations can be made 360 days in advance	Reservations can only be made 30 days, or less, in advance
Reservation priority	No priority
Eligible for foreign tourist quota	Only eligible for foreign tourist quota at some stations if pay in foreign currency
No restrictions in travelling short distances on any train	Restrictions on travelling short distances
Can break journey anywhere	Restrictions on breaking journey
Can use waiting and retiring rooms anywhere, any time	Can only use rooms if holding day's ticket
No supplements payable	Supplements payable
No surcharges payable	Surcharges payable
No reservation fees payable	Reservation fees payable
No minimum distance charge	Minimum distance charge
No need for platform ticket	Platform ticket needed for platform visit if not travelling
Can board any train	Must buy a ticket before boarding any train
Recognised as a Very Important Traveller	No special recognition
Reduced queuing	Frequent queuing

Where to buy the Indrail Pass outside India

General sales agents (GSAs) for the sale of the Indrail Pass out of India have been appointed in Australia, Bangladesh, Canada, Finland, France, Germany, Japan, Malaysia, Mauritius, Oman, Sharjah, South Africa, Thailand, UK and the USA.

Australia Adventure World, PO Box 480, North Sydney, NSW 2059, Australia; tel: 02 9567766; telex: AA 22680; fax: 00 612995 677 07

Bangladesh Omnitrans International Ltd, National Scouts Bhaban (4th Floor) 70/1, Inner Circular Road, Kakrall, Dhaka, Bangladesh; tel: 834401 (4 lines); telex: 63224; fax: 00 880281 3003

Canada Hariworld Travel Inc, 1 Financial Place, 1 Adelaide Street East, Concourse Level, Toronto, Canada M5C 2V8; tel: 366 2000; telex: 0623918; fax: 00 146660 20

Finland Intia Keskua Ltd, Yrjonkatu 8-10, 00120, Helsinki, Finland; tel: 90 851066; telex: 12 5087; fax: 00 3580611970

Germany Asra Orient, Kaiserstrasse 50, D-6000, Frankfurt M1, Germany; tel: 069 253098; telex: 41345; fax: 00 496923 2045

Japan Japan Travel Bureau, Overseas Travel Division, 1-6-4 Marunouchi, Chiyoda KU, Tokyo-100, Japan; tel: 81 031 284 7391; telex: 28648; fax: 033 0208014

Malaysia City East West Travels, No 23, Jalan Yap Ah Shak, 50300, Kuala Lumpur, Malaysia; tel: 2930569, 2910872 and 2918070; telex: BICCI 33526; fax: 00 60329 09214

Oman National Travel & Tourism, PO Box 962, Muttrah, Muscat, Sultanate of Oman; tel: 561377; fax: 00 96 8566125; telex: 5501

South Africa M K Bobby Naidoo Travel Agency, PO Box 2878, Durban, South Africa 4001; telex: 620 358; fax: 00 273130 936 28

Thailand S S Travel Service, 10/12–13, S S Buidling, Convent Road, Bangkok 10500, Thailand; tel: 2367188, 2360285, 2339478, 2339813, 2351195, 2350557, 2350558; telex: 87450; fax: 00 662236 7186

UAE Sharjah National Travel & Tourist Agency (Pvt) Ltd, PO Box 17, Sharjah, UAE; tel: 351411; telex: 68021 STTTAEM; fax: 06 374968; fax: 00 971436 7966

UK S D Enterprises Ltd, 103 Wembley Park Drive, Wembley HA9 8HG, Middlesex, England; tel: 0181 903 3411; telex: 940 12027 SDEL G; fax: 00 44 181 903 0392

USA Hariworld Travels Inc, 30 Rockefeller Plaza, Shop 21, North Mezzanine, New York NY 10112, USA; tel: 212 957 3000; telex: 4952383; fax: 00 121299 733 20

The ticket doctor

If you can get to London during the planning stage of your trip, there is a remarkable man who will answer all your questions and help plan the itinerary. He is Dr S Dandapani who has his office in a corner shop near Wembley Park station, on the underground Metropolitan and Jubilee lines. The full address is S D Enterprises Ltd, 103 Wembley Park Drive, Wembley, Middlesex HA9 8HG, England, tel: 0181 903 3411, fax: 0181 903 0392; telex: 94012027 SDEL G. Dr Dandapani is the GSA in Britain for the Indrail Pass and for the *Palace on Wheels*, but he and his family do much more than that.

"Selling a ticket is child's play," he told me. "I'm preparing people to visit a great country and come back happy." Dr Dandapani overflows with sound advice, not just on places to visit, but on how to make the most of the trip and even what underwear is best (cotton; jockey shorts for men).

He is a sociologist who worked for Indian Railways for 25 years and for 15 years as a UN adviser, as well as being an author of more than a dozen books on business management. His son, who helps him in the business, has inherited his father's enthusiasm for, and knowledge of, Indian Railways' journeys.

Dr Dandapani is the ever-cheerful pioneer of promoting the Indrail Pass. Even if you can't get to London to meet him, a phone call or fax will bring immediate advice on your trip. Whenever you buy an Indrail Pass or a ticket from him you will be able to benefit from his years of experience, and be deluged with tips on what to take, how or where to go and how to get what you want out of India.

If you have a specific reason for wanting to visit India, tell Dr Dandapani. It's amazing what he can arrange. The parents of a friend of mine wanted to visit a small town named after my friend's grandfather who had lived in India. Dr Dandapani not only plotted the whole rail itinerary, he also arranged for the station superintendent to greet the couple on arrival and for a surprise civic reception for them.

Should you have doubts about travelling by train, even after reading this book, discuss them with Dr Dandapani. His desire is for passengers to be satisfied with their train travels and he has thousands of letters of appreciation to prove they are. He likes to say that he has two million railwaymen working with him and when he promises something, you can depend on him.

"Everything is possible with Indian Railways," he once told me, "but you must allow adequate time."

To help travellers who have a vague idea of where they would like

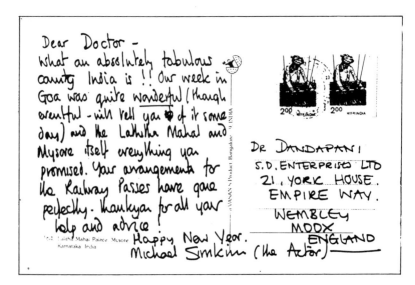

to go, but have neither the time nor the inclination (nor the right timetable), to plan their own itinerary, Dr Dandapani's staff have prepared over a dozen itineraries. These are based on the kind of journey the majority of visitors to India want to experience, including visits to Agra, Rajasthan, Khajuraho, Shimla, Darjeeling, Goa, Ooty and Mysore from either Bombay or New Delhi, utilising trains with practical departure and arrival times.

Dr Dandapani sells more Indrail Passes than anyone else in the world. If you can't visit him, give him a call or write with your itinerary and purchase the pass by post since he will send it by airmail to any prospective rail traveller anywhere in the world. (I once had a pass sent to me by Dr Dandapani when I was in the Maldives as I wanted to fly from there direct to Trivandrum and catch a train to Delhi. Everything worked perfectly and when I got to Delhi I found all my onward reservations were confirmed too.)

British travellers form the vast majority of purchasers of the IRP followed by French, Australian, Japanese and German. The most popular is the 30-day 1st class pass which also permits travel in AC 2 tier sleeper. Next in demand come 21-day and 15-day 1st class passes.

In India

Indrail Passes can be bought at the following stations: Ahmedabad, Agra Cantt, Amritsar, Aurangabad, Bangalore City, Bombay, Calcutta, Chandigarh, Gorakhpur, Hyderabad, Jaipur, Madras, New Delhi, Puttaparthi Town booking agency, Rameswaram, Secunderabad, Trivandrum, Vadodara, Varanasi, Vasco de Gama and Vijaywada. They cannot be bought at Tiruchchirappalli station, even though that city has an international airport which is a gateway for travellers arriving from Sri Lanka.

Indrail passes are also available at Delhi, Bombay, Calcutta and Madras airports and from some travel agents.

Pass details

The Indrail Pass looks like an airline ticket and is issued for three different grades of train travel:

1) Blue or white ticket	AC 1st class
2) Green ticket	AC sleeper (2 tier), AC sleeper (3 tier), 1st class, AC chair car
3) Orange/yellow ticket	Sleeper class (2nd class)

The front cover bears the pass number and indicates its total validity periods. The pass is valid for one year from the date of issue and its validity period starts from the day the first journey begins to midnight on the final day.

The terms and conditions, kept very simple, are outlined inside the front cover. Journey and reservation particulars are noted by carbon duplicate on what is called the "passenger foil". There are two of these, with the second one forming the back cover of the ticket. The GSA keeps the original of the ticket's "foils" on which he has entered the passenger details. Also recorded on the foil are the passenger's name, nationality, passport number, fare paid, signature and stamp of the GSA, and the date of issue. The validity of the ticket showing the first and last day of usage is noted in a space at the foot of the ticket. There is space on the rest of the ticket for endorsements showing the train number, date, from/to and remarks concerning every train trip included on the itinerary.

Armed with this you have a permit to travel "wherever you like, whenever you like and by whatever train you like" within the period of its validity. The words are those of Indian Railways: a remarkable concession. However, the pass does not guarantee reserved accommodation, unless you confirm all your arrangements with the GSA at the time of purchase. Even so, onward reservations should be confirmed in India by verifying them at the reservation office on arrival at each destination.

The Indrail Pass can be purchased up to 360 days before travel, and reservations can be made at the same time. Reservations by local travellers within India can only be made up to 30 days in advance, so a foreigner requesting a reservation between 31 and 360 days before a journey is competing only with other foreigners for a seat or berth. Even within the 30-day period before travel, a foreigner booking from overseas gets priority. The reservation (for which there is no charge) will be confirmed by telex to the GSA within seven days.

Ron and Sarah Keen bought a 30-day Indrail Pass (green) – for AC sleeper (2 tier) before leaving New Zealand. "We had a little trouble with pre-booking the rail segments as obviously what we were doing was unusual for New Zealand. The agent for rail travel (not our travel agent) got confused with place names – though I consider Bombay and Bangalore to neither look nor sound alike. Fortunately, we knew what we wanted and with the assistance of your book and perseverance, we got our bookings sorted out. One segment took three attempts before they got it right!"

In India, the process of making a reservation is greatly simplified by the pass. It entitles you to berths from the foreign tourist quota, and will also bring out the best in station staff willing to help. There are none of the reservation charges or supplements that are levied on single-journey tickets.

The Indrail Pass can be bought by foreign nationals who are not resident in India and by Indians residing outside India. A foreign national resident in India is regarded as Indian for the purpose of train travel and is not entitled to reservations from the foreign tourist quota. Correspondingly, an Indian resident abroad, with passport to prove it, is regarded as a foreign tourist.

When buying an IRP (or seeking a reservation from the foreign tourist quota) in India, take along your passport to prove that you have not been in India longer than six months and are not officially resident in India. The IRP issued in India is a folded card with holder's name entered on the front together with country of passport origin and passport number. There is no space on it to enter reservations so it is more flexible than a pass purchased overseas that has an itinerary scrawled on it.

A pass can be purchased out of India by mail, with an accompanying draft in US dollars, from the International Tourist Bureau (ITB), New Delhi Railway Station, New Delhi 110055, India, fax: New Delhi 343050. However, if you are going to purchase by mail, I suggest you do so through Dr Dandapani who is accustomed to sending passes by registered airmail to most countries of the world (see page 53).

To quote the SR (Southern Railway) timetable, "the Indrail Pass ticket will also be issued for: (1) a foreign tourist demanding an Indrail Pass for his Indian wife; and (2) a foreign tourist preferring to take a guide instead of depending on local assistance." The reference to a guide means someone officially recognised by an Indian tourism authority, so you can't take along an Indian chum, unless he's licensed, of course.

The pass is not transferable and the traveller should be prepared to show passport as proof of identity.

What it costs
The tariff on page 58 was effective from August 1 1996, with fares given in US dollars. The passes for half-day, one day, two days and four days are only sold out of India; other passes are available in India as well as overseas.

A child is between the ages of five and 12 years. Children below five can travel free on the Indrail Pass of their parents.

Short-term passes
The short-term passes of half-day, one day, two days and four days were introduced for sale overseas only, to help travellers who want to make a short journey on arrival in India and would not have the time to plan a long journey. The short-term passes are popular for one-day journeys such as from Delhi to Agra or Jaipur, or for an overnight trip to another city. Their value is not so much in what they cost but in the aggravation they save; in knowing that you have a confirmed reservation on the train of your choice before you even arrive in India.

All passes, including the one-day pass, are valid for the class for which they are sold, except on *Rajdhani Express* trains where since these are special trains, with meals included, the short-term passes are valid for the class below the one you've paid for. The AC 1st class one-day pass entitles the holder to travel in AC 2 tier on the *Rajdhani*. (I once used my 30-day AC 2 tier IRP to travel in the luxury of *Rajdhani* 1st class but I had to pay the difference on the single journey AC 2 tier fare and the AC 1st class fare in US dollars to get the upgrade.)

Period of validity	AC 1st class		AC 2 tier AC 3 tier AC chair car 1st class (non-AC)		Sleeper class (2nd class non-AC)	
	Adult/child		*Adult/child*		*Adult/child*	
Half day	52	26	24	12	10	5
1 day	86	43	39	20	17	9
2 days	160	80	70	35	30	15
4 days	220	110	110	55	50	25
7 days	300	150	150	75	80	40
15 days	370	185	185	95	90	45
21 days	440 *270*	220 *135* →	220	110	100	50
30 days	550	275 *168*	275	140	125	65
60 days	800	400	400	200	185	95
90 days	1060	530	530	265	235	120
Fares in US$						

Pass refund

Regular passes have to be used within one year of date of issue. The cost can be refunded, less 15% of the face value, if it is returned to the office of issue unused at least eight days before the commencement of its validity. There is a deduction of 20% after that period, and also of any cancellation charges for abandoned reservations. There is no refund possible after commencement of the pass's validity, if it is lost or stolen, or if the journey is undertaken in a lower class of accommodation.

The pass holder with a pass purchased outside India who decides while in India not to use it should present it to a stationmaster to have it cancelled and to obtain a dated cancellation certificate. The cancelled pass and the certificate should be kept to claim a refund eventually from the overseas office that sold the pass.

An Indrail Pass can be revalidated to commence on a different date by the overseas office of issue on payment of US$10. Cancellation of confirmed reservations and substitution of new ones incurs a penalty of US$10 outside India, or Rs10 per change (up to a maximum of Rs50) if changes are made in India.

Extension of the validity period of the pass can be made in India by the nearest area officer or gazetted station superintendent if it becomes necessary due to circumstances beyond the control of the pass holder, such as train delay.

Pass value

Is buying an Indrail Pass worth it? The answer is a big YES, but you have to take more than the cost per kilometre into consideration. On a straight comparison of costs (distance travelled on single journey tickets versus distance travelled on a Pass) there is little financial advantage, unless you spend all your time in India on trains just to clock up excess kilometres. It is being able to avoid the boring rules and surcharges that give it real value.

There is no financial advantage in buying a Sleeper class pass. Anyone who is prepared to travel at length in that class is likely to be young (in mind if not in age) and not impressed by the convenience and prestige that make an Indrail Pass worth having. The financial savings come with the 1st class pass with its entrée to superior accommodation on 1st or AC coaches. Its value is not only in kilometres travelled but also in the (free) nights spent on board in comfortable berths. The pass pays for itself in a few nights from the savings made on hotel accommodation alone.

The most expensive pass of all, the AC class (ie: 1st class air conditioned sleeper) Indrail Pass, brings a greater saving on buying single-journey tickets since those tickets are themselves much more expensive. There is also the bonus of privileged accommodation in the luxury of AC 1st class. Unfortunately, only about 80 trains (listed in *Chapter Twelve*) have AC 1st class, so only buy that pass if most of your long journeys will be on trains that do.

I was taken to task by Rendell A Davis, an attorney in the USA, for seeming to lack enthusiasm for the AC 1st class Indrail Pass in the first edition. He wrote: "I suggest you might want to recommend AC 1st class more highly. By Western standards, it is not very expensive. The cost difference between a three-week AC 1st class pass and a three-week ordinary 1st class pass was about the cost of staying in certain '5-star' hotels for one night. Yet the comfort of AC 1st class can make an enormous difference.

"I took a two-night and a day rail trip from Madras to Calcutta on the *Howrah Mail*. At the end of that trip, I got off the train totally rested and ready to go. If I had spent two consecutive nights sleeping in a lower class, I would probably have wasted my first day in Calcutta recovering from the rail trip. For that trip alone, the extra cost of AC 1st class was worth it.

"AC 1st class is more widely available ... the various *Shatabdi Expresses* now carry an airline-seat style of AC 1st class that is much more comfortable than the ordinary AC chair car seating on those trains."

Having used a 30-day AC 1st class pass in 1996 (when it cost about US$9 a day more than the ordinary 1st class/AC 2 tier IRP) I can vouch for what Rendell A Davis says. It is by far the less stressful way of train travel with the extra attention of beds made up with clean linen, stimulating travel companions, civil service, showers in the loos and access to any part of the train. The food, however, is the same as in all the other classes.

The ordinary 1st class long-period pass represents the best bargain financially. With a pass for 21 or more days you don't have to travel day and night to get full value from it. You can linger in different places and still be able to travel more kilometres than if you'd spent the same amount of money on single-journey tickets.

With an Indrail Pass you will have freedom of the Indian Railways network. It is important, though, to remember that, because of the demand for space on Indian trains, it is not always possible to jump on a train at random and expect to find a berth. You *have* to make a reservation, usually a few days in advance, if you want to be sure of travelling on a particular train, no matter what class of rail pass you have.

A fixed itinerary is what many rail travellers are keen to avoid, but the Indrail Pass helps the impulsive traveller too since, with it, you can turn up at a station four hours before a train's departure and try to get a reservation. Or you can simply find the conductor when the train comes in and try to arrange everything with him. The authorities hate these last-minute arrangements, and so will you if there is no berth available, but you stand more chance with an Indrail Pass than without it.

RESERVATIONS

It was raining when I arrived in Secunderabad. My train from New Delhi had been delayed and I had missed my connection so the itinerary, painstakingly prepared for me by the staff of the ITB, was now useless. The SS sent me out of his station into the dark, wet night and I carried my two cases past the bus stand to the reservations office 600m away around a corner.

After a day of travelling, I felt dreadful; I was soaked to the skin and fed up. The prospect of queuing for a reservation made me feel worse, but I had to leave for Madras the next day. The reservation office was like a council hall with rows of seats in which people were waiting. There were no queues. I asked at the enquiry desk what I should do. The clerk told me to fill in a requisition slip.

The slip was headed "Requisition for Reservation/Cancellation/ Return/Onward Journey" and contained spaces for "Station from ... to ... Date of Journey ... Train number" and for the names of up to six passengers with age and sex columns. The name of the applicant, address and signature with date were also needed.

I returned the slip to the clerk and was given a number and told to sit and wait. I sank into a chair gratefully and composed myself for a long wait. Looking around I saw numbers flashing above the different ticket counters; to my amazement my own number was being displayed. The clerk at the counter took my Indrail pass, scribbled "R" on it and some numbers, and gave it back.

My reservation had been made and it was not the exacting process I feared. I was in a strange city, without friends and at my lowest ebb, expecting the worst. Yet the system worked perfectly, and I can only guess it was because I had an Indrail Pass.

Making a reservation

If you don't have an Indrail Pass you must buy a journey-cum-reservation ticket. In the advance reservation centre fill in a requisition slip with details of when you want to travel, by what train and in what class, adding your name, age, sex and address. This has to be handed in at the appropriate reservations counter. When the reservation is confirmed, the journey-cum-reservation ticket issued by a man-operated reservation counter is endorsed on the reverse with the reservation details. It is only valid for the particular train and day for which it is endorsed. For a 1st class booking it will have the letter "R" written on it and the actual allotment of seat/berth will be done on the day of travel; you will see your allotted number on the lists posted in the station lobby and on the platform of your departing train. In the case of a reservation in sleeper class, the seat/berth number will be quoted, such as S3-45 which means seat 45 in Coach S3. If the reservation office does not have a quota for the journey you will have to buy a ticket and wait at least three days for messages to be sent and replies received to confirm the reservation. If it can't be confirmed, the ticket cost can be refunded, as detailed under *Refunds* below

If the process described above sounds rather old fashioned, don't worry, it is, and has mostly been replaced by computerisation. The system is much less trying now. The computer will have access to berth availability and the wait for telegrams back and forth is a thing of the past at most stations. When the advance booking is done at a computerised reservations centre, a single coupon instead of a cardboard ticket is issued by the computer and this serves as your ticket.

If you have an IRP, details of your itinerary will be entered on it for your information, but the journey-cum-reservation coupon is what will get you your berth when you are on the train.

John Gleeson, writing from Cork, commented, "While any station can theoretically make a reservation on any train, they can only give you a confirmed reservation while you wait if the station has an allocation of seats on the train. If it doesn't have an allocation then a message must be sent to the originating station to secure a seat from there.

"I found, when I arrived at the originating station, that on four out of five occasions no message had been sent by the station at which I made the reservation. Thus no seat!

"On the one occasion that a message was sent, it was only because I went directly to the CRS (at Siliguri) and begged him to ensure that the message was sent.

"I think it would be a good idea if you advised travellers to ascertain if the situation mentioned applies in their case and to ensure (perhaps by going to the CRS or SS) that the required message is sent."

The best solution, of course, is to use an IRP and plan your journey so that you can make reservations in advance at the major stations, where computerisation will take care of your requests.

What happens if you can't get the reservation you want? Rob Dobson tried and says he was "bounced from reservation desk to supervisor, in the end I had to go and see the assistant commercial superintendent. The quota system has gone crazy if you have to go so high up the tree to get a seat. It took an hour to get a ticket to Madras."

His experience proves that the system does work – but start at the top. If there is a foreign tourist counter at the reservations centre, the clerk there will advise you on what to do. If you actually want to buy a ticket and have no foreign exchange – or there is no counter especially for foreigners – you will be competing with everyone else for space. Even so, being a foreigner, you can still ask the CRS for help or the SS or the officials who control the emergency quota, usually the assistant or divisional commercial superintendent. Buy a "wait list" ticket, so you've got something to show, and ask them to sort it out.

If the worst comes to the worst and you simply have to travel that day and you don't have an IRP, buy a 2nd class ticket at the current (trains departing that day) counter. You'll have to try your luck when the train comes in, paying the TTE or the train conductor the extra fare for any upgrading, reservation fee, supplements, etc. If there is no space at all, you'll have to squeeze into the general, non-reserved 2nd class carriage. An official at the ITB told me: "Share with our problems like others. The capacity of the train can't be increased, you must avail yourself of the existing capacity."

Don't despair though! Pat Moyniham, also of Cork, wrote of her trip using single-journey tickets: "I had to buy a 2nd class ticket at Cudalore as they had no 1st class quota to Bangalore. When I got on the train, I was able to upgrade to 1st class, and had a two-berth coupé to myself."

Chris Smith with a 15-day IRP was on the last leg of his journey when I met him on the *Tamil Nadu Express*. He said that he wondered about spending so much money on trail travel but he found his pass absolutely worth it. He travelled only between the major cities (with a side trip to New Jalpaiguri from Howrah for the toy train to Darjeeling). He spent lots of nights on the train "because I found the sleeping accommodation much cheaper and safer than in cheap hotels".

He was amazed at the efficient running of the trains and so impressed by the system he wished he had taken a longer pass to travel more. Since he wanted to travel without an itinerary, he used to turn up at the foreign counter of the main station's reservations office on the day of a train's departure and get put on the waiting list. "Somehow," he said, "berths were found from some quota."

Computer coupons

The computer-generated ticket/reservation coupon is approximately 15 × 9cm in size, white and blue in colour and contains several numbers. The most important is the PNR (passenger name record) number as this identifies the passenger. The passenger's name does not appear on the ticket although it will appear on the reservation chart pasted on the side of the train and on the station noticeboard showing berth allocations.

The coupon contains details of the class of travel (in English and Hindi), the train number and date. The boarding and destination stations will be indicated together with the distance between them in kilometres. It will state whether the ticket is for an adult or child, the sex and age of the passenger (to prevent fraudulent use), as well as the seat/berth number if allocated in advance. Additional information, such as where the train comes from and the journey routing, will appear at the bottom of the ticket. Also at the bottom of the ticket is something referred to as "Key No:", representing the key number which has to be quoted whenever you are checking on the reservation for some reason.

Illustrated on page 64 is a reservation slip for a journey taken on 16 July 1996. The numbers on the top line, from left to right, show the PNR number as 210001. 2432 UP refers to the train number, while 3111 is the number of kilometres the journey covers. 1 shows one adult and 0 means no children. *Rajdhani* is the train name. 1A is the class and the train is shown as running from H Nizamuddin (Delhi) to Trivandrum. The handwriting indicates that the passenger will board the train at Madras.

No coach or seat number is shown but the vital word "CONFIRM" means that the reservation is secured. M99 indicates a male of 99 years – not the truth, however old I felt at the time! Since my Indrail Pass did not state my age and the reservation was made on my behalf, the formula 99 was used instead. NDLS 239 refers to the authority to travel, in this case my Indrail Pass which bore the number 000239.

Because I was using an IRP, the rupee cost of the journey is not shown. The worrying comment "food cost not included" has been

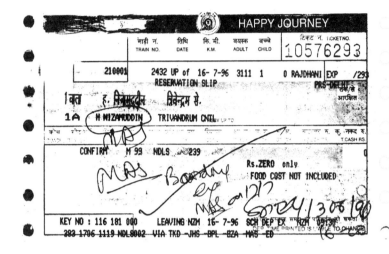

added because, although on the *Rajdhani* trains between Bombay and Delhi and Calcutta and Delhi the food cost is included, on other *Rajdhani* trains it is extra.

The notation following the key number relates to the date and time of departure and the route.

The reverse of the computer coupon usually contains a slogan of some sort, and general information. On a coupon I used in 1996 appeared the words:

"A puff, a pinch, a bite can push
You into the dark of Night
Shun Drugs."

Defining the codes appearing on the coupon, it stated that "first wait list/RAC (see *Types of reservation*, below) number is your serial number. The second number is your status at the time of booking."

The class codes are also given:

1A   First ACC
FC   First class
CC   Chair car
2S   Second sitting (the kind of accommodation, not meal
     arrangement)
2A   AC 2 tier
3A   AC 3 tier
Sl   Sleeper class

Types of reservation

There are two kinds of reservation: Confirmed and RAC. Confirmed passengers are allocated berths/seats at the time of booking and the details are endorsed on the tickets. RAC (reservation against cancellation) provides a limited number of passengers, at the train's originating station only, with seats on the train in all classes. A berth is promised if one becomes vacant due to a cancellation or no-show.

RAC passengers are entitled to board the train at its originating station and to occupy the seats assigned to them. If an RAC passenger is actually provided with a berth, the sleeper surcharge and the difference in reservation fee is collected by the TTE.

If all berths and the RAC quota have been filled, the name of passengers with journey tickets are entered on the waiting list. Wait list passengers are accommodated in the order in which their names appear on the list, subject to space being available, within the ten minutes before the departure of the train. Sometimes, extra carriages are added to a train, so it is worth having your name on the list.

Check the computer reservation coupon carefully when you receive it to see that you understand what it means, so then you can ask what to do if it says RAC or WL. Rob Dodson thought that WL on his coupon meant he was seated in coach WL for his journey from Agra to New Delhi. When he turned up for the train in the evening, he found he was wait-listed (WL) and had no right to travel on the train at all. So he stayed in the retiring room and got a seat on a less popular train the next morning.

Wait list does not mean you can board the train and hope to find a seat in the manner that RAC gives the right to travel. You can only board the train with the knowledge and consent of the train conductor or TTE (and then you'll have the various surcharges to pay unless you have an IRP). If you do have an IRP, your chances of getting a berth, even though you're wait-listed, are increased since you qualify for accommodation from the emergency quota (see page 70).

If you purchase a journey ticket and are assigned to the RAC quota or wait list, then decide not to travel, you can claim a refund on your ticket. No cancellation charges will be levied unless a confirmed reservation was actually provided before you cancelled, but a clerkage charge of Rs10.00 will be deducted.

An RAC passenger is entitled to board the train at its originating station and to occupy the assigned seat, even if a berth does not materialise.

Based on his own experience, Samit Roychoudhury comments that RAC travel, without a berth, in sleeper class in a broad gauge train is comfortable enough, except on very long journeys. A lower outside berth is shared between two passengers.

On a metre gauge train it is a different story. In one compartment, the upper berth is confirmed while the lower is used as seats for four people, which means the passenger holding the upper berth reservation doesn't have much seating space during the way (when the upper berths are supposed to be stowed) and he has to squeeze in with the RAC seated passengers.

Return reservations
Return journey reservations can be made at the originating station by filling in the requisition slip and purchasing a return journey (card or blank paper) ticket which will cost twice the single journey.

NO PROBLEM?
"No problem," said the reservations clerk at the Indian Railways Computerised Foreign Tourist Bureau in Fairlie Place, Calcutta.

I should have known that those words, when uttered in India, do not mean what you think. To the clerk they meant "Please stop asking me difficult questions and get out of the office."

To me, they meant that yes, we would be able to get two 1st class berths five days hence from Bhubaneswar to Madras on the *Coromandel Express*, even though our computer-generated "reservation-cum-journey" coupon bore the dreaded designation "WL", meaning "wait-listed".

At Bhubaneswar, when the express drew in, the conductor consulted his list and denied any knowledge of our "no problem" reservation. Instead, he told the Indian who had accompanied us to the station that he would arrange something for an appropriate tip. Shamelessly, we agreed, just to get on the train.

The conductor claimed some passengers would be getting off before nightfall and we could have their two upper berths. He hovered for his tip. "No problem," I said, deliberately reneging on the deal to tip him and pretending not to understand. He slunk away and we never saw him again.

Our triumph was short lived as the conductor did not enter our names on the passenger list which he passed to his colleague when he got off at the next station. Negotiations began again. Since my companion and I both had an Indrail Pass which meant we had tickets to travel, we refused to move or pay a bribe.

The very fact that the conductor was prepared to find berths for us in return for a bribe meant that there were berths available. Our bloodymindedness won in the end but we were lucky that there were, indeed, berths available, otherwise we would have had to stand all the way to Madras.

There are several lessons to be learned from that incident about rail travel in India, even though it does not put me in a very good light, behaving like the typical arrogant "Brit Abroad". It was, in fact, my first experience of bribes being solicited by rail personnel, although Indian rail travellers tell me the practice is common. The main lesson, of course, is not to try to short-circuit the system. What we should have done was to have checked with the reservations office at Bhubaneswar station and had our reservations changed, through an appropriate quota, from "wait listed" to "confirmed".

Adapted from Royston Ellis' article in *Wanderlust*, January 1995

A telegram is sent, at no charge to the passenger, to request accommodation from the return journey station, or it is done by computer link. Some return journey quotas have been set aside on popular mail/express trains and berths can be allocated from the originating station.

Space

Stations have advanced booking counters, sometimes in a separate building adjacent to the station, where reservations are made. Many of these buildings are agreeable places in which to wait, and have coffee counters and magazine stalls. The availability of space on the train will be indicated by coloured discs or lights so you can see if there are berths available on the train you want. The colour indicates the following:

green   space available
yellow RAC space available
pink   wait list available
red   no space, fully booked

If the train of your choice is shown as fully booked, don't despair. As a foreigner you have access to seats issued under different quotas (see page 70) and should apply at the separate counter for foreign tourists or to the CRS.

If you leave making your reservation until the day of departure, requests at the reservation counters are usually accepted up to four hours before the scheduled departure of a train. After that you must try the ticket collector (TC) or conductor at the train's originating station during the hour before the train's departure.

Reservation charges

Where computerised reservation facilities are available, there is an extra charge to pay for reservations. The fees (not applicable to IRP holders) are:

Class	Reservation fee
AC 1st class	Rs 30
AC 2 tier sleeper	20
AC 3 tier sleeper	20
AC chair car	20
1st class (mail/express)	20
1st class (ordinary)	20
Sleeper class (mail/express)	15
Sleeper class (ordinary)	15
2nd class (mail/express)	10
2nd class (ordinary)	10

(*The fees are the same for adult or child*)

Refunds

For single journey tickets, the minimum cancellation charges are
shown on page 46. The original reservation fee is not refunded since
this is included in the ticket price. The levying of cancellation
charges when an alternative booking is being made instead seems to
depend on circumstances. Refunds can also be sought on partially
used tickets or due to the failure of a train's air-conditioning
equipment (if the ticket is for AC accommodation).

NB: Foreigners who have reservations from the tourist quota should
always cancel them if they cannot travel, as this releases the berths
for other tourists who may be on the waiting list.

Lost reservation

It could be useful to record the various numbers and date of your
ticket in a safe place in case it is needed for future reference, as well
as the number of the train, berth allocation (if any) and date of
travel. However, if you lose a reserved berth ticket and there is a
record of your name as being its purchaser, you can still travel on
the same reservation. A payment of up to 25% of the original fare
paid will be levied for this duplicate ticket.

Special requirements

Reservations can be made only up to 30 days in advance of
departure for all classes and on all trains except for some special
expresses on which the advance reservation period is reduced to 10
days or even less. This restriction does not apply to Indrail Pass
holders, who can reserve up to 360 days in advance.

An individual can book only up to four berths in the case of a
party or a maximum of six berths for a family on the same train
travelling to the same destination. It is sometimes possible to
request a particular berth or seat: for instance, an outsider lower
berth or a berth in the ladies compartment, subject to availability.
Reservations are not transferable.

For reservations from an intermediate station, the passenger must
apply at least 72 hours before the departure of the train from its
starting station. Reservations are not accepted by telephone. They
are done in order of receipt of requisition slips.

Boarding the train

To make sure your reserved berth isn't given to someone on the
RAC or waiting lists, be at the station at least 30 minutes before the
train is due to leave. This will give you time to find the platform,
the train and your berth.

Passenger lists are posted in prominent places in a station before a
train's departure, and on the side of carriages themselves. The lists
show the passengers' names, sex and ages with numbers of allotted

berths and carriage number. Each carriage has its numbers painted on its side and also an indication of where numbered berths are to be found.

If you are confronted with a passenger list that's only in Hindi, you could find your berth by checking the list for your ticket number. Don't be surprised to see your name written in some novel forms. I've been listed as Ston Elli and a friend of mine called Christine invariably found she was travelling as Christ.

If you are boarding the train at an intermediate stop, arrive there with enough time to find out from the passenger lists which is your carriage and where it will be when the train pulls in. Some trains have 21 carriages so you will need to position yourself properly for boarding as there won't be time to run the whole length of the train searching for your carriage before it leaves.

Gary, an Australian I met at Karjat, was puzzled about how to find out where to stand on a platform so he was near the carriage in which his berth was booked. This is especially important when the train only stops for a few minutes and has no vestibule. The helpful assistant stationmaster at Karjat explained that 1st and AC coaches are normally located near the pantry car which is usually in the centre of the train.

To find out the exact location for Gary's train he consulted a booklet that every SM or SS has that shows the composition, marshalling order and accommodation of every mail, express and passenger train. Gary's ticket indicated FC3 (1st class, third coach) so the ASM counted down the coach order until he found the position of the relevant coach, in this case number eight from the engine. Gary waited under the sign (they exist at most major stations) which showed where that particular carriage would be when the train stopped. The system worked and he boarded the train without panic. So, if in doubt, ask the SS or SM where your carriage will be.

Reserved sleeping accommodation is provided between 2100 and 0600. During the day (0600 to 2100) overnight passengers must make room for seating passengers in the compartment, up to the number it is marked to carry.

If you are travelling in sleeper class, the same rule applies although you might find the carriage packed with more people than it should carry. They like to claim that reservation to travel is only applicable at night. That's nonsense. Those passengers should not be there if there is no seat available for them within the carriage's daytime capacity, but it's difficult to know what to do about it if the train staff are in cahoots with them. Even in AC 2-tier class, passengers who are travelling only a short distance will board the train and fill the seat space with more than six passengers to a bay. They are able to do this either with the connivance of the train staff or because they reach their station before they are discovered.

The quota system

Many foreigners wonder why accommodation can be found for them on trains which are shown as fully booked. They suspect some inefficiency or corruption. In fact it is due to the miracle of the quota system.

Railway officials turn coy when you ask them about the various quotas and how the system works. Basically, it is an arrangement which enables a reservation clerk at a station to allot berths on a particular train without reference to the headquarters controlling the sale of berths on that train. This is done by headquarters assigning the station a specific number of berths, more than which cannot be sold by that station.

Lists of berths available at various stations appear in zonal timetables. For example, from the South Central railway timetable, we discover that on train number 7029, the Cochin to Hyderabad Tri-Weekly Express, Nellore station has an allotment of two AC sleeper class berths, and in sleeper class Chirala has two berths, Gudur five, Ongole four and Tenali five.

Foreign tourist quota

Trains which are popular with foreign travellers have a foreign tourist quota set aside for reserving at tourist-frequented stations. Any foreign traveller can request a berth from that quota, where it exists. If there isn't one, the foreigner must try to get a berth out of the general quota which is open to all passengers.

What happens if the general quota is sold out, as is often the case? That is when the system gets interesting and the officials get coy.

There are over a dozen different quotas formulated over the years to cover the needs of special passengers. As well as the general, return journey and foreign tourist quotas, there are the parliamentarian, defence, VIP, outstation, railway employees and emergency quotas. (Outstation means a station – or a town without a station – where the train does not stop, usually because it is on another line.)

Berths from all quotas which haven't been taken up by the time the train departs are released to the conductor to allocate according to priority on the RAC and waiting lists. Where there is no foreign tourist quota, the SS or the CRS can apply to the area manager to have a foreign tourist accommodated on the emergency quota. Preference is given to Indrail Pass holders over purchasers of single-journey tickets and even over railway officials.

A reservations guide is published in some daily newspapers showing the earliest date on which berths are available on trains from major stations. Trains are listed with class of accommodation alongside and the dates from which there are vacancies. Some trains, such as weekly expresses, are very popular and are likely to be fully booked from the day reservations open.

With the introduction of computers, even though you may be among the first in the line at one counter on the day reservations open, you may still find all berths from the general quota have been allocated, since people queuing at other counters with access by computer to the same quota have already reserved all the berths.

Reservation assistance in India

If your itinerary, arranged weeks in advance by Dr Dandapani or another GSA out of India, changes, or you are setting up your journey in India, you will need assistance from competent, trained personnel. Fortunately, many reservations offices are geared to dealing with foreign rail travellers. The best service is provided by the ITB (see page 72) and by reservation offices with foreign tourist guides, whose authority is required by reservations clerks to seek reservations from the foreign tourist quota.

Northern Railway (which actually administers the IRP) has offices with foreign tourist guides at New Delhi station (ITB on the first floor), Jodhpur (first floor), Varanasi (off the main lobby) and at Jaisalmer (off the main platform). Central Railway has a counter in the Bombay VT station reservations complex. Western Railway has a desk and an expert guide on the first floor of the reservations complex at Churchgate, Bombay.

At Madras, there is an efficient, separate foreign tourist "cell" on the first floor of the reservations complex alongside Madras Central station. In Calcutta, foreign travellers can make reservations at the complex on the first floor of the Fairlie Place building, Calcutta. At other stations, according to their importance, there are counters dealing specifically with foreign tourists. Where there is no dedicated counter, deal directly with the Chief Reservations Supervisor (CRS). If the station is too small to have a CRS, then introduce yourself to the stationmaster.

Computerisation

The spread of the computerised reservation system throughout India did not seem possible when the first, and even the second, edition of this book was published. In 1992 there were only 32 stations able to offer the facility and a plan to introduce the computer system to 70% of the rail network. The Computerised Reservation Network now covers all important, and some completely unknown, areas (see map, inside back cover). It is even possible to make a computerised reservation in Port Blair in the Andaman Islands.

Although computerisation does not much benefit the ordinary passenger in terms of the time it takes to book a ticket (as was promised), it is a boon to people who want return or onward reservations. These can now be made instantly through computer link-ups with the original reservations centres.

There are five central computer systems (nodes), situated in

Bombay, Calcutta, Delhi, Madras and Secunderabad. Any centre offering the computerised reservation facility is actually an extension of one of those five nodes. For example, Ahmedabad is an extension of the Bombay terminal, and Bangalore is an extension of the one at Madras.

If you go to a reservation office and book a ticket for any train originating in a station of that zone (of the same node), it will be treated as a normal ticket. If you require a ticket for a train originating in a different zone, it will be treated as a return or onward ticket. For that you would be required to approach the extension counters which have special links to other nodes. These are available in the larger reservation centres. (However, where there is a counter dedicated to foreign tourist bookings and you have an IRP, all reservations can be done at that counter.)

Because of computerisation, new reservation centres have been built at many stations, and the whole reservations process has been streamlined. Since computers require careful maintenance in a dust-free, air-conditioned atmosphere, passengers are benefiting with climate controlled, clean and comfortable areas in which to sit and await their turn. With less harassing conditions in which to work, the booking clerks have become customer-friendly too.

Computerised reservations offices are generally open from 0800 to 2000 hours on weekdays, and from 0800 to 1400 on Sundays and national holidays (January 26, August 1 and October 30).

The system switches off automatically at the stipulated closing time, so it's no good hoping to complete a complicated itinerary by starting just before 2000 hours since the operator, however helpful, can do nothing about it when the computer has closed down.

International Tourist Bureau

The International Tourist Bureau (the ITB) is the flagship of Indian Railways' bureaux for dealing with foreign tourists. It is allocated on the first floor of New Delhi station, opposite the restaurant, and was opened in 1987 to cater exclusively for foreign travellers to make reservations. It sells single-journey and point-to-point tickets and reservations, as well as the Indrail Pass.

The ITB, sometimes known as Central Space Control, is the nerve centre of the Indrail pass scheme which is coordinated by the Northern Railway. When a pass is sold by an overseas GSA (or by an agent in India), the GSA telexes the name, nationality and passport number of the purchaser, with the Indrail Pass number, class, itinerary and reservations required. A file is opened for the passenger at the ITB.

Apprehensive foreigners just arrived in Delhi who visit the ITB with their foreign-bought Indrail Passes are delighted to discover that not only are their reservations confirmed as promised, but their full itineraries have been carefully recorded. This is possible because each GSA has an experienced reservations officer at the ITB who looks after the GSA's clients. When the telex containing the reservation request is received it is processed swiftly and confirmed by telex within seven days. Even if your Indrail Pass itinerary doesn't take you to Delhi, the details are recorded there.

The ITB is a brightly lit, cheerful office, open from 0730 to 1700 every day except Sunday. The staff take a break of 30 minutes for lunch from 1330 but tourists can wait in the office during that period.

Two tourist guides are available at a separate desk in front of a showcase of books about India. If in doubt, start there either for help with your itinerary or advice as to whether point-to-point tickets or an IRP is best for you, and which counter to go to. The counters opposite the entrance, with chairs in which to wait your turn in comfort, deal with point-to-point reservations and are equipped with computers to issue the coupons. Payment is accepted in dollars or pounds (in which case change is given in the same currency) or in rupees against the original and photocopy of your foreign exchange encashment certificate. If you have only rupees and no exchange certificate, you'll have to buy your tickets from the general quota at the reservations complex next to New Delhi station. (The reason is that foreign tourist quota tickets should be purchased with foreign currency.)

A notice indicates that "foreign students studying in India or Indians studying abroad are not dealt here". Your passport and visa will be checked to see you have not been in India for more than six months, since the ITB facility is only for genuine tourists.

If you want to buy an Indrail Pass it can be done swiftly here, at a dedicated counter. Payment for this has to be in dollars or pounds, so if you plan to buy an IRP at the ITB do not change all your travellers cheques in advance as you'll need them to buy the pass. Actually this is a pleasant way to cash your travellers cheques as the rate is calculated at the day's bank rate and the change is given in Indian rupees. Credit cards are not accepted "because the card companies require commission which is not built into the existing cost of the IRP", according to an ITB official. This comes as a shock to sophisticated tourists used to paying with plastic.

Another counter deals with travellers who have bought their Indrail Passes overseas and it has signs indicating the countries represented. The staff, who are delightfully helpful, speak Japanese, German and French as well as English. If you have arranged your itinerary in advance through a GSA, you will be able to pick up the reservations coupons, have your IRP endorsed and be on your way.

Whenever I go to ITB I always have a new and complicated itinerary, changing the one I'd first thought of. With computer link-up throughout India, most bookings can be made promptly, and other requests are telexed. It's amazing what the staff can achieve.

Since I usually spend three or four days in Delhi, I call in at ITB on the first morning and then call back on my last evening and find all the reservations are confirmed. It's the same for all IRP holders, since we are VIPs on Indian Railways.

A word of advice: if you've just stepped off the plane after an overnight flight, you'll be exhausted by the time you get to ITB – the heat, the crowds, India generally, will be overwhelming. So know what you want before you get there; it will make everything much smoother and you won't test the clerk's patience too much.

SS: The Sensible Solution

If something goes wrong while you are travelling, you could try the station superintendent (SS).

Station superintendents are usually men of great charm and personality who use tact and wisdom to soothe the irate traveller. Any foreign tourist who is bothered by an aspect of rail travel should go straight to the SS first. However, a man of such stature is not on duty 24 hours a day so you might meet his, usually less impressive, deputy instead. Shuttling around from one junior official to another will only compound your dissatisfaction. Save your temper and from the outset seek out the SS: he's the Sensible Solution.

Every station has a stationmaster (SM) who deals with the operation of trains, while the SS is the manager responsible for overall supervision. Smaller stations will only have an SM.

In colonial times stationmasters were considered as very important personages. One retiring viceroy is said, either at Bombay or Delhi (there are several versions of this story) to have thanked the stationmaster for his courtesies over the years, to which the man replied: "Not at all, Your Excellency, it has always been a pleasure to see you go."

Chapter Four

Class Distinction

"You must," said my publisher, "travel 3rd class. That's all that many rail travellers can afford and they'll want to read about it."

The good news is that there is no "3rd class". First class is being phased out too. A divisional railway manager told me this is being done as part of a scheme to create a classless railway. It's not true, I discovered, but it sounded right.

There are now in fact ten different classes, defined by ticket cost, with variations in style and comfort depending on the age or status of the train and whether it's day (sitting) or night (sleeping) travel. What used to be considered "3rd class" became "2nd class 3 tier non-AC class". That has now been upgraded in designation to the grandly named "sleeper class".

The nearest equivalent to 3rd class would be the general carriages on slow, rural passenger trains, or those non-reserved general carriages found at the rear of mail/express trains and referred to here as 2nd class Mail Express, seating only. Any class that is not 2nd or sleeper class is regarded as upper class. If the list seems complicated, it's going to seem worse as you read on.

In rising order of speed and comfort, if not expense, the classes are:

1. 2nd class ordinary (passenger train seating only)
2. Sleeper class ordinary (passenger train)
3. 1st class ordinary (passenger trains, seating only)
4. 2nd class mail/express (seating only)
5. Sleeper class (mail/express) (SL)
6. Air-conditioned chair car (mail/express) (ACCC)
7. Air-conditioned 3 tier sleeper (mail/express) (3A, 3rd AC, AC 3 tier)
8. 1st class (non air-conditioned sleeper) (mail/express) (FC)
9. Air-conditioned 2 tier sleeper (mail/express) (2A, 2nd AC, AC 2 tier)
10. Air-conditioned 1st class sleeper (mail/express) (1A, 1st AC, ACC)

Train type

Trains are either mail/express or passenger. Mainline mail/express trains will consist of sleeper class and one or more of the other classes on the above list, unless they are "Janata Expresses" when they have only sleeper class reservable. There are some "Janseva Expresses" (notably the Amritsar-Barauni, the Bhagalpur-Muxaffarpur, the Surat-Varanasi and the Puri-Ahmedabad expresses) that are fully unreserved trains.

Passenger trains are slow, stop at every station and village halt and will sometimes have ancient 2nd class carriages with wooden seats, but they will usually have some 1st class accommodation, even if it's only two compartments in a combined 2nd or 1st class coach. Incidentally, what I call a carriage or coach is also called a bogie in India.

For fast-travelling, you need an express or mail train, preferably a superfast one since there are few expresses that manage to go very far – or fast – without stopping at a station. "Superfast" (for which there is a supplement payable, see page 47) implies an average speed for the entire journey of over 55km/h. Broad gauge trains are capable of greater speed than metre gauge ones and, indeed, most metre gauge lines are being converted to broad gauge for more convenient travel.

CLASS STRUCTURE AND ACCOMMODATION

The regional timetables show what classes a train has, using abbreviations that are not always the standard ones quoted on page 64. For instance, you may come across ACC, representing air-conditioned class, which actually means 1st air-conditioned class. The IRP I travelled on in 1996 showed on its front cover "Air Conditioned (ACC)", which one ticket inspector seemed to think was not the same as 1st AC class (it is) but meant air-conditioned 2 tier sleeper. Needless to say, I was quick to put him right.

The 3144 *Darjeeling Mail* is listed in the Eastern Railways timetable as having this accommodation: "ACC, AC2, I, SL, II". It means that as well as having 1st AC and AC 2 tier, it also has non-air-conditioned 1st class (I), sleeper class (SL) and 2nd class (II).

Now that AC 3 tier has been introduced on some trains, it makes understanding the air-conditioned sleeper accommodation much more straight forward: 1st AC is what it says, AC 2 tier is equivalent to 2nd AC and AC 3 tier follows as 3rd AC. (Note that the official abbreviations support this with 1st AC being 1A, AC 2 tier as 2A, and AC 3 tier as 3A.)

1. 2nd class ordinary

This refers to an ordinary passenger train 2nd class carriage without sleeping berths. The bench seats may be ancient and wooden in remote rural areas. It has descended from the old 3rd class accommodation.

2nd class mail/express is exactly the same, but fares might be higher if a supplement is involved for superfast travel. One or two carriages are attached to mail/express trains and are often called the general (ie: non-reserved) coaches.

These carriages usually have a side aisle giving access to the open-sided compartments of two bench-style seats facing each other, and seating four (or many more) people on each bench. The luggage racks, of wooden slats, hang from the ceiling, giving extra space for passengers to sit or sleep (although signs say they are only for luggage). The luggage racks block out the light and add to the gloom of the compartment, as do the horizontal iron bars across the windows. Each compartment has two fans. On trains with a vestibule running its length, the linking door from the general carriage to the rest of the train is kept locked to prevent passengers slipping into the reserved carriages.

There are also 2nd class carriages referred to as chair cars which means they have dedicated seats, not bunks. Seats are likely to be of wood in bench sections of 3 × 3 (although some older coaches have 2 × 4 seating) facing each other. There could be a total of 108 seats, plus two jump seats by the centre doors. Seats can be cramped when more than three people squeeze on to them and leg room is limited when there are passengers on the facing seat. New coaches in this style have padded seats and fluorescent lamps. There are Indian-style toilets at both ends of this kind of coach.

2. Sleeper class ordinary

This is the same accommodation as described below (5: Sleeper class mail/express) but is to be found on passenger trains, hence it is regarded as a separate class.

3. 1st class ordinary (seating only)

Since this kind of accommodation is to be found on passenger or daytime trains, it is also referred to as chair car where dedicated seats, not berths, are available.

This accommodation is very comfortable for daytime travel but is, unfortunately, being phased out. There are versions with 60 reclining seats in a 2 × 2 layout, with the aisle passing between the two pairs. There are fans and the windows open. Curiously, a seat in such a carriage can cost up to 60% more than one in the newer AC chair cars.

Seats in the 1st class, non AC coaches have a width between armrests of 44cm and a cushion width of 50cm. The armrest dividing the seats is broad and fixed. Leg space (pitch) from the back of one seat to the back of the one in front is 55cm. There is a footrest, a pocket for papers in the seat back, and an ashtray at the

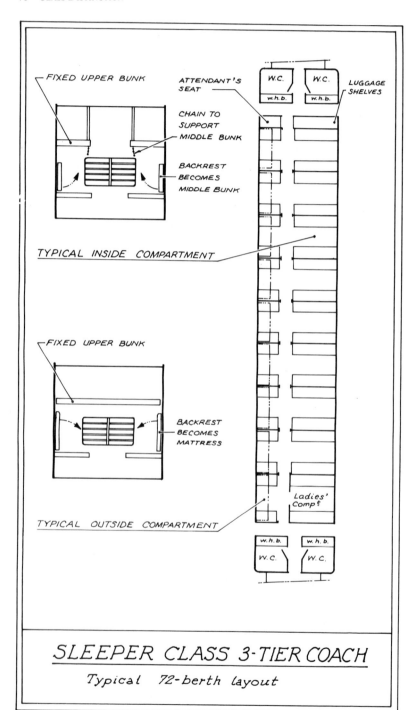

SLEEPER CLASS 3-TIER COACH

Typical 72-berth layout

side. All seats are forward facing except for a pair either side of the aisle at the end of the coach which face the others.

4. 2nd class mail/express (seating only)

Accommodation is similar to 2nd class ordinary but is in the "general" carriages attached to mail, express or superfast trains.

5. Sleeper class *(see plan opposite)*

Long distance expresses and mail trains have sleeper class which means 2nd class carriages with sleeping berths in three tiers: lower, middle and upper. There are 72 berths; the daytime seating capacity is supposed to be 72 but usually expands beyond that.

The windows are always open in hot weather and closed tightly as soon as it begins to rain, hence the carriage gets stuffy. The windows have bars across them, like a mobile jail, although both doors at both ends of the carriage are usually left open so anyone can jump in, or out, as the train stops. There are three fans to each compartment (no AC) and they can be airy in the cooler months. In hot weather, nothing tempers the heat, and the dust billowing in through the open windows adds to the swelter.

The carriage is divided into nine open-sided compartments. Each one has bench-type seating for three people facing another bench for three people. On the other side of the aisle is one single seat opposite another. The seats and benches have been converted from the old wooden ones and have been firmly padded and upholstered in rexine.

The padded back of the lower bench is raised to become the mattress of the middle berth, supported there by chains hanging down from the upper bunk. This upper bunk is a fixed, padded ledge suspended by permanent supports from the ceiling. The bunks formed in this manner have a width of 55cm and a length of 184cm.

Across the aisle are the "outside" berths, converted out of the two single seats facing each other. The cushioned backs of these seats drop forward flat across the seats themselves to touch in the middle and form the lower bunk. The upper berth is fixed. These berths measure 55cm in width with a length of 166cm.

Thus, "3 tier" refers to what are known as the inside berths, while the outside berths (those parallel to the outside of the carriage wall) are two tier. This makes eight berths per compartment, all open to the aisle that splits them. Sometimes passengers hang clothes and towels as curtains but with so many people in a small space, there's not much privacy.

Each compartment has nightlights and clothes hooks. Access to the upper bunks is by scrambling up the metal hoops by the aisle; these also serve as handholds for people passing through the coach.

There are two toilets at each end of the carriage, but no shower. There are also mirrors and washbasins in the lobby by the entrance doors. At one end of the carriage there is a seat for the attendant and shelves for luggage. On a long trip the inside of the carriage gets dirty when people throw their rubbish on the floor.

Because the top bunk is fixed, it is frequently used for passengers' luggage. A family or friends travelling together might also keep the middle bunk in place during the day which adds to the lack of headroom and comfort.

The choice of where to sleep usually depends on the luck of the draw at the reservations centre. You can request an upper/middle/lower berth but there is no guarantee you'll get it. The lower bunk, being used as a seat, is only available for sleeping when the other passengers have retired to their own bunks. Similarly, the middle bunk can only be used when the seated passengers have finished sitting since it is their backrest. The upper bunk is available all the time, but requires agility to climb in and out and it's close to the fans and the lights. This is where an eye mask helps for sleeping.

Women travelling alone can request accommodation in the ladies' compartment, which is a separate cabin, with a sliding door, at the end of some sleeper class carriages. It sleeps six. While men are not allowed in, they often spend time there during the day. Boys up to the age of 12, if accompanying a lady, are permitted. This ladies' only facility is not available on trains where the ladies quota has been abolished. On expresses with a train superintendant on board, the ladies' cabin closest to the 1st class is reserved for him as his quarters.

6. Air-conditioned chair car (ACCC)

This is a class of its own, whereas non-AC chair cars are either 1st or 2nd class, and are referred to above. Air-conditioned chair cars are becoming more common and whole trains (like daytime expresses) are composed of them. The most famous are the *Shatabdi Expresses*; accommodation in those trains is described on page 225.

ACCC accommodation can also be found on some overnight routes although they are gradually being phased out in favour of AC 3 tier. A list of trains with ACCC appears in *Chapter Twelve*.

The AC chair cars seat from 56 to 73 passengers in a 2 × 3 layout. As well as the AC unit, there are plenty of fans. The windows are sealed and the glass is tinted a sunset bronze so the carriages are a bit claustrophobic.

Seats have tables which fold down from the chair back in front, and a magazine pocket. They recline slightly. Be careful in locating your seat since when you think you've found, say, seat 45, because it says so above the fold-down table, you are actually sitting in seat 40 because that's the number on the back of the seat you're sitting in. Western and Indian style toilets are available.

7. Air-conditioned 3 tier sleeper *(see plan page 82)*

This is the latest class introduced to Indian Railways and is closely modelled on what is now sleeper class. After the conditions of sleeper class, the AC 3 tier carriages look quite luxurious. However, as they are air-conditioned the windows cannot be opened and anyone desperate for a cigarette has to go to the entrance lobby for it. The carriages do pong a bit after a day and night thanks to the variety of food carried and consumed by long-distance travellers.

The nature of the compartments, with passengers stacked in threes, makes for cramped conditions but nothing as squalid as in sleeper class. There are eight bays in each carriage with six passengers in three tiers accommodated in the inner bays, and two in two tiers in the outer bays, taking a total of 64 passengers. The outside bays have the tiers running parallel to the side of the carriage; the inside bays have berths that are perpendicular to the carriage's side.

The three tiers (tier is frequently pronounced "tire") are neatly designed to make the most of the limited space available. The lower berth has a backrest which is supposed to be locked back to the bay wall during the day as the lower tier is the seat for passengers. At night, the backrest drops down to form a mattress over the seating bench.

The second tier is also locked back to the wall during the day, dropping down from it as a shelf for sleeping during the night. It is supported by chains from the upper tier. Whoever has the middle tier has no territory during daytime travel as the shelf needs to be locked back so people can sit up properly on the lower tier.

The upper tier, on the other hand, is fixed and could be occupied by its passenger even during the daytime. However, that would be a bit confining since the bunk is quite close to the roof of the carriage, the AC vents and the fans.

There are no curtains so the bays are open to anyone passing down the aisle. At the other side of the aisle are berths for two people. The upper one is fixed and the lower one is formed out of two seats whose backrests drop down to make a mattress with a join in the middle.

The carriage has lots of hooks for hanging clothes, and hoops for holding on to when trying to walk through the carriage while the train is on the move. There are two toilets, with washbasins outside them, at each end of the carriage. Interior doors at either end help to keep the air conditioning in and interlopers out.

8. 1st class (non air-conditioned sleeper)
(see plan page 83)

Forget the glamour and luxury associated with 1st class travel; on Indian trains those comforts are now only to be found in the air-

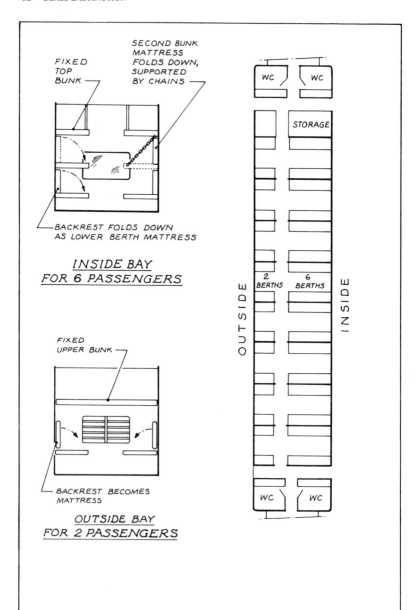

FIXED TOP BUNK

SECOND BUNK MATTRESS FOLDS DOWN, SUPPORTED BY CHAINS

BACKREST FOLDS DOWN AS LOWER BERTH MATTRESS

INSIDE BAY
FOR 6 PASSENGERS

FIXED UPPER BUNK

BACKREST BECOMES MATTRESS

OUTSIDE BAY
FOR 2 PASSENGERS

WC   WC

STORAGE

OUTSIDE

2 BERTHS   6 BERTHS

INSIDE

WC   WC

AC 3 TIER SLEEPER

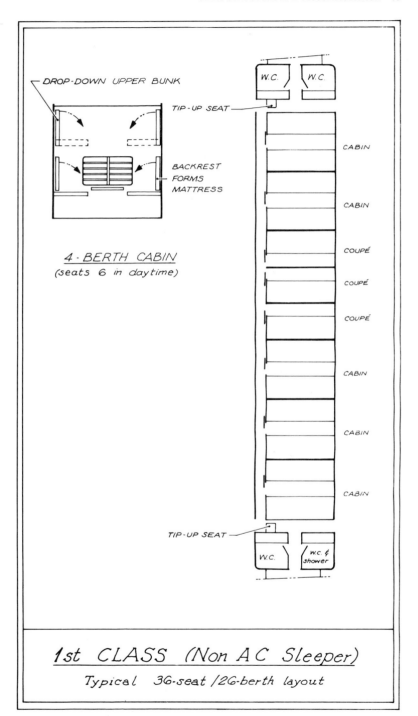

DROP-DOWN UPPER BUNK

TIP-UP SEAT

W.C.   W.C.

CABIN

BACKREST
FORMS
MATTRESS

CABIN

4·BERTH CABIN
(seats 6 in daytime)

COUPÉ

COUPÉ

COUPÉ

CABIN

CABIN

CABIN

TIP-UP SEAT

W.C.   w.c. ¢
shower

1st CLASS (Non A C Sleeper)

Typical 36-seat /26-berth layout

conditioned coaches. It is hard to know what to call 1st class when it ranks third in expense after AC 1st and AC 2 tier.

Where possible, 1st class carriages are being replaced by the AC sleeper 2nd class coaches since 46 people can be accommodated at night in those two-tier coaches, compared with 26 in the same amount of carriage space in 1st class. As a result, many 1st class coaches are being allowed to deteriorate. They are often shabby with hard, bench-type seats covered in grimy, patched, grey rexine.

Passengers who don't like travelling in air-conditioned isolation, or in the cramped conditions of sleeper class, have only these neglected carriages to ride in. However, the situation may be improving as a number of these coaches have been rehabilitated and others are being rebuilt. This is not because of passenger demand (although this is acknowledged to exist) but because there are certain routes where 1st class cannot be replaced by AC coaches for technical reasons, and also because insufficient AC coaches are being built each year to replace all the 1st class rolling stock.

Unless it's a chair car, all 1st class coaches have sleeper accommodation. A typical 1st class carriage is spit into five compartments with four berths in each, and three two-berth "coupé" cabins. There are four fans in the four-berth cabins and two in the coupés. The glass windows open upwards and there are metal screens which can be lowered at night while the window remains open to let in air. There are bars across the windows, as in sleeper class.

There are window screens that can be raised on the aisle side of the cabin too, and a sliding door which can be double-locked by bolts from the inside to keep out intruders. There is a metal loop fitted on the aisle side of the door (at its base) that enables the door to be secured with a passenger's own padlock. Some doors have a namecard holder on them, a relic of the style of the old days.

The upper berths in these cabins can be raised during the day and bolted flat against the compartment wall. Many passengers keep them lowered, though, which obscures what little light there is, reduces the space available and becomes an obstacle when getting up from the seat below. (Mind your head.)

There are two footrests that flip down from the cabin wall to help the passenger get into the upper bunk. A reading light and a pocket for personal items are fixed to the wall just above the bunk, and there is a shelf over the window.

The main disadvantage of being assigned an upper berth, apart from the process of getting in and out, is that it is close to the fans – fine in hot weather but they are noisy – and to the ceiling lights. Although these aren't very bright they can be annoying if the passenger in the lower bunk doesn't switch them off. There is a blue nightlight over the door.

The lower berth is formed by unbolting the cushioned backrest

Above: *Train approaching Matheran, with rider sanding track* (GA)

Below: *On the way to Ooty* (GA)

Above: *Bombay Victoria Terminus (VT) station* (GA)
Below left: *Sleeper class*, Kerala Express (GA)
Below right: *Children on the steam train to Ooty* (GA)

Above: *Platform catering*
  Left: *Omelette vendor, Vijayawarda station* (GA)
  Right: *Coimbatore station* (GA)

Below left: *Collecting water from steam loco, Trichy/Thanjur line* (GA)

Below right: *Platform vendor, Balharshah station, with* Kerala Express (GA)

The Taj Mahal, Agra, Uttar Pradesh (PB)

and letting it drop forward to make a wider mattress than the seat of the bench. At the aisle side it has a ledge for personal belongings and a holder, for glasses or bottles, to which suitcases can be chained. There are also coat hooks, ashtrays, a pocket attached to the wall above the bunk and a reading light. There is a small table between the two lower berths, under the window.

The lower berth is easier to use but the occupant may feel obliged to wake early if the person in the upper bunk wants to sit on it, or to go to sleep late if the upper berth occupant stays up. During the day the bench seats can accommodate three sitting passengers, which raises the total complement in the carriage to 39.

The upper berth is 64cm wide and 188cm long, with the lower berth being 57cm wide and 192cm long.

The advantage of 1st class travel, despite its recent deteriorations, is its spacious privacy. The cabins have enough room for four people to spend nights together in security and for six to travel companionably in the day. Women travelling alone may not be too comfortable if sharing such a cabin with male strangers, so should probably opt instead for AC 2 tier sleeper with its dormitory-style accommodation.

The coupés, while being perfect for a couple or loner who gets one for sole occupancy, are a bit depressing with only the cabin wall to face. 1st class is as hot and dusty as sleeper class, as the windows are always open, but it's not so dirty or noisy.

There are two toilets at each end of the carriage; at least one of these is Western style. A marvel is that one of them will have a shower, such a boon on a long, hot journey. At one end of the coach is the attendant's seat, positioned so he has full view of the aisle. There is shelf space too for meal service.

9. Air-conditioned 2 tier sleeper *(see plan page 86)*

This kind of accommodation is actually a superior dormitory class, similar in basic layout to AC 3 tier and sleeper class since a lot of passengers share carriage space. However, there is some privacy provided by the curtains which have been introduced to hang over inside bays and outside bunks. Its air conditioning, cleanliness, facilities, fixtures and fittings have made it superior to 1st class (and more expensive). It has become the most popular with Indian upper class travellers.

The coaches have 46 seats/berths. Entrance is by doors at either end into a lobby which is cooled by a ceiling fan. At one end there are two toilets, a washbasin, the control panel for the air-conditioning unit in a glass-fronted cabinet, shelves for storing meal containers and flasks, a jerry can of drinking water, and a seat for the attendant. A shelf drops down to serve as the AC unit technician's bunk. At the other end of the carriage there are two more toilets, a washbasin, more electrical controls and a cupboard

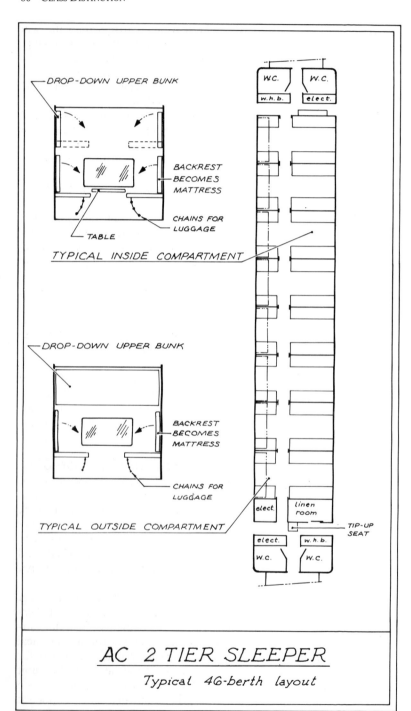

DROP-DOWN UPPER BUNK

BACKREST
BECOMES
MATTRESS

CHAINS FOR
LUGGAGE

TABLE

TYPICAL INSIDE COMPARTMENT

DROP-DOWN UPPER BUNK

BACKREST
BECOMES
MATTRESS

CHAINS FOR
LUGGAGE

TYPICAL OUTSIDE COMPARTMENT

W.C. W.C.
w.h.b. elect.

elect. linen room

TIP-UP
SEAT

elect. w.h.b.
W.C. W.C.

AC 2 TIER SLEEPER

Typical 46-berth layout

for the storage of bed linen, which also serves as the attendant's cabin.

Self-closing doors lead into the air-conditioned dormitory part of the carriage which has an aisle running its length. On the outside of the aisle are single seats, facing each other in seven pairs. Bunks hang down above them from the ceiling, although they can be raised and bolted back to the cabin wall.

Each pair of seats converts, by lowering forward the chair back, into a lower bunk. At one end of the carriage there is only one lower bunk and no upper, making a total of 15 "outside" berths. One of the seats used to make this sole lower berth is actually an extra one. The worst berths are numbers 5 and 6, which are by the door, and number 46 by the other door and under an ever-humming AC unit.

At the other side of the aisle are the "inside berths" grouped in compartments of four each (two upper, two lower), with a curtain that can be pulled across to close the open space to the aisle. The upper bunks can be raised and bolted back flush to the wall to give greater space and light, but most passengers prefer to keep them down for daytime sleeping.

The lower berths are formed by letting down the cushioned backrest. The seats/berths are covered in a blue-grey rexine and are comfortable even on long journeys. A prominent sign says: "Please pull up the backrest-cum-bed during 6am to 9pm to avoid inconvenience to sitting passengers". Few people bother.

There is a shelf serving as a table, and two glass holders, below the windows. The windows have curtains; they are sealed, double-glazed and tinted, sometimes yellow, adding to the gloom within the carriage.

There is a strip light with push-buttons to switch it on or off by the window, and another strip light above the aisle, controlled by the passenger in the lower outside berth. Reading lights above each bunk are switched on automatically when the covering shade is raised. There is a fan above the aisle for each compartment, with a switch under the mirror on the inside wall.

Carriages have seven four-berth compartments with one having only three berths; two lower and one upper. Berths have different measurements. The outside lower one, converted out of two single seats, is 186cm long and 53cm wide. The berth above is 184cm in length and 54cm wide. Inside, the upper berth measures 184cm long and 61cm wide, while the lower berth is shorter, at 173cm long, but wider at 65cm.

Of the coach's four toilets, at least one is Western style and one might be for ladies only. The "ladies" has side as well as full-face mirrors. Newer models of these carriages have fans in the toilets, too, but there are no showers.

Carriages built since 1988 have several improvements over the original models. The end side seat, number 5, has a partition wall by it that protects its occupants from the ceaseless opening and shutting of the access door. Curtains have been added to the side bunks giving privacy and, since each bunk is curtained off individually, those adjoining the aisle are actually more private than those in the four-berth compartments. Chains to which luggage can be padlocked have been fixed under the seats.

These AC coaches have two attendants (one is the technician who looks after the AC unit) so they are usually well-maintained. Some passengers like the AC unit set at maximum, perhaps feeling that if they are not cool, they are not getting their money's worth. The usual temperature is around 72°C.

Attendants have different views on keeping the carriages clean. I've been in one carriage where the attendant was scrupulous in his job, crawling around on his hands and knees with a dustpan and brush and a damp cloth, and in another where rubbish was allowed to accumulate until passengers complained. There is a rubbish bin in the lobby at the end of the carriage, under the washbasin. The toilets are generally kept clean. Each AC carriage is issued with an opinions book in which the attendant will try to get two entries every trip, preferably complimentary ones.

I've noticed in this class of coach that Indian passengers tend to spend the day lolling in their bunks in apparent boredom, whereas they seem livelier and more friendly in the non-AC 1st and sleeper class carriages. I was curious to see several fellow passengers who were very old men, with companions of equally advanced years. They turned out to be Freedom Fighters, pensioners who have been given an annual pass by the Government of India to ride free in 1st or AC 2 tier class with a spouse or companion.

There are no separate compartments for ladies in this class although women can request to be accommodated with other women. An appeal on board to whoever is in charge of berth allocation will usually be successful in achieving any necessary change. In theory, a woman travelling alone in this class is safer with 45 other passengers and two attendants than she would be alone in a 1st class coupé.

Smoking is prohibited in the AC part of the coach: smokers congregate in the lobbies at either end.

The main appeal of this type of accommodation is the air-conditioning. With the windows permanently closed, the dust and noise are kept out as well as the heat. However, you also miss much of the scenery since you can't see through the tinted windows clearly and can't open them to buy snacks and knick-knacks from platform vendors without leaving your seat.

There is no spare space in the compartments and I personally find them claustrophobic and a bit dismal. However, if you can't stand the heat, this is an ideal way to travel. But if you want the windows open so you can see, feel, and smell, the India you are passing through, then a non AC coach is better.

10. Air-conditioned 1st class sleeper

Since it costs about double the price of a berth in the AC 2 tier sleeper and about eight times one in non-AC sleeper class, you expect something splendid in AC 1st class. I wasn't disappointed. The difference was apparent the moment I set foot in the carriage, with attendants eager to help and inordinately proud of their jobs serving in the best accommodation available to passengers on Indian railways.

The division of cabins and berths in this class differs according to the carriage and route. Where demand is small, berths are limited to ten; two cabins of four berths each, and one coupé.

The floor of each cabin is carpeted and the upholstery is a soothing brown. The upper bunks are bolted flush to the cabin wall during day time, with the lower berth serving as a comfortable rexine-covered seat for two. The seat converts into a berth at night by lowering the cushioned backrest down over it to serve as a mattress.

This mattress has been ingeniously designed with flaps down the length of its sides forming an envelope into which the bedding can be tucked. (This refinement, incidentally, is also to be found in the new generation of AC 2 tier coaches.) Freshly laundered bedding – and a hand towel – is included in the ticket price and the bed will be made up by the attendant.

Cabins have a washbasin and a small table top and a collection of switches for lights, fans and summoning the attendant. Bed tea (the early morning cuppa) is usually served at 0700 and other meals served to the cabin throughout the day. While the accommodation is vastly superior to other classes, the food is not; it's the same in every class. Service in AC 1st class can be amateurish or lethargic, the same as in other classes, unless an "old school" bearer is on duty or tips are in the offing.

The toilets (two at each end, one Western, one eastern) aren't too clean, although some might have toilet paper tucked behind the water pipe (or available on request). In this class, both kinds of toilet have showers and fans. A sign in some loos says: "To stop train, pull the chain". It refers to the emergency cord, not the toilet flush.

Each cabin has a sliding door, which can be locked from the inside, with a curtain to hide it. The windows, also with curtains, are sealed shut because of the air conditioning which is kept at an unobtrusive level; there are fans as well. Cabins have a drop-down table; some coupés have a miniature washbasin. There are ashtrays and a rubbish bin, a pocket for papers, and holders for glasses which are provided. Cold water is available.

A narrow, shallow closet contains a ladder to be removed for reaching the upper bunk, and some coat hooks, but no coat hangers. There is a range of buttons for putting on or switching off the strip lighting and night lights, or for summoning the attendant.

The only disagreeable feature of this cosy accommodation is a sign which says "Drinking of alcohol drinks prohibited", which tends to spur all but the devout to disobedience.

AC 1st class is only available on some 80 trains, not all of them daily, and only on major routes (see *Chapter Twelve*). Despite the cost, it is popular, and for any but the most dedicated rail traveller, the only way to travel for long periods in India by train. Fellow passengers, if they have acquired their tickets legally in advance, are likely to be men of stature: politicians, military officers, businessmen. Since upgrading from 2 AC to 1 AC is possible on the train, others not on the passenger list may turn up. For the less adventurous tourist, this is the best way to travel by train, especially if using an Indrail Pass which makes this top class a low cost bargain.

Double decker carriages

A novel feature in some trains operating to/from Bombay and to/from Calcutta are the double decker carriages introduced in 1978 for 2nd class travel. The *Panchavati Express* running daily between Manmad and Bombay VT, a five-hour journey, has some of these.

By deft design, 144 to 148 people are accommodated in two decks of a single coach. The lower deck, to which passengers descend by a few steps after entering by a door at the end of the carriage, holds 69 people. They sit on bench-type seats, some of which are upholstered, with space for four on each. There are single seaters at the other side of the aisle.

The upper deck has seating in a 2 × 3 layout as well as singles, like thrones, and pairs, at the top of a tiny flight of stairs. When these carriages are empty, the clever use of space is impressive, When they are full, they are chaotic, hot and stuffy despite the fans. There are two toilets at both ends of the carriage.

Metre gauge accommodation

There are many combinations of berths and seats on MG trains which have had carriages custom-built for them. You will come across two-tier sleeper coaches (non AC) with 16 upper berths and 64 seats and even three-tier sleeper coaches with 48 berths and 64 seats. The MG *Vaigai* and *Pallavan Expresses* are 2nd class chair car, but with one AC chair car. In AC class the layout differs from that of BG trains. For instance, the *Pandyan Express* (see *Chapter Eleven*) has 1st class AC cabins in a carriage which also has AC 2 tier berths in cabins, instead of in the usual BG dormitory layout.

Metre gauge trains are renowned for their leisurely pace. There is a story about a travelling ticket examiner on an MG passenger train who asked an old man with a beard for his ticket. The old man gave it to him.

"This is a child's ticket," said the TTE in surprise. "You can't travel on that."

"Believe me," the old man replied, "when I started on this train journey, I *was* a child."

TRACK AND TRAINS
Gauge conversion

Much of the Indian Railways' network of metre gauge track is being torn up and replaced by broad gauge.

A page headed "Uni-Gauge – A Step Towards Socio-Economic Revolution In India", in the timetable of South Central Railways, explains "the uni-gauge system once established will bring immense benefit to the community at large and will correct regional imbalance in the development and growth of the country".

The idea behind uni-gauging is to create a system so that passengers and, of more revenue-importance, freight, do not have to be transferred from trains where a metre gauge track links with a broad gauge one.

A lot of the conversion is being done in the South Central, Southern and Northern (Rajasthan area) zones. Gauge conversion from metre to broad gauge involving 6,000km of track was underway during 1996–97. At that time metre gauge represented about 30% of the total route network, generating 4.95% of freight output and 10.9% of passenger output. (Figures from the *Indian Railways Year Book* published in 1996).

Some of the more interesting of the metre gauge routes, like Mysore to Bangalore, Allahabad to Varanasi and Jodhpur to Jaisalmer, have already been broad gauged.

Sections scheduled for broad gauging during the 1996–1997 period are:

Viramgam-Mehsana (65km)
Mehsana-Marwar-Ajmer (423km)
Jodhpur-Marwar (103km)
Guntakal-Nandyal (136km)
Wadsa-Nagbir (28km)
Arsikere-Hassan (47km)
Hossur-Salem (151km)
Sagauli-Narkatiaganj (59km)
Hotgi-Bijapur (97km)
Castle Rock-Vasco (87km)
Furkating-Mariani-Lekhapani (193km)
Tinsukia-Dibrugarh (48km)
Tinsukia-Lekhapani (63km)

Rolling stock

Many trains on Indian Railways are very long, sometimes longer than the platform, and consist of at least 20 carriages. A major express will be made up of one AC 1st class carriage (sometimes combined with AC chair accommodation) and an AC 2 tier carriage next to it. This will be joined to the pantry car with a 1st class carriage the other side. The remaining carriages will all be sleeper class 3 tier sleepers with two unreserved passenger coaches, one at the front and one at the rear, making up the rest of the train.

Individual carriages on long distance mail and express trains are manned by railway staff. They will close and lock the doors five minutes before a train is due to depart, leaving one door open on the platform side of each coach so they can check late-comers. Doors open inwards.

The worst long distance trains are those without a corridor. It's

LIVERIES

Indian Railways do not offer the range of livery seen in other countries. Following the demise of steam locomotives which had distinctive liveries, standardisation has meant drab colours with madly painted rolling stock and at times illegible graphics.

Most of the diesels today are an ubiquitous muddy brown, with a yellow stripe along the middle, sometimes sporting speed whiskers. You may see a few examples in blue or other colours, but these are usually dedicated to certain trains which themselves sport those colours. A few colourful ones turn out to be privately owned by mines, factories or power generation units.

Electrics show a bit more variety, though many of these are a duller version of the brown (with the yellow stripe). Some will have a maroon red instead of the brown. Diesels and electrics usually remain unnamed.

The less said about coaches the better: most of them are painted a dirty brown-maroon colour. This is to reduce the effect of dust and grime but even the clean coaches look dirty and uninviting. The insides are just as bad, with an overuse of dull ochre in second class coaches.

Some of the special trains are better. The *Rajdhanis* sport a standard vermilion orange base with a yellow stripe; the *Shatabdis* have a common deep blue with a light cream stripe. In both cases, the locos match. The *Palace on Wheels* is completely white. The *Pink City Express* is turned out in pink (what else?) and lemon.

Other combinations also exist, many of them found off the beaten track. Most of the hill railways (including Darjeeling, Nilagiri, some Shimla rakes, etc) are blue with a cream stripe. This combination, used on other services too, makes a train look brighter, cleaner and more attractive. Even the crack Bombay-Pune services are finished with a blue base, and a white top with a continuous red stripe, which is quite pleasing to the eye. (SR) difficult to know in advance whether a train will be vestibuled or not. Even when they do have a linking corridor, the attendants seem to delight in locking the doors so people can't walk up and down.

Why should you need a vestibule? Precisely so you can walk the length of the train to stretch your legs and to meet new faces in different carriages. And if the train stops in the middle of nowhere for 20 minutes you can get out and walk its length and not worry about hurrying back to your compartment when the train moves off, since you can board it anywhere and walk back along the corridor at your leisure.

When getting off a train, do remember to face the engine so if the train moves suddenly, you'll be able to recover your balance. Of course, never get off a train when it is moving, and always make sure the tracks are clear if you are clambering down on to them.

Train numbers

Train numbers were changed in November 1989 to four-digit numbers so that each train has its own number which the computerised reservation system can understand. The first digit indicates the zone that operates the train, unless the digit is "2", which indicates the train is one of the 70-odd superfast ones where a surcharge is levied and the numbering is controlled by the Railway Board.

The second digit indicates the division where the carriages for the train are maintained. In the case of superfast trains only, the second digit shows the zone that operates the train. The last two digits correspond to the last two digits of the train's previous number.

Thus, the 131/132 *Madras-Jammu Tawi Express* became 6031/6032, which shows it is a Southern Railway's (6) train based at Madras (0). The 125/126 *Kerala Mangala Express* became 2625/2626 because it is a superfast train (2) operated by SR (6) with its last two digits 25/26 corresponding to its former number.

First digit

1 =	Central Railway	6 =	Southern Railway
2 =	Superfast	7 =	South Central Railway
3 =	Eastern Railway	8 =	South Eastern Railway
4 =	Northern Railway	9 =	Western Railway
5 =	Northeast & Northeast Frontier Railway		

Second digit
Central Railway (1)

0 =	Bombay	2 =	Bhopal
1 =	Jhansi	4 =	Others

Superfast Trains (2)
In the case of these trains only, the second digit shows the railway zone (see first digit key above) that operates the train.

Eastern Railway (3)

0 =	Howrah		3 =	Dhanabad
1 =	Sealdah		4 =	Malda
2 =	Danapur			

Northern Railway (4)

0 =	Delhi		5 =	Ambala
1 =	Allahabd		6 =	Firozpur
2 =	Lucknow		7 =	Bikaner
3 =	Moradabad		8 =	Jodhpur
4 =	Others			

Northeast and Northeast Frontier (5)

0 =	Lucknow (BG)		6 =	Lumding (BG)
1 =	Varanasi (BG)		7 =	Kaithar and
2 =	Samastipur (BG)			Alipurduar (MG)
3 =	Lucknow (MG)		8 =	Lumding (MG0
4 =	Varanasi (MG)		9 =	Tinsukia (MG)
5 =	Samastipur (MG)			

Southern Railway (6)

0 =	Madras (BG)		4 =	Not allocated
1 =	Madras (MG)		5 =	Bangalore
2 =	Mysore (MG)		6 =	Palghat
3 =	Trivandrum		7 =	Others

Southern Central Railway (7)

0 =	Secunderabad		5 =	Hyderabad (MG)
1 =	Others		6 =	Not allocated
2 =	Vijayawada		7 =	Guntakal (MG)
3 =	Hubli (BG)		8 =	Hubli (MG)
4 =	Guntakal (BG)			

South Eastern Railway (8)

0 =	Kharagpur		4 =	Khurda Road
1 =	Chakradharpur		5 =	Waltair
2 =	Bilaspur		6 =	Adra
3 =	Others			

Western Railway (9)

0 =	Bombay Central		5 =	Others
1 =	Vadodara		6 =	Ajmer
2 =	Bhavnagar (BG)		7 =	Jaipur
3 =	Ratlam		8 =	Bhavnagar (MG)
4 =	Kota		9 =	Rajkot

At the time of going to press it was not known if train numbering would be changed with the introduction of new railway zones.

Up or down trains

Railway staff refer to a train as being an "up" or "down" one, a familiarisation too complicated to fathom as it seems derived from different reasons in different zones. A helpful assistant stationmaster at Karjat tried to enlighten me by saying that, in Central Railway, a "down" train (one with an odd number) has departed from Bombay; "up" trains (those with even numbers) are bound for Bombay. A commercial inspector based at Calicut agreed that even numbers are usually "up" trains, and odd numbers are "down". Trains, he said, heading to and terminating at division or the zonal HQ are even numbered (ie: "up") unless they are only touching their HQ and terminating at Delhi in which case they are odd numbered (ie: "down"). In Calcutta I was told it depends on the route of the train compared with the flow of the Ganges.

FROM RAIL TO JAIL

Is where you will end up if you buy a ticket from a tout.

When you buy a ticket from a tout, you are buying somebody else's ticket.

Do you know?

* Fraudulently travelling on a transferred ticket is an offence for which you may be imprisoned and/or fined.

In 1994, in Western Railway alone over 9,500 persons travelling on transferred ticket were detected and prosecuted.

So, play safe. Buy tickets only from the Railway Booking/Reservation windows.

* As per Indian Railways Act 1969, Section 137 fine upto Rs. One Thousand and imprisonment upto six months for fraudulently travelling or attempting to travel without proper ticket or on a transferred ticket.

"LEAVE NO DOUBT - Never buy a ticket from a tout"

Any person giving information leading to arrest of touts will be suitably rewarded.

Please give information about touting of tickets to Chief Vigilance Officer (T), Western Railway, Churchgate, Bombay.

WESTERN RAILWAY
Concerned for Your Safety
1995 - Year of the Rail Users

Chapter Five

On the Move

There's an air of excitement on the platform as the train's departure time draws close. You've found your name on the passenger list, together with the names of those in the compartment with you, so you already know your fellow passengers' names, ages, sex and destination. People are pushing past you to get on as you show your coupon to the conductor and he tells you to board.

Your fellow passengers are settling in, staking out their claims to territory with too much luggage. A bell clangs but there is no slamming of carriage doors, no blowing of whistles and no shout of "All aboard!" as in the States. The train simply draws out of the station while people stroll alongside and, with studied nonchalance, clamber on one after the other through the still-open doors.

You claim your own seat, pleased to be on the move. Since you have a long journey ahead in the company of strangers, what happens next will govern your enjoyment of the trip. You can start up a conversation and make friends, allies, quickly, or be anti-social and lonely for the whole of the journey. Of course, it depends on your personality but if you are travelling alone you'll need an ally, someone you feel you can trust to watch your luggage when you go to the bathroom. You can't isolate yourself completely on a train so if that's your style, train travel isn't for you.

I get a thrill out of the start of every train journey in India. It's not just the excitement of moving on to a new place, there's the anticipation of what's going to happen on the journey; the pleasure at the new acquaintances I'm going to make; the dissolving of city skyline into lush, rural landscape beyond the windows; and the heightened emotions of everyone on board. Indians love to travel by train; they are used to it and prepare properly so it becomes a picnic on wheels. I get a charge out of being part of it; you will too.

With Indian Railways, like everything else, you get what you pay for. In India, though, there is a bonus. If you choose the unreserved carriage in the slowest passenger train, you can be sure of an unpleasant overnight ride. In retrospect, it may provide you with amusing anecdotes at the expense of your Indian fellow travellers.

But you're not seeing any more of the "real India" than if you reserved a berth in affordable 1st class on a superfast express with meals served at your seat and fellow passengers who are lively, intelligent company. That's the bonus.

Part of the excitement of train travel is meeting new people who will pass on tips. However, some will regale you with horror stories of their journeys, seldom realising that the fault could be theirs, or that of their guidebooks.

According to an article in an Indian journal, "Travel guides dish out advice: when in India, think cheap, dress cheap, travel cheap, eat cheap and count on local hospitality and kindness of strangers to get you through". The article urges foreign rail travellers to "try to balance their experiences of cheap travel, and do themselves a favour, by travelling in a more comfortable class".

For a foreigner, India is cheap but that doesn't mean you have to choose the cheapest and miss the best. Do the opposite. If you can't afford 1st class in your home country, give it a try in India. You'll meet a cross section of the 100 million Indians who travel in upper class from time to time. Never stayed in a five-star hotel? Now's the chance, since some of the world's best are in India.

Signals

The thrill begins with seven sharp rings struck on the warning bell (or sonorous piece of pipe) hanging outside the stationmaster's office. That means "only five minutes before the train leaves". At Bombay Central, though, seven bells indicates "ten minutes to wait". Two strokes on the bell means departure time.

The guard will wave a green flag, or a green light at night, and the journey begins.

When the train is passing through a station you will see a railway man on the platform holding out a green flag horizontally (at night

---

RUNAWAY TRAIN

According to a press report in August 1996, the red signal system helped prevent a collision with a runaway train.

The Nizambad passenger train was taken into a siding at Mirzapur after completing its second run of the day. As the driver and helper alighted, the diesel engine suddenly sprang to life. It picked up speed and was soon far away.

Astonished railway officials frantically sent messages to stations along the route and stationmasters used the red light and red flag signals to halt oncoming trains, which were swiftly diverted to clear the track and avoid a collision.

The train's two-hour journey over 100km finally ended when an uphill bend of the railway track was blocked with truckloads of wooden and iron sleepers.

he waves a green light). This signal tells the driver and guard that the train is "proceeding in a safe and proper manner". If the watcher notices anything unusual about the train, he will hold out a red flag so the driver or guard know to stop it immediately.

If you need to stop the train in an emergency there is a communication cord. It is activated by pulling down a handle very much like the end of an old-fashioned toilet chain, and seems to be a relic of the Raj. It is placed close to where a standing passenger is likely to grab if the train jolted and he lost his balance. Be careful, especially in the toilet where it is tempting to pull the cord to flush the loo. There is a penalty of Rs1,000 and/or imprisonment for improper use.

Train end
LV displayed at the end of a train means "last vehicle" (at night there is a red light). This indicates to those monitoring the train's progress that the entire train has passed them. If the last carriage does not have LV or a red light, then the train watcher will know that the rear section of the train has become detached, so he will flash a signal to the driver. On the other hand the sign, or the watcher, might have dropped off.

Passenger rules
Compartments contain many notices advising passengers how to behave, such as "Switch off lights and fans when you don't need them", and "Discourage beggars", and "Smoke only if other passengers don't object".

There is a rule about alcohol on trains. The Western Railway timetable says "No passengers should consume alcoholic drinks in II AC sleeper, II class, and AC chair car coaches or be in a state of intoxication in any railway carriage". The inference is that in 1st class carriages, drinking is OK. But I've seen signs in 1st class that state alcohol is prohibited there too. In practice, if it is done discreetly and without causing offence to other passengers, alcohol is consumed and even sold to passengers by trackside vendors, especially on the line to Goa.

Central Railway has a rule saying "Case of transistor radios in an air-conditioned chair car is not allowed except with an earphone".

Train staff
Some expresses are under the command of a train superintendent (TS) who travels from the originating station to its destination. He is the train's manager and will take a keen interest in foreign travellers requiring help. His office is likely to be a requisitioned ladies only cabin in the sleeper class carriage near the pantry car.

A conductor travels in the 1st class coach and joins the train only for the few hours it is in his railway zone, not for the entire journey.

At wayside stations he helps joining passengers in all classes with their accommodation. He carries a reservation list as well as a complaints book. The conduct ensures that passengers are evenly distributed, and prevents overcrowding. He has been instructed to "exercise tact and firmness in dealing with passengers occupying more than their fair share of space in I and II class compartments either for themselves or for their luggage".

A conductor's duties also include checking on the train's cleanliness, waking passengers who have to leave the train during a night halt, and taking orders from upper class passengers for meals where these have to be ordered in advance. Conductors usually wear black jackets with a white shirt and tie, and often with white trousers too. They are supposed to have a name badge.

Corridor coach attendants are less smart although they do have a khaki uniform of shirt and trousers, and name badge. They act as support for the conductor in 1st class and have a passenger list and can help with berth location and check tickets if the conductor or TTE aren't available. They are supposed to "keep a good lookout on the corridor of the coach from the attendant's seat, particularly during night time" and to see that everything is in order. Whereas the conductor will have a seat in a compartment, the attendant uses the tip-up seat in the corridor of the 1st class coach.

There will be several travelling ticket examiners (TTEs) on a train in sleeper class who join at different stations for a few hours. As well as the obvious duties of checking passengers' tickets and assigning vacant berths, they also take orders for meals, see the carriage is kept clean, and "look after generally the comfort and convenience of passengers". They are supposed to see that upper berths are folded up and locked during the day.

TTEs usually wear uniforms of dark jacket and tie, and will sit in the coach they are in charge of. Travelling ticket inspectors in plain clothes will also be encountered occasionally. Since they are looking for fare dodgers, they are unlikely to be as affable as the TTEs or conductor.

The *Indian Bradshaw* contains hints for travellers, one of which says: "Civility on the part of railway travellers to the railway staff who have frequently unpleasant duties to perform will, as a rule, command civility in return. Discourteous conduct on the part of railway servants should be reported to the authorities".

Other train people you will meet are the pantry car staff. Bearers will come through the corridors with meals, snacks and drinks for sale. They are usually dressed in a drab grey uniform and tend to look scruffy. Since they have to live on the train in cramped conditions while it travels to its destination and back, this is not surprising.

The pantry car is under the control of a catering supervisor who has a white uniform but he sometimes wears his own clothes because of the difficulty in keeping the uniform clean.

The effectiveness of train staff differs by railway zones. Some trains do not seem to have enough TTEs to cope. In the north especially, 1st class can become just as crowded as 2nd class with ticketless interlopers and bogus free-pass holders. There are no restrictions on the beggars, pedlars and shoe-shine boys who invade the train and push their way through a carriage seeking money.

Keeping clean

You'll be amazed at how dirty you get on a train, especially if you travel in a carriage where the windows are open. You can wash, and shower, in the toilets, but doing your laundry is not practical because of the drying process. That has to be done during overnight stops. Clothes dry quickly in India. Laundry is cheap and you can sometimes find someone at the railway retiring rooms who will arrange to have your clothes washed, pressed and returned before you move on.

When a train stops for a long period, you could even have a shower on the platform. Station waiting rooms have showers attached to them and there are also separate shower cubicles on many platforms, for which no charge is made. Take with you your own soap, and towel, and valuables in a plastic bag to place where you can keep your eye on them.

The cleanliness of the carriages themselves is fairly good although it depends on the attitude of passengers. The AC sleeper class coaches are usually the cleanest while 1st class is somewhat shabby with compartment walls that are in need of a good scrub since repainting seems unlikely.

Freelance cleaners will hop on board some trains and make desultory sweeps with a broom of twigs and then pass around for tips. On the *Tinsukia Mail* from Patna to Malda Town there was a railway cleaner who swept out the carriage twice and then produced a book for passengers' comments, instead of asking for a tip. Since most people when confronted like that are unlikely to put down anything critical the cleaner was pretty safe. However, someone had the courage to write "foul".

Loo lore

Perhaps what most puts potential passengers off train travel in India are tales about the toilets. I've got good news: they are not as bad as the anecdotes of travel writers and horror stories of tourists pretend them to be.

There are usually four toilets to each coach, a far better ratio of loo per passenger than on a jumbo jet. Some coaches have ladies only toilets, and there is no graffiti. At least one of the toilets in the upper class coaches, and many in sleeper class, will be Western style. This means a flushable commode. Indian style is an aluminium trough with foot stands and a hole over which one squats.

For hygienic reasons, the Indian-style lavatory is preferable to the Western one. Often the Western one won't have a seat and when it does you'll hardly want to put your bottom on it. At least the Indian version does not demand bodily contact. You will have to learn how to hang on while the train, as well as you, are in motion. There are strategically placed bars and handles for that purpose.

I am not advocating that, as a Westerner, you abandon your personal toilet training and do it all Indian style. Carry your own toilet paper. (Contrary to popular belief, this can be bought in India.) There is a tap at knee level for personal hygiene and a lever to flush the trough.

If you are not sure how to use an Indian toilet, glance out of the train window as it goes through a town in the early morning and you will see people squatting with their backs to the tracks in the recommended position.

You will probably find train loos pleasanter to use than station ones. An article in *The Guardian* by Jugs Suraiya recalled the days when trains had no toilets and a passenger wrote in the complaints book: "Beloved Sir, I am arrive by passenger train and my belly is too much swelling with jack fruit. I am therefore went to privy. Just as I'm doing the nuisance that guard making whistle blow for train to go off and I am running with *lota* in one hand and *dhoti* in next when I am fall over and display all my shockings."

You need your own soap for handwashing and the basin will have cold water from a self-closing tap. There is a hand towel provided in every bed roll but this is small. If you are going to take a shower, you will need your own, larger towel. There are no showers in AC 2 tier class so if the train has a vestibule you'll have to use the one in 1st class.

In the toilet, be careful where you hang your clothes since the hooks are so positioned that water from the shower will soak whatever is hung on them. Take a plastic bag and bundle your clothes and valuables in it so they can be hung safely from the handle that flushes the latrine. The water isn't heated and comes from a rose set into the ceiling.

SLEEPING

Many foreign travellers sleep in their clothes, seeing this as the best way of keeping all their possessions intact as well as avoiding the confusion and embarrassment of undressing in a crowded compartment.

Indians sleep with their briefcases under their heads, using them as a pillow. They might change into a cotton pyjama-style suit on the train, or wear a *lungi*. On one occasion when I shared a compartment with an Indian lady (and two men, all strangers to each other) I noticed she dived under the blanket every night still swaddled in her sari.

In the sleeper class coaches, you have little option but to sleep in your clothes with your valuables close to your skin. This is where your own blanket will come in useful. One regular rail traveller from England told me that he buys a new blanket every time he arrives in India. He uses it as a seat cover during the day since he wears shorts and the rexine gets uncomfortable, and to cover himself at night. He takes the blanket back to England after each trip as a colourful souvenir.

Air pillows with a choice of attractive woven pillow cases can be bought at major stations. Without air they do not take up much luggage space and they can be blown up very easily. They are useful as cushions for padding hard seats during daytime travel as well as being better than a briefcase for resting one's head on at night.

When travelling in areas where nights are cold, it may be warmer in the air-conditioned carriages than in 1st class. This is because the temperature in AC is controlled, usually around 72°, and there are none of the draughts which can chill you to the bone overnight in 1st class during cold spells.

Another irritant to sweet dreaming will be fellow passengers. On a recent trip I began to believe the same man was at the other end of the carriage on every train I rode. He always spoke at the top of his voice far into the night, and woke me in the morning with his raucous hawking. You'll probably encounter him too, so don't forget the earplugs.

An Englishman told me he prefers to share a bay of four berths in the AC 2 tier compartment with women passengers. "They don't snore, they don't play music, they talk less and are less likely to be rogues."

Bed rolls

The old name of bed rolls has stuck, although now they are officially referred to as "travel bags". They are supplied free of charge to passengers travelling in AC 1st and AC 2 tier classes. They are also available, if ordered in advance, or by good luck, to AC 3 tier passengers and to those in non-air-conditioned 1st class.

Where they are not included in the fare, bed rolls have to be ordered in advance: when making the reservation is the best time. They cost Rs20 per journey. For this you get a large canvas bag containing two bedsheets, one blanket, one pillow with pillow case, and one hand towel. The linen is crisply laundered and the blanket clean.

Get a receipt listing the contents, which will be checked by the attendant when he collects the bed roll the next day. There is no deposit payable but there is a charge for anything missing.

एक बिस्तर नं. . . . . .प्राप्त हुआ, जिसमें
निम्नलिखित वस्तुएं हैं :—

Received One Bedding Set No. . . . .
Consisting of

1.   दो चादर/Two Bed Sheets.

2.   एक तकीये का गिलाफ/One Pillow cover

3.   एक कंबल/One Blanket

4.   एक गद्देदार तकिया/One Foam Pillow

5.   एक तौलिया/One Towel

6.   केनवस/रेक्ज़ीन बैग में पैक किया हुआ ।
     मैं बीच के कोई स्टेशन पर यात्रा विराम नहीं करूंगा ।
                           (कुल सात वस्तुएँ)
     Packed in Convas/Rexine bag.
                           (Total Seven Articles.)

         I do not intend to break Journey at any
Station en route.

दिनांक/Date   यात्री के हस्ताक्षर पत सहित ।
                    Signature of Passenger with Address.

If you forget to order one when you make your reservation, apply at the station at least three hours before the train's departure. Some zonal timetables show where bed rolls are available and there are about 100 trains which provide this facility.

Christine and Mike Wadsworth of Cumbria, UK, have become old hands at the bed roll game. They find it works only when you join the train at its starting station, not if you board during the journey, despite requesting bed rolls in advance. "We travelled on the 6028 Mangalore–Madras from Cannanore, an excellent journey but no bed rolls despite requesting them from the SS that morning who promised to relay the request," they wrote in 1990. In 1991, they wrote: "Yet again there were no bed rolls in a sleeper, this time on 6202 Vasco–Bangalore from Margao."

Both trains are run by Southern Railway whose timetable says:

"Passengers travelling in 1st class will be supplied with bed rolls – if requisition is placed two hours in advance before the scheduled departure of the train at the station from where reservation is obtained."

Berth control

If you have a lower berth in 1st class or in an AC sleeper coach, you will have to fold down the backrest over the bench seat to form the bunk's mattress. By laying your trousers and flat valuables on the seat before lowering the backrest mattress on top of it, you can keep them safe during the night, and your trousers get pressed too.

In full compartments you will have to develop an economy of movement in making up your bunk without disturbing other passengers. The upper bunk is the most difficult as you either have to reach up to make the bed or scramble around in the small space between it and the roof. As yet I have no reports from passengers who have drawn the middle berth, sandwiched between lower and upper in the newly introduced AC 3 tier layout. It seems to be the one to avoid.

In hot weather, the blanket provided in the bed roll can be used to sleep on. However, the temperature of the air-conditioned coaches is usually so cold you'll need the blanket on top of you instead of underneath.

Is it possible to get a good night's sleep on a train? When you think of the jolting, the constant stopping and starting of the train, the sudden shrieks of engines passing in the night, the insistent shouting of platform vendors when the train halts, the disturbance caused by passengers getting in and out during the night, and the worry about the safety of your belongings, it seems unlikely. Earplugs and an eye mask will help. Since there are less people in the cabins of AC 1st class, you stand a better chance of sleeping in them than in the various dormitory classes. This is another argument in favour of not travelling the cheapest way but going for the best value.

Incredibly, after a day sitting on a train doing nothing very much, you will still feel tired at night. After a couple of night's practice, you'll be able to fall asleep easily, shutting out the noise and ceasing to worry about your belongings. I got so accustomed to sleeping on moving trains that occasional nights in a retiring room bed were sleepless ones because it was stationary.

Rob Dodson comments that "Indians love to travel *en famille* so they may request that you change your berth with another member of their party; the attendant may also make this request to accommodate travellers." He advises you to check the alternative berth before agreeing to move. You do have the right to refuse, especially if you've requested a lower berth and they are trying to shunt you off to an upper one.

When this happened to me and I declined to budge, the atmosphere in the cabin was frostier than the air conditioning but at least I was spared the round of interrogation about my private life that is customary with fellow Indian rail passengers upon first acquaintance.

SECURITY

The possible theft of belongings is a worry to foreign travellers but it need not occur if you take sensible precautions. Luggage in compartments should be padlocked to the chain under the lower berth or to a fixed fitting so it can't be removed if you leave it for a few minutes. On platforms, never leave bags unattended. Carry valuables, whether money or documents, on your person, and sleep with them too.

If you're in a compartment with a door to the corridor, lock it on the inside at night but check there's no one already in the cabin hiding under the seat who'll wait until you're asleep and then disappear with your unchained luggage. The four external carriage doors can be fastened and double locked from the inside to prevent unauthorised entry. The doors linking carriages on vestibuled trains are also locked at night.

A German traveller told me he felt safer on a train at night with his luggage locked and secured under his seat than he did in a cheap hotel room, having lost a camera from one hotel room when he was asleep.

Don't leave anything of value by open windows. Busy stations have gangs of urchins who cluster around trains as soon as they arrive. Many of them carry long sticks with hooks on the end with which they fish out discarded plastic cups from under the train. They could also catch your purse or bag if you're careless.

You will see notices on stations warning people not to accept food or drink from strangers. There are stories of passengers being given drugged food or drink and then robbed. It is hard to refuse an invitation to share a picnic lunch with a friendly Indian fellow traveller without causing offence. But if you are suspicious then plead an upset stomach.

Fellow travellers are just as likely to be thieves as urchins are, especially in dormitory style carriages where you are sharing sleeping accommodation with 60 or more strangers. There is no need to become neurotic about losing things; if you do, your attitude could attract the very calamity you are anxious to avoid. Good sense will save you from most awkward situations.

Delia Rothnie, writing in *The Independent*, reported: "Barely five minutes into the journey, we fell victim to an immaculate conman. We had booked a 1st class sleeper on the train from Bombay Central to the little station of Sawai Madhopur. There were the trains, but which was the right platform? Five queries elicited five different answers from porters and bystanders. At last a smart chap in white shirt and trousers bustled over.

" 'You are wanting your carriage?' Indeed we were.

" 'Please to be following me this way.' In minutes he had shown us to a berth.

" 'And you will be requiring lunch and dinner also?' enquired our saviour. Yes, most certainly.

" 'Please give me money for purchase of coupons. I will bring menu.' So we handed over Rs200 (then about £10) and off he went never to be seen again!

"When our fellow passengers heard the tale, they chortled. 'You are in India, my dear sir and madam,' they expostulated. 'Never must you give away your money without first having seen your purchase!' "

If you are robbed while on a train, contact the conductor or guard immediately you discover it. They have forms for theft reports so it is not necessary for a passenger to leave the train to lodge the report at a police station.

Some trains have police travelling on them, especially when they are going through areas notorious for *dacoity* (banditry) or demonstrations. The responsibility of providing security is undertaken by two agencies, the Government Railway Police (GRP) and the Railway Protection Force (RPF). The GRP works under the various state governments and looks after the security of passengers and their belongings. There are about 32,000 railway police and a further 64,000 in the RPF, which concentrates on the protection of railway property.

In an Indian newspaper, I saw an article about ticket collectors with canes trying to drive away young beggars who have made the railway stations their homes. Periodically these urchins are rounded up and despatched by lorry to an unknown destination.

"But lo", said the newspaper, "the brats make a stormy entry into the station like homing pigeons before even the lorry comes back."

Kids are attracted to the station because of the new packaging used by railway caterers. The discarded silver foil, casseroles and plastic cups can fetch their finders as much as Rs40 a day. Consequently passengers are urged to crush their cups before disposing of them to prevent them being used again.

MEALS ON WHEELS

The use of foil casseroles for different dishes instead of serving meals on the traditional tray-dish, *thali*, is spreading throughout the railways and enhances the hygienic serving of food. The method of preparation, too, has undergone changes in recent years. Only in occasional circumstances are entire meals prepared on a train.

Orders for meals are taken from passengers and a message is sent to the base kitchen scheduled to supply them. Meals are cooked in base kitchens on demand.

Many kitchens have been modernised with machines to churn dough and other innovations to make them capable of cooking the thousands of meals required daily. Major base kitchens are equipped with mobile heated cabinets in which the foil dishes are kept hot for delivery to a train's pantry car. If there is no pantry car, the meals are brought to each individual carriage to be distributed to those who ordered them.

A long-haul express of 21 carriages would probably carry about 1,100 people, at least a third of whom will want meals every meal time. Others make do with food brought from their own homes, which is what many Indians prefer. They will also buy from vendors on the platform.

There is a variety of snacks on offer at the major stations and omelettes can be cooked in seconds over a kerosene stove on a trolley outside the train window. The platform vendors are either railway catering department employees or they work for a licensee. They are subject to inspection and food handlers have a regular medical check-up.

Platform vendors sell on commission. In trains with a catering staff many of them are paid on a commission basis too, which is why there are frequent offers of refreshment by bearers passing up and down the aisle of every carriage. On trains without a pantry car, or a vestibule, unlicensed hawkers will board the carriage to ride it to the next stop selling snacks, or tea from a huge kettle.

Mike Wadsworth recalls how the conductor on the *Nandi Express* from Bangalore to Mysore used the bottom of the passenger list computer printout to note his tiffin order. "He then tore it off, rolled it into a ball and threw it out when passing through a station. Obviously it was picked up and telegraphed ahead as usual, because when he next stopped there was a man waiting with the meals, flasks and glasses."

A new development is the introduction of privately run pantry cars on a contract basis, on the same principle as the leasing of station restaurants to companies. Alas, according to all reports, the food is still awful.

Generally, better trains have better food. Samit Roycoudhury cites the *Howrah–Bombay Mail*, which goes via Nagpur, as even serving chicken cutlets, at Rs24 for two. However, he was told by the waiter that they were made from chicken left over from the lunch order.

He reports that food on the Pune–Bombay *Deccan Queen* is exceptional. "Chicken cutlets cost Rs36. They even have fish fry for Rs51 . . ." On some trains, he warns, the only non-veg meal available will be egg curry.

Special meals

If you are keen on food, you could meet the catering supervisor of the train and discuss special requirements with him, and be agreeably surprised. After a surfeit of standard, base kitchen fare, I fancied a good chicken curry on one long journey. It was prepared in the pantry car and was delicious. Then it occurred to me to ask how they had managed to store the chicken since there was no freezer.

"We didn't," said the supervisor. "When we stopped at a station this morning, I bought a live chicken and we killed it especially."

Bearer service

Where meals are put on the train from base kitchens, they will be served late if the train is late at the scheduled pick-up station. On some journeys, the train stops long enough for bearers from the station restaurant to bring meals to passengers' seats. A typical vegetarian lunch served in that manner, as a *thali* meal, would be helpings of four vegetable curries (such as cabbage, potato, ochra and dhal), chapati and rice with curd in a chrome dish. A spoon could be provided on request if you haven't got your own cutlery, or you can use your fingers like Indians do.

The bearers (the Indian Railways term for waiters) come in all shapes and sizes. One I encountered was especially proud of the hygienic packing of the food he served me, pointing out the advantages of the foil casseroles for foreigners with sensitive stomachs. Having laid out the dishes on a table made up of my briefcase cross my knees, he dug deep in his pocket and produced a plastic spoon. With a flourish, he polished in on the collar of his grubby uniform jacket before handing it to me.

His concern to give good service was impressive but it did make me wonder what sort of training he received.

"On-the-job training." I was told by a top railway official. "The bearer may not be sophisticated but he does know how to serve on a moving train."

A superfast express with a pantry car could have 20 bearers/vendors on board with two cooks, two kitchen helpers/cleaners, a supervisor and an inspector. Sometimes only breakfast and snacks are cooked in the pantry, over charcoal or gas stoves, with main meals coming from base kitchens.

There are trains with a pantry car but no vestibule. The bearers have to wait for the train to stop, at a signal or station, and then run down the outside to serve. Consequently meals arrive less than fresh and the service is unreliable since it depends on the train stopping and on bearers who have to work under impossible conditions.

Some trains which have a railway-staffed pantry car can also have a contractor service. This explains why nondescript vendors appear on trains, alongside railway uniformed bearers, offering coffee, soft drinks and snacks.

On a train with a pantry car the day starts with morning tea brought to the compartment about 0630 hours, as long as you've ordered it the night before. If, like me, you find the tea too strong when a bag has stewed in a flask of hot milk for a long time, request the flask of hot water and the tea bag to be served separately and make the tea to your own strength. Indians prefer tea strong and milky and very sweet.

Breakfast is served about 0800 to order. On the *Jhelum Express* to Pune I was even asked if I wanted my eggs single or double fried. They were served in a casserole with tomato ketchup in a small polythene envelope, buttered toast and chips. Two hours later, cups of tomato soup were on offer, while women with sacks of oranges sold them, one by one, to passengers.

I wish I could report that the food on Indian Railways is improving. Unfortunately, it isn't. If you have a chance to have a good meal before boarding the train, and can take picnic food with you, do so, unless you happen to be travelling 1st AC Class on one of the *Rajdhani Expresses* between Delhi and Bombay or Calcutta (but not the other *Rajdhanis*, see page 233).

My experience in 1996 in 1st AC class on the *Madras Mail* from Howrah seems typical. The breakfast omelette was presented on a filthy china plate, spilling over its edges, with four slices of very stale bread, a bowl of tomato sauce and a teaspoon. The black coffee I ordered turned out to be pre-mixed milk tea.

I should have expected something like that since the meal offered on departure was a concoction of rice and vegetables that looked like the scrapings from someone else's meal, served in a cardboard box. I was asked to pay Rs60 for that, reduced on protest to Rs30 although on the box was a printed price of Rs20. The extra Rs10, I was told, was for service. When I realised, from the writing on the inside of the lid, that the box had been used by someone as a scrap pad, I rejected the offer. Hence, no supper that night.

The next morning, while I was contemplating the breakfast, another bearer turned up to take my lunch order, demanding payment for it in advance, even before I had paid for breakfast.

Tariff

The price of meals served on trains is not the same in all railway zones, although the difference is slight. The menus are similar, with a choice: either vegetarian (V) or non-vegetarian (NV). In the south there are the special breakfasts, such as Iddli and Vadai and Masala Dosal, which are a popular part of south Indian cuisine.

Typical meals and prices
(Rates are inclusive of taxes)

Breakfast (V)
2 potato chops (100 gm)
Tomato ketchup (20gm)
2 bread/butter slices
Potato rounders (25gm)
  Price: Rs10.00

Breakfast (NV)
1 omelette (2 eggs)
Tomato ketchup (20gm)
2 bread/butter slices
Potato rounders (25gm)
  Price: Rs12.00

Lunch/dinner (V)
Rice (200gm)
Vegetables (100gm)
Dal (175gm)
Roti/chapati/paratha (100gm)
Curd (90gm)
Salad (20gm)
  Price: Rs16.00

Lunch/dinner (NV)
Rice (200gm)
Roti/chapati/paratha (100gm)
Egg curry (2 eggs; 125gm
sauce) (215gm)
Salad (20gm)
  Price: Rs18.00

Special meal (V)
Mixed veg pullao (150gm)
2 stuffed parathas/
  2 roomali roti (100gm)
Dal/rajmah (100gm)
Muter panner/vegetable (150–165gm)
Malal kofta,
  with 90gm sauce (75gm)
Pickle (5gm)
  Price: Rs16.00

Special meal (NV)
Rice (200gm)
2 Roomali roti/chapati
  paratha (100gm)
Chicken curry (225gm)
Salad (20gm)
  Price: Rs35.00

Beverages

Tea in pot (285ml)	Rs3.00
Tea in cup (150ml)	Rs1.50
Instant coffee in pot (285ml)	Rs4.00
Coffee in cup (150ml)	Rs3.00

Service times
Meals are normally served on trains and in refreshment rooms and restaurants on stations during the following times:

Morning tea	0600 to 0800
Breakfast	0800 to 1000
Lunch	1200 to 1430
Afternoon tea	1500 to 1730
Dinner	1800 to 2100

As well as the normal beverage available on board, there are fruit juices sold in cartons, the most popular being mango which costs about Rs7, as well as soft drinks, fizzy sweet ones, and sometimes bottled mineral water.

The main problem about train food is lack of variety, especially on a long journey when curried eggs for every meal can become boring. Meals can be brightened by fruit and other regional delicacies sold at wayside stations. If you do suffer from problems caused by food (or drink) while on a train, at least you are close to a toilet.

OTHER SERVICES AND FACILITIES
Medical aid
There is a first-aid box on every passenger-carrying train and guards have some training in first aid. If you're in need of assistance, ask the coach attendant or TTE to summon help. While it is not obligatory on the part of the railways to provide medical aid to passengers, a simple scheme has been introduced to help staff find out if there is a doctor on board. On the reservation requisition form doctors are asked to indicate if they could be of help in an emergency. An asterisk is then marked against the doctor's name on the passenger list so train staff can find who and where the doctor is whenever necessary.

In an emergency, train staff can arrange for a doctor to meet the train at its next stop. The doctor will supply medication or arrange for the patient to leave the train.

In the guardsvan for emergencies will be a box containing a telephone which can be plugged into wayside posts in the event of an emergency stop so that master control can be informed. There is also a high-power battery for energising lights, and a couple of stretchers.

Station facilities
Most stations have upper class and ladies' waiting rooms. These usually have a zealous attendant at the door who will only allow entry to authorised ticket, or Indrail Pass, holders. The rooms have fans and most have attached bathrooms, often with showers, and luggage racks to which you could padlock your suitcase. The waiting area for other passengers is sometimes a spacious hall or a room with an enormous table (used as a bed at night).

Facilities vary according to a station's status. Main stations have closed circuit TV (CCTV) with train announcements transmitted live in colour from a studio actually on the station. CCTV is very popular with waiting passengers, but adds to station noise when sets are at full volume. Another feature of big stations are the juice bars selling canned and bottled apple juice from Kashmir. If the juice is made with apple concentrate served from a dispenser, think of the water it is made up with.

Some stations have wheelchairs available for disabled passengers, and also self-help luggage trolleys.

The Railway Board has defined the basic amenities which should be at every "regular" and "flag" station as "adequate seating arrangements; a drinking water supply, minimum of two hand-pumps at wayside station; sanitised latrine with water arrangements nearby for hand washing purposes; electric light; proper booking facilities; shady trees.

At "halt" stations there should be a "rail level platform of suitable length; a small waiting shed which will serve as a booking office; electric lighting where trains stop at night; shady trees".

The following facilities are being provided, where justified as a priority: "waiting halls; pucka platform surface for whole or part length; platform covers of adequate length; raising of platform from rail level to medium level/high level; coolers where piped water is available".

A second priority programme is for stations to have "retiring rooms as required; upper class waiting rooms; bathrooms as per yardstick; enquiry office; refreshment rooms".

As well a these improvements, some stations in each railway zone have been designated as "model" stations, which means they are being rebuilt to cope with rail users demands in the 1990s. As well as improved passenger comforts, the booking facilities are being upgraded to match the sophistication of the computer age.

Station nameboards are located facing the end of the platform, perpendicular to the track so they can be read with ease from passing trains. As well as the station's name, they show the station's height above sea level.

Small stations, or halts, are let out to contractors who can earn as much as Rs1,000 a month on commission from ticket sales; for this they must maintain the station and booking office.

Enquiries

All railway stations have enquiry counters, some featuring microphones with loudspeakers. The purpose is to make questions and answers audible to people in the queue, so that another person with the same enquiry would not need to stand in line for his answer. This scheme has not had much success because of a deep-rooted mistrust that makes people believe things only when said directly to them.

Most major cities and towns have telephonic enquiry systems, with operators giving the current status on arrivals and departures. Some stations have recorded information.

Although the telephone numbers vary from city to city, they usually follow this pattern:

train enquiries   131
reservation enquiries   135

(SR)

Luggage

Main stations have 'cloakrooms' which are not toilets but where passengers may leave luggage for up to a month. The charge starts at Rs2 or more for the first 24 hours, then rises in day-stages according to the total time of deposit. There are also safe deposit lockers at some stations. A typical locker, such as those at Bombay Central station, is 90cm wide, 52cm in height and 42cm deep; big enough to take a small suitcase. An advance payment has to be made and the cost begins at Rs5 per 24 hours for the first day, rising each subsequent day.

There are regulations about the weight of luggage that may be carried into a train's compartment by a passenger. Although these should not affect a foreign rail traveller who is limited by the amount airlines will allow to be carried free of charge when flying to and from India, fellow passengers may try to overstep the limits. And that could block mobility within your compartment when you find you can't step over their excess luggage.

Passengers who exceed the following limits are liable to a charge of six times the normal tariff:

	Free allowance per passenger	Maximum weight allowed in compartment per passenger
AC 1st class	70 kg	150kg
AC 2 tier & 1st class	50kg	100kg
AC 3 tier & AC chair car	40kg	40kg
Sleeper class	40kg	80kg
2nd class	35kg	70kg

A size limitation also applies and there are restrictions on the carrying of "normal luggage' in AC 3 tier coaches. This must refer to the normal amount (ie: 40kg). Just what normal luggage is, I'm not sure.

Railway regulations are more definite about luggage that will not be accepted: "Offensive items such as wet skins, hides ... dry grass and leaves, waste paper ... dead poultry and game."

Excess luggage such as a bicycle has to be booked in the brake van, a tiresome process which, being a foreigner, you should commence well in advance of the train's departure, preferably enlisting (and rewarding) assistance from station staff.

From Western Railway comes the following information: "In the case of air-conditioned First Class passengers with tiffin baskets including small ice boxes, small handbags or attache cases (not suitcases), walking sticks and umbrellas, are allowed free and will not, therefore, be weighed. In the case of Second Class passengers walking sticks, umbrellas and such articles of food as may be required on the journey are allowed free and will not, therefore, be weighed".

Regular train travellers are emphatic that the least amount of luggage you carry, the better off you'll be. One told me, "the lack of luggage helps you to conserve energy, then you won't feel a need to drink so much water". Another believes that his small, tatty bag indicates that he has nothing worth stealing.

Porters

Luggage you can carry yourself means you won't need a "coolie", as porters are called.

Porters are licensed by the station authority and pay a fee for the privilege of carrying people's luggage. They are supplied with a uniform red shirt and with a brass armband showing their licence number. A system was devised for the porter to give a token with his number on it to a passenger in exchange for the passenger's luggage. Then the passenger would have proof of who was the porter if the luggage and porter disappeared. Instead, the token disappeared.

If you do have a porter, keep an eye on him. He is adept at loading your luggage into a taxi you don't want. On the other hand, although a porter's uniform of red shirt and red scarf tied around his head makes him look like a brigand, he can be useful in locating the right train, or even to guard your luggage. He'll want at least Rs10 from you because you're a foreigner, but the normal carrying charge is less.

Porters in larger cities expect even more. The official rates are never followed and although notices in some stations invite complaints from passengers dissatisfied with the porter service, it is probably a futile cause. Sometimes unlicensed porters are cheaper and more helpful, as long as you keep your eye on them.

Even Indians are overcharged by porters, and suffer more because they understand the abuse if they don't reward sufficiently. If you must have a porter, you'll have to accept paying the penance for having too much luggage to carry yourself.

Complaints

Complaints, or compliments, can be made easily and effectively while actually on board the train. "Suggestion-cum-complaint" books are carried by the guard/conductor of mail, express and passengers trains, and also in the dining or pantry cars.

A request for the complaint book can cause great consternation among the train staff because all entries are investigated and can result in disciplinary action. The complainant is required to record full name and address and ticket number as well as the train number and date. As a foreigner, you may be asked to write down your comments if the train or catering staff think you are likely to be appreciative.

Complaint books are available at large stations in the station master's office, in the goods shed or in the parcel office. Refreshment rooms and restaurants also have books. Suggestion-cum-complaint boxes are available at major stations for passengers' letters.

Many stations have "public grievance booths" where passengers can let off steam or register formal complaints to a railway employee. Letters of complaint can also be sent direct to the DRM or general manager of the zonal railway.

It is worth using the complaints machinery. Some foreigners keep their complaints to themselves, then malign the railway system when they return home. Only if they make their comments known to the railway management can there be any improvement. An Indian once urged me to complain because "a complaint from a foreigner can improve the system for all of us".

Complaints relating to bribery and corruption are investigated by a special vigilance squad run by each zonal railway. The complainant should be prepared to give evidence before the investigating officer and the original complaint should be sent by mail to the chief vigilance officer at the HQ of the railway concerned.

A traveller from the UK recently rooted out several instances of bribery and wrote to tell me, instead of the railway authorities. He claims his cabin mate (an Indian) on the *Howrah Mail* paid Rs750 above the ordinary ticket price to secure a berth, bidding against seven others. "Corruption underscores the importance of purchasing an Indrail Pass," he said. "In some ways the pass can be viewed as a legal pay off that gives westerners many of the benefits that Indians can get only through bribery."

Travellers' tips

Most foreigners you meet will be happy to share their tips. One told me that, since local trains are slow, he actually prefers bus for short trips, only taking superfast trains on major trunk routes for long-distance journeys. He travels 2nd class, unreserved, during the day, not in the general coach but in a reserved carriage in which there are seats, and he pays the extra reservation fee, and surcharge, on the train (see *Chapter Three* for how to do this). He travels during the day to see the scenery rather than at night. He was amazed by the number of rail routes in the eastern, Ganga, region where, he said, they probably only have a pair of trains a day.

Pat Moynihan wrote: "In the south of India, I used the local bus service quite a lot. They have the advantage of not needing advance booking, covering more destinations, and being very cheap. The disadvantages are obvious – overcrowding, discomfort and confusion. Often I was the only westerner on the bus, and therefore

SOUTH CENTRAL RAILWAY APPEALS
DO NOT DETAIN TRAINS

RAIL ROKO & RASTA ROKO are resorted to by organisors of agitations to press their demands.

SOME INSTANCES

1. "DATE: 15.7.88 PLACE: ONGOLE. Severe dislocation of rail traffic caused by agitators squatting on the track ... to highlight the grievances of Cotton Growers of Prakasam District!

2. "DATE: 27.7.88   PLACE: SECUNDERABAD.   VIJAYAWADA, NANDYAL Trade Union Organisations squatted on track as part of RASTA ROKO.. to press withdrawal of proposed changes in Industrial Disputes Act. etc.,

"PLEASE   DO   NOT   DETAIN TRAINS"

*   Detained   trains   set   off   "CHAIN   REACTION" by causing other trains to be detained.
*   Thousands of passengers get detained at locations far away from their homes.
*   Goods trains carrying essentia ommodities such as foodgrains, coal can not reach destinations affecting the Public L tribution System, power generation etc.

**ISSUED IN PUBLIC INTEREST
BY
SOUTH CENTRAL RAILWAY**

the object of much curiosity. This can get wearying but I certainly felt I was getting in touch with ordinary Indian people (often literally!)"

An English couple told me: "We travel by bus as well as train, but we don't like it. Not that it's crowded but it leaves you tired at the end of the day, and emotionally wrecked. The frenzy of driving, and the horror of watching near-misses the whole time, destroys whatever pleasure there could be."

I've never been on a long-distance bus in India and don't plan to. However, Samit Roychoudhury says that in areas served only by metre gauge trains, such as in Rajasthan, parts of Gujarat and some of southern India, buses are generally faster and have a more frequent service. I prefer to dawdle by rail than hurtle by bus.

Another traveller said: " To help avoid that feeling of lethargy that can be demoralising on a long-haul trip, I make a list from the timetable of all the scheduled stops and times of arrival and departure of the train I'm going to take.

"If the train leaves late, as often happens, I list my own idea of the ETA based on the amount of delay. In a third column I list the actual times of arrival and departure. It's amazing how some trains make up time despite inexplicable delays in the middle of nowhere."

He added: "I try to stick to a timetable of my own on a long journey, listening on my shortwave transistor radio to BBC World Service at 0730 and 1630 (Indian time) every day. A shower and a change of clothes works wonders for the self-esteem. The shower is usually empty during the hour before lunch or dinner since those passengers who use it at all are likely to do so in the early morning or late evening."

Another tip: "Conversing with fellow passengers really helps to pass the time, and relieves the isolation of being of no fixed abode. An eyemask (most airlines give them out free), is useful when you've had enough conversation and want to meditate or sleep without being disturbed. Indians usually respect such an extreme desire for privacy."

Someone else told me: "Earplugs are absolutely essential if you want an after lunch nap. It's not the noise of the train, which at least has a regular rhythm, that is disturbing, but the shrieks and caterwauling of the free-range children whose troublesome activities seem to be encouraged by their parents."

Other tips I've gleaned from travellers met in India:

- When arriving by train at a station you've never visited before, make for the station restaurant, not the exit, and relax over a cup of tea while the rush to get out of the station subsides and the touts take off. The local passengers you'll meet there, and the restaurant manager, will give better advice on where to say than the touts will.

- The best seats, or berths, are those in the centre of the carriage where they are not over the wheels.

- Use timetables as a guide rather than as a guarantee of departure time or train accommodation. A check at the station in advance is vital since departure times can even be brought forward.

- If you have problems with officials at a station at night, head for the nearest hotel, check in, sleep, and wait for the next morning to resolve matters. Getting a good night's sleep is important if you are going to be quick witted enough to deal with Indian bureaucracy. Besides, in the morning there should be different officials on duty who'll be more helpful.

- Try to adjust to the Indian tendency to make everything as complicated as possible. Remember there is no way to rush the system. You are the guest and don't have the right to dictate anything.

- Don't expect to get the correct answer; you are told what people want you to hear. Nobody wants to be the one to tell you bad news.

- Whenever you hear "No problem!" watch out – something is sure to go wrong.

The best advice I had was from a young Indian navy officer who wrote to me after our meeting on a train: "Things may be difficult but you will encounter many people, many things, which will linger in your memory for long. Everything has a bad side – you must take them as a bad experience. I can assure you that definitely with time you will love this country."

Chapter Six

Trains Past and Present

To Madras goes the credit for the first plan to have a railway network in India when, in 1831, a parliamentary committee discussing the affairs of the East India Company proposed the introduction of railroads to improve the deplorable communications. Although the idea was considered again in 1836, nothing happened for 20 years.

Instead, Bombay did something about it in the 1840s with the result that the formal inauguration of the first railway line in India took place on April 16 1853, when a train carried 400 passengers from Bombay to Thane. Actually, it had taken only 28 years after the start of the world's first commercial train service, between Stockton and Darlington in the UK, for India to have her own passenger trains.

Calcutta followed swiftly, inaugurating a 24-mile line from Howrah to Hooghly in August 1854. It would have happened sooner but the ship bringing the locomotives went to Australia instead. In South India, the first line opened in June 1856 for the Madras Railway Company: 65 miles of track (built in three years at a cost of £5,500 per mile) from Madras to Walajah Road.

Meanwhile, in the north, a length of 119 miles of line was laid from Allahabad to Kanpur and opened in March 1859. Three years later, a line between Amritsar and Lahore opened for traffic.

Engineering feats

The achievements of the 19th century railway engineers are remarkable. The laying of a rail line from Bombay across the Bhore Ghats to Pune and the Thal Ghats to Bhusaval was the most difficult then undertaken anywhere in the world. Work began in 1860 with 40,000 men labouring for four years. The average daily consumption of gunpowder was 2½ tons. The two lines were opened in 1864, having been built without dynamite, pneumatic tools or any of the equipment used today.

More remarkable still was the construction in 1874 of the 55-mile metre gauge line at Godspeed from the left bank of the river Ganga to Darbhanga, forerunner of the present day North Eastern Railway. Major F S Stanton, Superintendent Engineer of the Raijputana Malwa Railway, carried out the survey, acquired the land, moved material to the other side of the river, laid the track, commissioned the locomotives and opened the line for traffic, all in 65 days.

The government was anxious to attract private capital to develop the railways but private companies were cautious about the potential for their investments so a guarantee system was devised. After 1870, railway development became rapid.

For centuries, the growth of roads had radiated from the interior, from centres such as Delhi, Lahore, Allahabad and Agra, to the coast. With railways, the communications expansion was reversed with lines commencing at the major sea ports and penetrating inland. The line over the Bhore Ghats to Pune, for instance, was to serve as a connecting line with South India and the line over the Thal Ghats to Bhusaval went on to Delhi and Calcutta.

Rail fever

As well as tracks being laid throughout the country when rail fever took hold, stations were being constructed. The railway companies were the patrons of new architecture in the 19th century. Stations, big and small, were constructed in different styles: classical, Gothic Arabic, Indo-Arabic, traditional and 19th century contemporary. The stations are still in use, although the early locomotives have disappeared.

One such station is in Madras, at Royapuram, one kilometre by suburban train from Madras Beach, where there are a few remnants of the grandiose building opened in 1856 as the terminal station for the southern link by rail of India's east and west coasts.

None of the three locomotives used on the first line from Bombay, they were called *Sind*, *Saheb* and *Sultan*, exist now. *Sindh* did survive the two world wars and was kept on a pedestal at Matunga, only to be sold for scrap. The first locomotive which hauled passenger trains on the East Indian Railway between Howrah and Raniganj is still preserved, however, at Jamalpur.

Travel by steam train in the early 20th century was the height of luxury with the Great Indian Peninsula (GIP), the forerunner of Central Railway, the pioneer. A postal express ran weekly between Bombay and Calcutta providing sleeping and dining accommodation for 32 1st class passengers. Another GIP venture was the running of hotel trains complete with sleeping cars and restaurants vestibuled together from Bombay to various tourist spots. The weekly P & O ship from London to Bombay was met by the Special Boat Express which, with the opening in 1911 of the shorter route to Delhi, enabled the Bombay, Baroda and Central India Railway (BB&CIR) to run its boat specials in 24½ hours, while the GIP postal expresses did the journey in 28½ hours.

In the 1920s, the railways entered a new phase of development as the state began to take over the management of the various railway companies. A period of prosperity followed, including electrification which was introduced in 1925 by the Great Indian Peninsula Railway and in 1928 by the suburban section of the Bombay, Baroda and Central India Railway (BB&CIR – also known as the Bloody Bad and Can't Improve Railway). The Madras suburban section was electrified in 1931.

World War II brought a setback to the railways when some rolling stock and materials were shipped out for the war effort, and some lines were dismantled and workshops used for ammunition manufacture. After independence, the entire network of 42 separate railways systems came under state control. They were reorganised into six zones in 1951/52, which eventually became the nine zones in operation up to 1996.

Since the reorganisation of 1951/52 there has been a phenomenal growth in usage. In 1950/51, there were 1,284 million passenger journeys; in 1986/87 the figure was 3,580 million. The average distance travelled by a passenger in 1986/87 was calculated as 71.6km (compared with 51.8km in 1950/51) while the average per upper class non-suburban passenger was 528.4km. The route kilometres of the railways now is over 62,000; almost twice the length of the national highways, with an average 11 million people a day travelling on the fleet of 33,700 passenger carriages hauled by about 6,900 locomotives.

As Indian Railways prepares for the 21st century and the colossal increase in passenger and freight traffic, expansion is being planned at the same time as streamlining takes place in an effort to control runaway expenditure. There are plans to import new rolling stock including electric locomotives as well as to increase indigenous production. Essential to expansion are new tracks, as existing railroads already work to capacity. The railways are speeding up the conversion of all metre gauge (MG – one metre wide) lines to broad gauge to keep pace with India's rapid industrialisation, as a unified system is seen as a must for development.

Railroad gauges throughout the world vary due to 19th century political or economic decisions. Broad gauges support heavier trains, narrow gauges are cheaper. India's trunk lines are mostly broad gauge (1.676m, 5ft 6in wide) which is also common in Bangladesh, Pakistan and Sri Lanka. The original British "standard gauge" of 1.43m (4ft 6in) is used in North America, most of Europe and China; Finland and Russia use 1.5m (5ft) gauge.

Future plans

"The railways have to meet the requirements of passengers which include safety and high speed travel, as well as the requirements of

THE "FAMILY TREE" OF THE NINE RAILWAY ZONES

1853–1872	1873–1892	1893–1912
Eastern Punjab E I R (Lucknow Moradabad & Allahabad Div	Rajpura Bhatinda Jodhpur: Binaker state: BBCI (Delhi Rewari Fazilka section)	Ludhiana Dhuri Jakhal Kalka Simla
	Assam Bengal BBCI: Kanpur/ Achnera section Bengal & NW Tirhut. Lucknow Bareilly Rohilkund. Kumayon Darjeeling Himalayan	Coochbehar State
East Indian Eastern Bengal	Tarakeswar Dildarnagar Ghazipur State	South Bihar
	Bengal Nagpur	East Coast Northern Rupsa Talband Naupada Gunupur Purulia Ranchi branch Raipur Dhamtari Satpura
Madras Railway Southern Mahratta Rly South Indian South Indian (MG)	Madras Railway Southern Mahratta Rly Kolhapur State Pondicherry Branch French Mysore State	Kolar Gold Fields Shoranur Cochin Sangli State Nilagiri M&SMR Travancore Peralam Karaikka
Great Britain Peninsula	Scindia State Bhopa Itarsi Nizam State	Bhopal Ujjain Bina–Goona Baran Nizam State Dholpur state Matheran Hill Scindia
BB&CIR Holkar State (MG)	Petlad Cambay BBCI Gaekwards Mehsana Bhavnagar State Gondal Porbandar State Junagadh State Gackwars Baroda	Tapti Valley Nagda– Ujjain Ahmadabad Dholka Branch Ahmadabad Prantij Palanpur State Jetalsar Rajkot Jamnagar Morvi Drangadra State Jaipur State Rajasthan Gujerat–Champaner Rajpidla State Morvi Tramways. Cutch

1913–1932	1933–1951	1958
Hosiarpur Doab Ranch Jind Panipat Sirhind Rupar Kangra valley	Rupar Nangal Dam	Northern Railway
Chaparmukh Silghat Katakhal–Lalabazar	Assam Bengal Assam	North Eastern Railway North East Frontier Railway
		Eastern Railway
Central India Coalfields		South Eastern Railway
Bangalore–Chick Ballapur Light	Cochin Harbour Branch	Southern Railway South Central Railway
Dhond Baramati Ellichpur Yeotmal Pachora Jamner Pulgaon Arvi		Central Railway
Boriavi Vadtal Jamnagar Dwarka Okham Andal Bodeli Chotaudaipur Gujerat–Godhra Lunavada Nandad Kapadbhan Piplod–Devgod. Baria Bhavnagar–Talja Mahuja Tramways	Jodhpur–Marwar Phulad Section	Western Railway

industry for transportation of both raw materials and finished products."

The quote, perhaps surprisingly, comes from the Delhi telephone directory which has a page devoted to development in the railways. We learn "the railways have taken a major initiative in introducing electronic signalling ... and electrification of major routes. Electrified routes of the railway comprise 20% of the total network ... Worn out electro-mechanical telephone exchanges of the railways are being replaced by digital electronic exchanges."

More relevant is the acceptance by the Railway Board that rail tourism should be encouraged. In a "Brief On Rail Tourism Policy" document, it states: "The Ministry of Railways (will) provide catalytical support for achieving the National objective of increasing the foreign tourist arrivals from the level of 2.1 million in 1995, and in foreign exchange earnings of Rs6,000 million, to 5 million foreign visitors and earnings of Rs14,000 million in foreign exchange by 2000AD."

The document outlines some ways this is to be done. A plan is to introduce tourist trains "on popular tourist circuits to provide comfortable and convenient access to seven major tourist destinations on a "travel at night and sightsee by day" concept of fully packaged tours of one week's duration."

Perhaps recognising the importance of railway retiring rooms as low-cost accommodation for adventurous rail travellers, the Ministry of Railways plans to set up 100 Rail Yatri Niwas (budget hotels) at selected locations, in cooperation with private investors.

Rail weekender tickets covering defined destinations "with hassle-free single-window booking of rail reservation, boarding and lodging and sightseeing at nearby tourist destinations" are being introduced.

Recognising the area in which most improvement is required to make rail travel more palatable, the Indian Railways Catering & Tourism Corporation (IRCTC) is being set up. It will take over all private railway catering services by the year 2000.

The *Asian Age* newspaper in July 1996 said: "The Railway Board is setting up the corporation following complaints against the quality of catering which has been deteriorating over the years and the catering departments have failed to provide economic, hygienic, complaint-free food."

Other plans for the future include the complete elimination of steam locomotives from the railways. This is surely an example of killing a golden-egg-laying goose since, for many tourists, a ride on a real steam train is one of the main reasons for trying Indian Railways.

Rail museums

The history of Indian Railways can be traced in the excellent Rail Museum in Delhi (see page 148). A lesser-known museum exists at Mysore, and this is described on page 211. More rail museums are planned at Madras and Varanasi.

STEAM IN INDIA

Steam has all but disappeared in India (see page 129). In earlier editions of this book steam rail enthusiast Hugh Ballantyne detailed meticulously what steam locomotives still existed and where to find them. Only a few paragraphs of his earlier notes remain valid now, and probably for not much longer:

"India once had a bewildering variety of locomotive types, but now there are no more steam locomotives on broad gauge lines and, on the diminishing metre gauge lines, only standardised classes exist.

"The two standard types on the MG railways look identical at a quick glance. They are the YG class 2-8-2 for goods and the YP class Pacific 4-6-2 passenger locomotive. A total of 1,076 YG class were built between 1949 and 1972, and 871 YPs between 1952 and 1972."

My source at the Railway Board unearthed a document that would cause severe depression to even the modest lover of steam: it lists the exact number of working steam locomotives left in India. In the short span of 48 months they have been reduced from 2,500 to less than 200.

Northern Railway Even as recently as 1993, a broad gauge steam locomotive used to be a daily visitor to New Delhi station. Now there are only two steam locos left, both YG on the MG line, based at Rewari. These are used to haul the *Royal Orient Express* on its start and finish at Delhi Cannt station.

North Eastern Railway Hugh Ballantyne has written: "It is probably the best railway in India for overall concentrated steam activity." A total of 54 steam locomotives remain, with the most (17 YPs and 12 YGs) at Saharsa. Other loco sheds with MG steam are at Mau Junction with 7 YPs and 2 YGs, Samastipur with 1 YP and 3 YGs, and Darbhanga with 2 YPs and 9 YGs.

Northeastern Frontier Railway Hugh Ballantyne has written: "This operates mainly in a security area and is difficult to visit. The world famous Darjeeling-Himalayan Railway is a .610m gauge line in this region and, if it is operating, you are strongly recommended to travel on it. This railway suffers frequent washout damage nearly every year during the heavy rains which close the railway to through workings. When this happens, enquire if the Kurseong to Darjeeling school train is running as this is not usually affected.

With its spirals and zigzags, this amazing railway climbs to a summit of 2,259m at Ghum before descending by means of a double loop into Darjeeling, all steam worked with its beautiful B Class 0-4-0STs."

The good news is that the DHR is not being deliberately scrapped, perhaps because its tourist value is appreciated. However, it is not always working. A new addition to the garden outside the Railway Board headquarters, Rail Bhavan in New Delhi, is a B799 steam locomotive withdrawn from service on the New Jalpaiguri to Darjeeling line in 1992. It was built in 1925 by North British Loco Ltd. A notice says it has a weight of 11.25 tons and its wheel arrangement is 0-4-0.

As at March 31 1996, there were 17 NG steam locos and 37 MG locos in the Northeastern Frontier Railway. At the loco sheds, in NG, there were 7 Bs at Tindharia, 6 Bs at New Jalpaiguri, 2 Bs at Kurseong and 2 Bs at Darjeeling. In MG, Badarpur had 3 YPs and 9 YGs, with Tinsukia having 6 YPs, 9YGs and 1 WD. At Mariani there were 7 YPs and 2 YGs.

Eastern Railway Once famous both for BG and NG steam, particularly on the Burdwan-Katwa section, the Eastern Railway no longer has any steam locos.

South Eastern Railway There are six NG systems, all .762m, and all but one are diesel. Hugh Ballantyne reported that the Bankura–Rainaga service used CC class Pacifics dating from 1906. Ninety years later there were four logged at the Bankura loco shed.

Southern Railway The romance of steam on MG has evaporated, with only two YGs remaining; these are stabled at Madurai and no longer in operation. However, a vestige of the popular steam loco ride on the unique rack and pinion line between Mettupalayam and Udagamandalam (the erstwhile Ooty) remains. This MG line is operated (at least up to Coonoor) by X class compound 0-8-2T built by Swiss Loco and Machine Works from 1920. Eight of these locos remain at Coonoor, representing a thrill to see even to someone who couldn't care less about steam.

South Central Railway has no steam at all.

Central Railway has no steam at all.

Western Railway Numerically this seems to be the most rewarding in terms of existing steam locomotives. Probably by now the five remaining attractive NG standard class ZB 2-6-2s at Baroda have gone (they were listed as "awaiting for condemnation" in March

1996). However, 74 MG locos are on the books with 9 YPs and 4 YGs at Mhow, 8 YGs at Wankaner, 12 YPs and 7 YGs at Sabarmati, 15 YPs and 2 YGs at Jetalsar, and 7 YPs and 8 YGs at Ranapratap. Also included in the total are the 2 YGs used for hauling the *Royal Orient* train which have already been included in the Northern Railway tally.

In the end, then, even these figures seem suspect. It is sad, after the part steam railways played in the development of India, that their passing goes unnoticed by the majority of rail travellers.

The trains now leaving – for ever

Without a trace of sadness, the man from Indian Railways announced the passing of an age. "We are eliminating steam." he told me. In 1992 there were 2,500 steam locos left in India; by 1997 there will be virtually none.

"Immediate dieselisation of steam throughout the railways" was the call that went out from the railways headquarters in Delhi to every railway zone and division. This was Dr Beeching's axe wielded with an Indian vengeance, chopping steam engines not just because they were poorly maintained and uneconomical (which most of them were at the end), but also, it seems, through shame that they existed at all.

In India the last steam locomotive was manufactured in the 1970s. Speaking about their elimination, the then chairman of the Railways Board, Dr Y P Anand, said, "They are too old and can't pull much. We have stopped carrying goods with steam; steam is used for shunting or to haul slow passenger trains." He did acknowledge that some passengers might actually like to travel by steam but added this clincher "Steam locos are very expensive to run."

Although steam had become more of an endangered species in India than the tiger, no-one except nostalgic foreigners seemed to care. So I made a pilgrimage to ride a steam train before it was too late.

I journeyed first to Gwalior to discover that the only steam locos there were long dead in the railway shed, bar a pair of distinguished antique engines in the garden of the palace of the erstwhile Maharaja, Madhavrao Scindia, a former railway minister. But I did get to ride the quaint narrow gauge train that makes the twice daily jaunt from Gwalior to Bhind.

Someone told me that broad gauge steam engines were still in use further down the line at Jhansi. I rushed there and felt my journey was nearing success when I glimpsed the bullet shaped nose of a steam locomotive protruding from the brick-built Victorian engine house.

The stationmaster confirmed that a regular passenger train leaving Jhansi in the morning would be steam-hauled. The train was at the platform on time and I walked its length to study the locomotive, but stopped in dismay. It was a diesel. "Oh yes," said the driver. "We changed yesterday. We won't be using steam again."

I continued southwards to where I knew that at least one steam engine, the *Blue Mountain* passenger train to Ooty, would be operating.

I believed it was technically impossible for a diesel engine to replace the vintage steam loco that puffs and pants as it pushes four carriages up the steep (1 in 12) gradient from the plains of southern India to the hill station of Ooty, 7,349 feet above sea level. I was wrong, but I was in time.

Was this line – served by steam since the beginning of the century – really going to be dieselised? At Tiruchchirappalli (Trichy), the senior divisional mechanical engineer at the Southern Railway Golden Rock workshop told me, "Every passenger I've met from abroad likes the smell of steam, the sound of steam, the look of steam. They tell me we shouldn't get rid of steam. But we must..."

So a diesel loco was introduced to run between Coonoor and Ooty, where the gradient is not so steep. The rack-and-pinion coal-fired engine was to be converted to oil-fired to serve the section to Coonoor from Mettupalayam. "The tourists will see steam, even if it isn't genuine," the engineer said.

At Trichy the next morning, I caught one of the last steam trains in India. Tata YP steam engine number 2752 was freshly greased and ready to go when I saw it at the platform. At 0750 precisely a shrill whistle, rounded off with a sharp "pip pip" announced its departure.

The sound of steam adds to its fascination. This one sighed and chugged before picking up a steady puffing rhythm as it surged through paddy-fields and palm trees with a ribbon of smoke streaming its length.

The passengers, travelling from one halt to another, sat on the slats of the wooden seats while I relished the whiff of coal smoke drifting in through the open window. Specks of soot peppered my shirt. In the paddy-fields, children waved and, between stations, we paused to pick up passengers who flagged the train to a halt. At Sologampatti we all disembarked while the train took on water.

With a deep sigh, the engine lumbered on, picking up pace with a whoosh, whoosh, letting out a shriek like a moan of anguish at the sight of buffaloes ploughing, women crouching over waterlogged fields and a child daydreaming along the line.

In the first carriage behind the engine, the sounds and smells were special: suddenly there was a damp shirt being ironed, a nostalgic hint of a coal fire in winter, as well as the rumble, toot and racket of the speeding train.

We stopped again and women and children gathered around the loco to fill pails with water from its tank, children exchanged banter with the driver, and someone handed him a cigarette. He blew his whistle and then, with a sudden belch of black smoke, the engine set off again. In a siding on the single track, we waited for another passenger train which had priority to steam past us.

Steam locomotives may have been old, slow and uneconomical, but they were the thread that bound rural India together. It is hard to believe that they have gone, shunted off into history, every one.

SUBURBAN SERVICES

The railways run Electric Multiple Units (EMU) trains on the suburban sections of Western, Central, Southern, Eastern, South Eastern and South Central Railways. The largest number of EMU trains are to be seen in Bombay where about 2,000 EMU services a day are in operation.

A recent extension of EMU services has resulted in the creation of MEMUs (Mainline Electric Multiple Units). These are exactly the same but run on non-suburban routes, such as Ahmedabad-Anand-Vadodara and Asansol-Dhanbad sections. They provide fast, efficient service in areas which have intensive commuter traffic.

Another new breed of train is the DMU, or Diesel Multiple Unit. These have been introduced on some non-electrified suburban sections of the larger cities. DMUs are characterised as having faster

---

DID YOU KNOW THAT...?

- Five of the longest railway platforms in the world are at Kharagpur, Sonepur, Lucknow, Bezwada and Jhansi stations.
- The station with the longest name is Srivenkatanarasimharajuwaripeta, in Andra Pradesh.
- The station with the shortest name is Ib, in Orissa, on the South Eastern Railway.
- You can go to Her, a station on the Vikarabad-Parli-Vaijnath line, but there is no station named Him. The A to Z of India's railway stations starts at Abada and ends with Zorawapura. Perhaps the oddest station name is Tin Mile Hat at Northeast Frontier Railways. The most romantic is surely Lovedale on the Nilagiri Line, while the funniest must be Punpun, on the Patna-Gaya line.
- The highest station in the Indian Railways system is Ghoom, on the Darjeeling Himalayan Railway, at 2,258m or 7,408ft above sea level.
- The slowest trains are those on the Darjeeling Himalayan Railway where one train takes 8hr 25min for the 87km run to Darjeeling, thereby averaging 10.14km/h.

acceleration and deceleration, more passenger-carrying capacity, cushioned seats and tinted glass windows, and a vestibule for moving from one carriage to another.

DMUs have the advantage of being able to operate on electrified routes as well. They are equipped with the latest twin-pipe graduated release air-brake system and a 700 horse power engine. DMU is a three-car set: one power car, one trailer car and one trailer car with driving cab. Passenger capacity is 288 seating and 504 standing. They are designed for maximum speeds of 100km/h and cost approximately Rs2.20 crore.

Chapter Seven

Where to Stay

RETIRING ROOMS

Guidebooks for the budget-conscious tourist and the travellers' grapevine concentrate on low-cost hotels and guesthouses in most towns in India, yet usually overlook a cheap place to stay within metres of the station platform: the railway retiring room.

From Rs100 for a double room with twin beds here is the best, cleanest and most secure accommodation you'll find at the price. It's also the most convenient since you don't have to traipse around town with your luggage looking for a place to stay.

Don't be put off by the term "retiring rooms". These are adequately, if eccentrically furnished guest rooms, nearly all with attached bathrooms. The most luxurious are suites with sitting room, bathroom, pantry, TV, fridge and air-conditioned bedroom. Rooms are usually located off the main platform or on the first floor above the booking office.

Railway accommodation conforms to minimum standards that include adequate bedroom furniture and a rule that the bed linen be changed after every occupant. If you find the sheets are grubby when you arrive, ask for them to be changed. It will be done without rancour.

Towels are also supplied on demand. The bathrooms will have a shower (sometimes with hot water) and sometimes a Western toilet, but no toilet paper. You will usually be given a padlock with a key to lock the door, or you can use your own. Many of the attendants are eagle-eyed women (wearing light blue saris) who won't let a miscreant near your door, so security is good.

The rooms in British-built stations are large and airy, with fans. Many of them open on to terraces that overlook the station forecourt. Limited room service is usually available, such as bed tea and soft drinks; sometimes tea, soft drinks and a newspaper are included in the room rate.

There are twin-bedded rooms (known as "doubles"), single rooms and dormitories. Dormitories will have their own shower and toilets attached, with a locker for each occupant to store his belongings in. If you are travelling alone and are wary about sharing a room, or dorm, with strangers, doubles can be let for single occupancy but you must pay the double rate.

Many rooms are air-conditioned with huge boxes containing alternators chugging away during the night to pump in cold air. I prefer a fan at night but I discovered that at some stations the air-conditioned rooms are much larger and, since they are regarded as prestige accommodation, they are cleaner and better serviced too.

I've only once found beg bugs under my mattress in a retiring room, in the same room where the attendant locked me in and wouldn't let me out, after waking me at 0300 hours to catch my train, until I'd given her a tip. I was pleased to notice on my second visit, after I'd complained to the DRM, that both bed bugs and attendant had gone.

Retiring rooms are charged per 24 hours. No matter what time of day or night you arrive, the room is yours for 24 hours from time of check in. Payment is made on arrival to the attendant in charge, or to the SS. Some stations increase the room rate by 25% or 40% for the second 24 hours. Occupancy is only permitted to rail travellers with tickets, or to Indrail pass holders.

Apart from the cost advantage, railway retiring rooms are ideal for those with pre-drawn departures. Their proximity to station facilities such as restaurants and, at New Delhi station, to the ITB, also adds to their appeal. A disadvantage can be the noise of the CCTV and of diesel engines hooting in the night.

A major snag is that, while foreign rail travellers may not know about railway retiring rooms, Indians certainly do, so they are very popular. At busy stations, you need to arrive early in the morning to secure one. Only one room per station can be reserved in advance, otherwise rooms are allocated on a first-come, first-served basis.

To reserve a room, when you arrive in India write to the SS of the station, enclosing a rupee money order in favour of the SS for the cost of the room, giving details of date and time of arrival.

Rendel A Davis agreed that retiring rooms are great value and wrote: "When I talked with officials at New Delhi station about the problems I had in getting a retiring room, they advised me to (in the future) go to the station superintendent, wave my Indrail Pass, and insist on being treated like a VIP. I tried that technique and it worked."

Since Indian railway travellers are well versed in using influence of their own to secure a room, do not be reluctant to take advantage of the privilege the IRP brings, but its importance is only likely to be recognised by the SS, not by the retiring room caretaker.

Ian Scrimgeour of Thunder Bay, Canada, recalled his stay at the retiring room, Reningunta. "I was stationed there in 1945–46 and life in the area was so dreary that it was not unknown to have parties in the refreshment room at Renigunta with some of the more overcome by Parry's gin ending up upstairs!"

Even though alcohol is no longer available in the refreshment rooms, the retiring rooms are still there. The rates are to be found in the zonal timetables. They range from Rs20 for a dormitory bed to Rs500 for a twin-bedded air-conditioned room. Some stations, like Jaipur, even have a dormitory exclusively for women (at Rs35 per bed inclusive of tea and a newspaper).

Stations with retiring rooms
Some stations have only one retiring room and others (where indicated) have only a dormitory. Facilities are sometimes only basic.

Abohar	Asand	Bellampalli
Abu Road	Asansol	Bellary
Adra	Aurangabad	Berhampur Court
Adoni	Ayodhya	(dorm)
Agra Cantt	Badarpur Jn	Berhampur (Ganjam)
Agra Fort	Badaun	Bhadohi
Ahmedabad	Badnera	Bhadrachalam Road
Ahmednagar	Bagaha	Bhadrak (dorm)
Ajmer	Bagalkot	Bhaga
Akola	Baheri	Bhagalpur
Aligarth Jn	Bahraich	Bahratpur
Alipurduar Jn	Baidyanathdam	Bharuch
Allahabad	Baijnath Paprola	Bhatni
Allahabad City	Balasore	Bhavnagar
Alleppey	Ballia	Bhilwara
Alwaye	Balotra (dorm)	Bhimavaram
Alwar	Balrampur	Bihwani (dorm)
Ambala Cantt (dorm)	Balugaon	Bhopal
Amethi	Banda	Bhubaneswar
Amlai	Bangalore City	Bhuj
Amritsar	Bankur (dorm)	Bhusaval
Anand	Barajamda (dorm)	Bijapur
Anandnagar	Barauni	Bikaner
Anantapur	Barddhaman	Bilaspur
Ankleshwar	Barmer (dorm)	Bina
Annavarum	Bareilly	Bishnupur (dorm)
Ara	Barpeta Road	Bokoro Steel City
Arakkonam	Basti	Bolpur
Araku (dorm)	Bathinda (dorm)	Bombay Central
Aravanakadu	Begusarai	Bombay VT
Arsikere	Belgaum	Bongaigaon

Burnpur (dorm)
Buxar (dorm)
Bettiah
Betul (dorm)

Calicut
Cannanore
Chakradharpur
Champa (dorm)
Chandigarh
Chandrapur
Chaparmukh
Chenganur
Chenganacheri
Chhapra Jn
Chidambaram
Chinnaganjam
Chirala
Chitrakutdham
Chittaranjam
Chittaurgarh
Chittoor
Coimbatore
Coonoor
Cuddapah
Cuttack

Darbhanga
Davangere
Daund
Dauram Medhepura
Dehra Dun
Dehri-on-Sone
Delhi
Deoria Sadar
Dhanbad
Dharmanagar
Dharmavaram
Diamond Harbour
Dibrugarh Town
Dimapur
Diphu
Dongargarh
Durg
Durgapur
Dwarka

Eluru
Ernakulam Jn
Erode Jn

Faizabad

Fakiragram Jn
Falna
Farukhabad
Fatehpur
Firozabad
Firozpur
Forbesgani

Gadag (dorm)
Gandhidham
Gandhigram
Gaya
Ghazipur City
Godhra
Golagokarannath
Gomoh
Gonda
Gondal
Gondia
Gopalganj
Gooty
Gorakhpur
Gudur
Guna
Guntakal
Guntur
Guwahati
Gwalior

Hajipur
Haldwani
Hanumangarh (dorm)
Harpalpur
Hardoi
Haridwar
Harmuti
Hassan
Hazaribagh Road
Hojai
Hospet
Howbagh
Hubli
Hazrat Nizamuddin

Indore
Itarsi
Izatnagar

Jabalpur
Jagi Road
Jaipur
Jaipur-Keonjhar Rd
(dorm)

Jaisalmer
Jalandhar City
Jalgaon
Jamalpur
Jammu Tawi
Jamnagar
Jasidih
Jaynagar
Jhanjharpur
Jhansi
Jharsuguda
Jiribam
Jodbani
Jodhpur
Jolarpettai
Junagadh

Kadur
Kakinada Town
Kalka
Kamakhya
Kanniya Kumari
Kanpur Anwarganj
Kanpur Central
Karaikkudi Jn
Karimganj
Karwi (dorm)
Kathgodam
Katihar
Katni
Katpadi
Kazipet
Khagaria
Khalilabad
Khandwa
Karagpur
Khurda Road
Kishanganj
Kiul Jn
Kodaikanal Road
Kolhapur
Kota
Kotdwara
Kottayam
Krishnanagar City
(dorm)
Kumarghat
Kumbakonam
Kurnool Town

Laheria Sarai
Lakhimpur

Lar Road
Lovedale
Lucknow (NR)
Lucknow Jn (NER)
Ludhiana
Lumding Jn

Madgaon
Madhubani
Madhupur
Madras Central
Madras Egmore
Madurai
Mahesana
Maihar
Makrana (dorm)
Malda Town
Mangalore
Mankapur
Manmad
Mantralayam Road
Mariani Jn
Mathura
Mathura Cantt
Mau Jn
Mayiladuturai
Meerut City (dorm)
Merena
Mettupalaiyam
Midnapur
Miraj
Mirzapur
Moradabad
Morbi
Motihari
Mughal Sarai
Muri
Murshidabad
Muzaffarpur
Mysore

Nagappattinam
Nagda
Nagercoil
Nagore
Nagpur
Nainpur (dorm)
Najibadad (dorm)
Nanded
Narkatiaganj
Nasik Road
Naugarh

Nautanwa
New Alipurduar
New Bongaigaon
New Coochbehar
New Delhi
New Jalpaiguri
Nidadavolu
Nidubrolu
Nirmali
Nizamabad
North Lakhimpur
Ongole

Pakur
Palakollu
Palani
Palanpur
Palasa
Palghat
Palimarwar (dorm)
Parbhani
Parlivaijnath
Pathankot
Patna Jn
Patna Sahib
Pendra Road (dorm)
Pilibhit
Pipariya
Pollachi (dorm)
Pondicherry
Porbander
Pune
Puri
Purnea Jn
Puruliea

Quilon

Rae Bareli
Raichur
Raigarth
Raipur (dorm)
Rajahmundry
Rajgir
Rajkot
Rajnandgaon
Ramagundam
Rameswaram
Rampur
Rampurhat
Ranchi
Raurkela

Renigunta
Ratlam
Raxaul
Rayagada (dorm)
Renigunta
Rewari (dorm)
Roorkee

Sagarjambagaru
Saharanpur (dorm)
Saharsa Jn
Sakri
Salem Jn
Samastipur
Sambalpur
Sanchi
Sasaram
Satna
Sawai Madhopur
Sealdah
Secunderabad
Shahganj
Shahpur Patoree
Shahjahanpur
Shantipur
Shimla
Sidhawalia
Silchar
Siliguri Jn
Simaluguri Jn
Sitamarhi
Siuri
Sivakasi
Siwan
Sitapur
Solapur
Sonagir
Sonpur
Sriganga Nagar
Srikakulum Road
Srirangam
Supaul
Surat
Surendranagar
Suri

Tarakeswar
Tatanagar
Tenali
Tenkasi
Thanabihpur
Thanjavur

Thiruvarur	Tuticorin	Vindhyachal
Tinsukia Jn		Viramgam
Tiruchchirappalli	Udagamandalam	Virudhunagar
Tiruchendur	Udaipur City	Visakhaptnam
Tirunelvelli	Ujjain	Vizianagaram
Tirupati		Vriddachalam
Tirur	Vadodara	
Tiruppur	Valsad	Wadi
Titlagarh	Varanasi Jn	Warangal
Trichur	Vasco da Gama	Wardha (dorm)
Trivandrum Central	Veraval	Wellington (dorm)
Tulsipur	Vijayawada	
Tundla	Villupuram	

RAILWAY HOTELS

Not strictly hotels, but neither are they retiring rooms, are two of the best places to stay for convenience, comfort, security and price in Delhi and Calcutta: Rail Yatri Niwas (rail travellers' inn).

The one at New Delhi station is three minutes' walk from the Ajmeri Gate (not the main) exit. Dive through the scrum of taxi drivers and touts and head for the puce, granite building of some eight storeys that you can see on your left. It is best to make a reservation in advance since there is a big demand for rooms there. Reservations can be done through the ITB or direct by mail to Rail Yatri Niwas, New Delhi Railway Station, Gate Number 2, New Delhi 110002, tel: 3313484, enclosing a money order for the full amount with details of your arrival and departure days and times, plus ticket (PNR) or IRP number. Only rail passengers with tickets for a journey of at least 500km, or IRP holders, can stay there, for a maximum of three nights.

If you don't have a reservation, you'll stand a better chance of a bed at weekends, and if you arrive around 1000 hours, the hour of check in or check out. (If you check in between 0600 and 1000 an extra 20% is payable.) The charm of the place may escape you during the chaos of registering (full fee is demanded in advance plus Rs100 key deposit) but this can be a fun place once you've established a rapport with the staff.

There are 71 rooms with 244 beds, fans, no air-conditioning. The best are the rooms (at Rs250) with twin beds and ensuite showers/toilets and morning tea service. Dormitory beds were Rs70 in 1996. Not many foreigners stay there and I don't know why not since it is clean and convenient, with Connaught Place only minutes away by cutting through the station. There is a restaurant where you have to pay the cashier before getting your meal; it's a bit gloomy but the food is much better than the usual railway catering.

I made the mistake on my last visit of trying to get my laundry done officially, which took three days. A Brit who was staying there was smarter. He gave the dormitory attendant 12 items including his precious jeans and got them back washed and ironed in four hours.

The Rail Yatri Niwas at Howrah station is built on a grander scale as part of the extension housing platforms 18 to 21. Even if you don't stay there the Yatrik restaurant is worth a visit. The architects have joyfully followed old traditions with a high ceiling, a vast room and a sophisticated decor of murals and pastel panels.

There are 115 beds on two floors in air-conditioned and non air-conditioned rooms and dormitory beds in five- and seven-bedded dorms. No advance reservations are accepted but you can arrive in the morning and pay the full room rate to secure a room later the same day. Rooms are let on a day-to-day basis from 1000 to 1000. The stay can be extended from 0800 each morning up to three nights. The room rate is payable on check-in, together with a refundable deposit. Bed tea and a newspaper is included, and there is a left-luggage storage facility. You must hold an IRP or a current inward or outward ticket for a journey of at least 500km.

Many of the rooms have balconies and are superb for watching the sun rise over the Hooghly River and seeing the city of Calcutta from a safe distance. Not so safe are the metal arms at eye level at both ends of the beds, designed for draping mosquito nets over, but more dangerous to your eyes and head than a mosquito would be.

Two splendid old-style hotels are operated by South Eastern Railway (SER). There is one at Ranchi, established in 1915, and another at Puri, built in 1925. Both are worth a visit for the pleasure of staying in them.

At Ranchi, the hotel is a sprawling bungalow type with 22 rooms and shuffling waiters wearing the livery of the former Bengal and Nagpur Railway. The waiters at the Puri hotel, which is in a garden setting near the beach, dress and serve in the same old world manner.

CITY HOTELS

When I want to stay away from railwayland in a town I've not visited before, the only option I consider viable is a good five-star hotel. There are practical reasons for this. After several nights on a train, there is nothing better than to check into the best hotel and be pampered. You'll feel you deserve a comfortable hotel in which to sleep properly, have the laundry done, luxuriate in a hot bath, watch TV, indulge in a wide choice of good food, and drink a cold beer. (A five-star hotel is about the only place where you'll get a drink on a "dry" day.)

With rates at US$200 a night, and even more, five-star hotels are not for every traveller nor for every night, but the best are worth the extravagance, especially when set against the savings being made through travelling by rail.

For older train travellers who are suffering from lack of their usual comforts, a good five-star hotel is the best antidote. Even one night tended by caring, alert staff who know their job can be a restorative and fortify for the journey ahead.

For younger rail travellers, some five-star hotels are an experience not to be missed, as much for the beauty and grandeur of their buildings as for the luxury of their service. It all costs less than comparable hotels at home. Being able to pay with a credit card, including Visa and Access, is useful, too, since it preserves rupees for train expenses.

Sometimes an Indian five-star hotel is not from the same constellation as international five-star properties, but those of the major chains like Oberoi, Taj and Welcomgroup usually are. Oberoi Hotels have a pleasing mix of modern amenities and old world charm and tradition. (The modern New Delhi and Bombay Oberoi hotels actually have a team of butlers attending every room around the clock). Oberoi was the first Indian hotel company to hire educated people for such run-of-the-mill jobs as waiters and bellboys, and to employ women in housekeeping and as receptionists and guest relations staff.

Welcomgroup run the remarkable Umaid Bhawan Palace Hotel, where any visitor to Jodhpur should try to stay for a taste of the Maharaja lifestyle. They also operate the custom-built colonial delight, the Windsor Manor Sheraton in Bangalore, where the Oberoi group have also opened a splendid property.

One of the most recognisable hotels in India belongs to another luxury hotel chain, the Taj group. Photos of the Lake Palace Hotel at Udaipur, as it seems to float on the blue waters of Lake Pichola, are one of the enticements to visit India. It's not far from Udaipur railway station.

The luxury hotel and the ordinary retiring rooms (always the best bet for the low-budget passenger) where I've stayed are mentioned in detail under the destination headings. Low- and medium-budget hotels exist in every town and city and information on them can be found in the general guides to India (such as Lonely Planet's) and from state tourist offices.

HOTEL RESERVATIONS

In many cases, the published telephone and fax numbers of both official institutions and hotels in India have proved inaccurate as these are frequently changed. The Government of India tourist offices in various countries should be able to help but even the list of their own telephone numbers issued in June 1996 by the head office in Delhi was out of date.

More reliable for up-to-date information on hotels before you travel would be such agencies as WEXAS (see page 17), which publishes a handbook for members that includes the latest contact numbers for many hotels in India. WEXAS members are entitled to discounts on accommodation. The agents for Indian Railways in England (S D Enterprises, see page 53) would also book accommodation and provide current telephone numbers.

Asia-Pacific Business Travel Guide 1997/98

The business and independent travellers's essential guide to the 36 countries of the Pacific-Asia area.

Doing Business, Etiquette, Tourism Update, What to See, Key Facts, Useful Addresses, over 1000 hotels from Karachi to Honolulu.

"Any business traveller heading east for the first time can be confident with this in his briefcase" - Executive Travel, London
"The most comprehensive, yet compact, Far East guide on the market" - Lloyds List, London
"A fund of information" - Check-In Magazine, Munich
*"**The** Book on business travel"* - Recommend Magazine, USA

328 pages, full colour paperback ISBN 1-871985-25-0   £9.95

(Also now available on the Internet under **http://travel.cm-net.com/pata**)

SYRESHAM, BRACKLEY
NORTHANTS NN13 5HH
TEL 01280 850603/850218
FAX 01280 850576
E-MAIL priory@dial.pipex.com

Chapter Eight

The Journey Begins

Since most visitors to India arrive by air at the airports of Delhi, Bombay, Calcutta or Madras, their rail journey is likely to begin from a station in one of those cities. This chapter looks at the facilities in those cities, and in two other cities with airports served by flights from abroad: Trivandrum and Tiruchchirappalli. Goa is covered in *Chapter Ten*.

DELHI

For many readers of this book, their first experience of Indian railways will be at New Delhi or Delhi stations. That is unfortunate because both stations give a dreadful first impression with which to begin your journey. They are quite unlike Delhi itself which is pleasant and enjoyable.

Much of the negative reaction inspired by Delhi's two main stations is due to a traveller's own frame of mind. If you go to the station straight off the plane after a long-haul flight, you're bound to be appalled by the heat and squalor. Allow yourself a chance to adjust to the time change, jet lag and culture shock before attempting to buy a ticket. At least the ITB (see *Chapter Three*) relieves most of the hassle, but you'll need to be in top form for the station itself.

There is a desk operated by Northern Railway at Delhi's Indira Gandhi International airport where reservations can be made by arriving passengers. It is open from 0000 to 0800 hours, the period during which many long-haul flights arrive.

Delhi is the headquarters of Northern Railway (NR), the biggest zonal railway in the country. Its 10,977 route kilometres serve a population of nearly 200 million in Punjab, Karyana, Uttar Pradesh, Rajasthan, Himachal Pradesh, Jammu and Kashmir, and parts of Gujarat, as well as Delhi and Chandigarh. Stretching 1,168km from Amritsar to Varanasi, NR also connects with the Pakistan rail network at Atari and Munnabao. NR runs more than

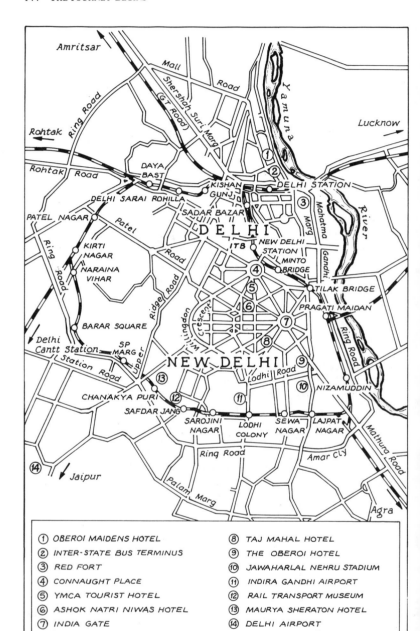

① OBEROI MAIDENS HOTEL
② INTER-STATE BUS TERMINUS
③ RED FORT
④ CONNAUGHT PLACE
⑤ YMCA TOURIST HOTEL
⑥ ASHOK NATRI NIWAS HOTEL
⑦ INDIA GATE
⑧ TAJ MAHAL HOTEL
⑨ THE OBEROI HOTEL
⑩ JAWAHARLAL NEHRU STADIUM
⑪ INDIRA GANDHI AIRPORT
⑫ RAIL TRANSPORT MUSEUM
⑬ MAURYA SHERATON HOTEL
⑭ DELHI AIRPORT

DELHI

270 mail/express and 650 passenger trains daily, carrying about 1,200,000 people a day.

The NR zone abounds in pilgrim places: Amritsar, famous for the Golden Temple; Haridwar, the holiest Hindu centre; Allahabad, the site of the Triveni Sangam, the confluence of the Ganga, Yamuna and the invisible Saraswati rivers; Varanasi, the oldest pilgrim centre. The Himalayan resorts of Shimla and, via Jammu Tawi, of Kashmir, are accessible by NR.

Trains from Delhi also give access to colourful historical centres: Agra, the capital of the Mughal empire, famous for the Taj Mahal; Fatehpur Sikri with its magnificent monuments of Mughal glory; Lucknow, the cradle of Muslim culture; Bikaner, a city renowned for Rajput chivalry; Jodhpur, famous for its massive fort; and even the unique desert outpost of Jaisalmer.

Since you'll have to pass through one of Delhi's stations to get to these exotic places by train, it's as well to be prepared for a low-key beginning.

New Delhi station

The station is not a major terminus in the grand style (like Bombay VT for instance) but a depressing transit station with overstretched facilities. The catering outlets are poor. At platform level, there is a snack counter staffed by people who make it obvious they have no interest in being helpful. The restaurant upstairs, opposite the ITB, is like the canteen of a small, rundown factory. The whole station has an unwelcoming atmosphere and it's a relief to jump on a train and get out.

There are waiting rooms for upper and 2nd class passengers, with a separate one for ladies, and there are toilets with showers. The general public have a waiting area with fans above their seats. There are cloakrooms, a telegraph office, phone booths for local and trunk calls and a post office.

There is a current reservations booking office for same day departures as well as ticket counters for non-reserved travel. On the left as you enter the station building is a lobby from where stairs (or a lift) lead to the first floor where the ITB is located. It's a haven from the chaos below.

On the second and third floors are the retiring rooms. A point in their favour is their proximity to the ITB, but they are not very nice. There is a view from the terrace of the small forecourt below, bright with colour from yellow-topped taxis and red-shirted porters.

Reservations for the retiring rooms are made on the ground floor where there is a desk behind the current reservations counter. They are usually fully booked, which shows that my own feelings about the station are not shared by everyone.

Actually, out of the station building and along the platforms, the atmosphere does change. It becomes almost rural. At the end of platform 1 there are plants in pots and hibiscus bushes in bloom. A gate leads to railway offices and housing, and there are intriguing coaches parked in an adjoining siding. You might spot the royal blue Ultra Sonic Rail Testing Car URT100 Matix System here. At the other end of the platforms, there are nine in all, is a temple, serenity amidst the shunting trains.

Near platform 9 is the base kitchen where cooks prepare over 3,000 meals a day to put on trains. Also near the platform, through the Ajmeri Gate exit and across a compound, is the Rail Yatri Niwas, a hostelry for transit passengers opened in March 1988 (see *Chapter Seven*).

Information on other places to stay can be gouged out of the staff at the Delhi tourist office tucked away in a corner close by the lift to the retiring rooms. The staff are so fed-up with being asked the times of trains, their response to questions is almost automatically negative. But they have booklets to sell.

It is not far from New Delhi station to Connaught Place, the hub of the city, and to the computerised reservation complex ten minutes' walk from the station. Tourists, however, should use the facilities of the ITB for their ticket purchase and reservations.

Among the major trains originating at this station are the seven *Shatabdi Expresses*: 2002 via Agra to Bhopal, 2004 via Kanpur to Lucknow, 2005 via Chandigarh to Kalka, 2017 to Dehradun, 2011 to Chandigarh, 2013 via Ludiana to Amritsar and the popular 2015 to Jaipur and Ajmer.

There are also five *Rajdhani Express* trains which leave from this station, emphasising that New Delhi's importance in the rail network is much greater than appears from the state of the station. The *Rajdhanis* are 2302 via Dhanbad to Howrah, 2306 via Patna to Howrah, 2952 via Vadodara to Bombay Central, 2422 via Howrah to Bhubasneswar and 2424 via Patna to Guwahati.

To Madras there are daily departures by 2616 *Grand Trunk* and 2622 *Tamil Nadu Expresses*. Over two dozen other expresses link the capital with Lucknow, Puri, Guwahati, Patna, Indore, Allahabad, Bangalore, Secunderabad, Trivandrum or Mangalore, Kalka, Amritsar, Jammu Tawi and Varanasi.

Delhi station

Delhi station (sometime called Delhi Main or Old Delhi) is to the north of New Delhi station and can be reached by train from there, either on suburban or main line services. It has a friendlier atmosphere than New Delhi but is bereft of more than essential amenities. Kiosks and snack counters are grouped along the length of the main platform where there is a charmless self-service restaurant. There are 18 platforms.

There is a counter where reservations can be made for the retiring rooms, which can be reached by lift. The retiring rooms – at least the one I had in 1992 – gave me the feeling that I would rather be elsewhere, and the attendants seemed to wish that too. There is a barber shop.

Reservations for departures from this station by foreign tourists should be made at the ITB.

Delhi used to be the main station for metre gauge train departures (a role now taken over by Delhi Sarai Rohilla). An interesting new train worth trying from Delhi station is the 9760 Delhi–Jaipur *Intercity Express*. There are other exotically named trains from Delhi, such as the 4647 *Flying Mail* (to Amritsar) and the 3112 *Delhi–Sealdah Express*. The 4033 *Jammu Tawi Mail* and the 4041 *Mussoorie Express* to Dehradun also start from this station.

It makes sense to double check your departure station when starting a journey from New Delhi just in case the train actually leaves from Delhi, and not New Delhi, station. If you go to the wrong one it will take at least 30 minutes by taxi to switch from one to the other.

Hazrat Nizamuddin station
To take the pressure of New Delhi this station, located in the southeast of the city, close to the luxury hotel area, has been expanded. It is also the major station on the ring railway. A computerised reservations complex is 500m from the station. Current reservations can be made in the booking hall which is a contrast to the scrum of New Delhi station. There is a left luggage cloakroom. Two retiring rooms and a dormitory are off platform 1, which also has refreshment and waiting rooms.

The forecourt is a bit haphazard in services for what has become an important station. While there are pre-paid taxis available (you queue at a booth and buy a ticket to your destination) there are also freelance taxis whose operators seem more obliging. The place is like a village park. In fact, the district was founded 600 years ago as a village around the shrine of the Saint Sheikh Nizamuddin Chisti; the area remains mainly residential.

The booking hall contains an ever-lengthening list of the day's departures including shuttle trains and EMU (electric multiple unit) trains.

A notice warns travellers: "For your kind attentions. Please do not accept sweets eatable or drinks offered any strange or unknown co-passenger in the train, platform or waiting room. Buy food and drinks and other eatable only from authorised stall or from licensed wenders otherwise you can be cheated."

Nizamuddin's new importance as a station is due to it being the start and terminus of the increased *Rajdhani Express* services. These are the 2954 Rajdhani to Bombay Central via Vadodara, the 2425 to Jammu Tawi, the 2430 via Secunderabad to Bangalore, the 2432 to Trivandrum via Madras and the 2634 to Madras. Other departures include the 4004 Agra Cannt *Intercity Express* and the *Taj Express* to Gwalior via Agra. Watch Nizamuddin; it seems destined to grow.

Delhi Sarai Rohilla station
What was previously a halt on the ring railway and on the metre gauge line has assumed prominence as the terminal for the metre gauge trains still serving Delhi. It lies west of Delhi station and a taxi would probably be the easiest way to get there. It is an open station with only basic amenities.

Metre gauge trains originating here include the 9901 and 9903 *Ahmedabad Mail* and *Express*, the 2905 *Ashram Express* to Ahmedabad, the 4893 *Jodhpur Mail*, the 2915 *Garib Nawaz Express* and the 9615 *Chetak Express*, both to Udaipur City, and the 4791 and 4789 *Bikaner Mail* and *Express*.

Ring railway
Delhi's ring railway gives a marvellous view of the backside of suburban city life, often literally as people use the line as a toilet. It was opened in 1982 and girdles the city, covering a distance of 35km.

The trains encircle the city clockwise and anti-clockwise throughout the day, from Hazrat Nizamuddin to 20 stations. These provide a link from New Delhi to Delhi.

This is an EMU service, which means an electrical multiple unit is used to pull it. It is supposed to stop for only 30 seconds at stations so passengers have to move sharply. It is very popular with commuters; if you want to try it, the best time is at a weekend when it is not so busy.

The seats are wooden and there are lots of handles for standing passengers, as well as plenty of fans. The doors are kept open all the time and no smoking is allowed. One of its stations, Safdarjang, is near the rail museum.

Rail Museum
The Rail Museum, set up in New Delhi in 1977, was the first of its kind in India. Engines and carriages, all refurbished and painted in their original colours, are exhibited on tracks of different gauges laid out in a ten-acre "railway yard". Six display galleries and a padlocked, glass-walled building housing the museum's star exhibit (the *Fairy Queen*), together with a toy train and a restaurant, are included in the museum grounds.

For those fascinated by the sight of old locomotives, the museum is delightful. When I was there off-season (in July) it looked a bit neglected with bored attendants and overgrown gardens, but nothing could detract from the majesty of the engines on view.

The *Fairy Queen* is claimed to be "the oldest surviving locomotive in perfect working order anywhere in the world". It was purchased by the East Indian Railway in 1855, two years after the inauguration of the first rail line in India. It was built by Kittson, Thompson & Hewitson of Leeds, UK, and looks eager to keep on running. However, the claim to be the oldest is disputed. In a letter to *The Guardian* in April 1989, George Shuttleworth of Leighton Buzzard says there are older locos in working order in Austria (*Liacon* built in 1851) and in England (*Lion* built in 1838). Close to her is half an engine, a locomotive built in 1891 in Glasgow for the Nizam's Guaranteed State Railway, and sliced lengthways to show its workings.

On tracks among the grass, where you can wander at will, are more than two dozen vintage locos and a score of carriages, including an armoured train. Such trains, with "Maxim guns", were extensively used up to the 1920s by the British Army. The metre gauge (MG) train in the museum was built in India prior to World War I on wagon stock of the 1880s. Each carriage is provided with an armoured plate ½in thick, with felt lining 3in thick and another armoured plate ¾in thick to protect the occupants against normal gun fire.

Other spectacular carriages are the white-painted Vice-Regal Dining Coach (1889), with its entrance platforms at both ends, and the saloon coach of the special train of the Maharaja of Mysore. This coach could be run on broad gauge as well as metre gauge with a change of bogies without disturbing the royal family during their journey from Mysore to Madras. The other two carriages which made up the Maharaja's train are in the rail museum in Mysore (see *Chapter Ten*).

The *Prince of Wales* saloon coach has its original fittings and furnishings. It was built for the visit to India of the *Prince of Wales* (later Edward VII) in 1876, and is provided with sunshades on both sides. A four wheeler sheep van (built in 1929) is divided into four compartments with two tiers to accommodate 176 sheep. It, too, has sunshades.

The wooden *Nilagiri* passenger coach (built 1914) used on the rack and pinion railway up the steep gradients of the Nilagiris has canvas curtains as protection against the sun, wind and rain, its only difference from the wooden coaches in use today.

A new addition to the museum is an X-class metre gauge loco of the types still used on the Nilagiri Mountain Railway. The Shimla railcar (built 1931) fitted with a 4-cylinder petrol engine and painted in white and light blue, is a small version of the railcars used on the Kalka/Shimla line.

Other delightful oddities include *Ramgotty*, with wooden brakes, built in France and converted from 4ft gauge to 5ft 6in in 1896, and the steam monorail engine which ran on a single rail with an outrigger wheel running on the road alongside the track. Originally monorail trains were pulled by mules of the Patiala State Monorail Trainways on a 50-mile track.

A behemoth hulking over pygmy locos is the *Garratt*, built by Neyer, Peacock of Manchester in 1930 for the Bengal Nagpur Railway. This engine could easily haul 2,400 tons of trailing load on a 1 in 100 up gradient. Not all the engines are steam. *Sir Roger Lumley* built in 1930 for the Great Indian Peninsula Railway, is electric powered. One of the first EMU coaches introduced on the Bombay suburban section of the Bombay, Baroda and Central India Railway (BB&CIR) in 1928 is also on display.

The galleries have a variety of mementoes and models of early as well as current Indian railway equipment. There is some of the Burmese teak furniture from the BB&CI Railway; the Miraj station clock (1926), engine plate, special coach fittings and displays showing the development of signalling and telecommunications.

An astounding sight in the middle of the technology is the skull of an elephant whose firm refusal to budge from the track caused the derailment of the entire seven-carriage Calcutta to Nagpur mail in September 1894.

Souvenirs on sale include original builder's plates and motor plates from scrapped steam locos at Rs300 to Rs400 each, some rail history books, a pack of ten colourful postcards of the exhibits, and a bottle opener/ice-breaker. There is a good, if out-of-date, guide to the museum available. The exhibits are well labelled with description, year built, builder and area of service.

Admission fees are low; there is a charge for every camera taken in. On Tuesdays, entry is free for children below 12 years old. The museum is open from 1000 to 1730 but the ticket office closes at 1700 hours. It is closed on Monday and on Republic Day, Holi, Idn'l Fitr, Independence Day, Mahatma Gandhi's birthday, Dussehra and Diwali.

The most appropriate way to get to the rail museum is by train. It is five minutes' walk from the ring railway station of Safdarjang, in the southwest of New Delhi. It is close to the Chanakyapuri Diplomatic Enclave, an easy ride by taxi or auto-rickshaw from the Welcomgroup Maurya Sheraton or Taj Palace hotels.

Rail Transport Museum, Shantipath, Chanakyapuri, New Delhi, 110021.

Delhi Cantt

This MG station could almost be part of the rail museum. It has the period look of the 1930s, heightened by seeing the *Royal Orient* train which departs from here; the setting is perfect for its antique-style carriages. The station is off the road to the international airport on the western outskirts of the city, beyond the Dhaula Kuan roundabout.

There are several stations with the word Delhi in their name, but they are halts on the main or suburban passenger lines: Delhi

Azadapur, Delhi Kishanganj, Delhi Safdarjang and Delhi Shahdara Jn.

Where to stay

Taj Mahal Hotel, 1 Mansingh Road, ND; tel: 3016162. Popular with New Delhi regulars, it has a lively bar off the lobby and a roof-top restaurant, where Italian/Indian buffet lunches are served. The rooms have twin beds and small bathrooms; there are 308 units including some magnificent suites. The practice of serving a tea bag in a plastic flask in my room for breakfast reminded me too much of railway retiring rooms, but a good feature is the illuminated "Do Not Disturb" sign outside each room.

Oberoi Maidens Hotel, Sham Nath Marg, Delhi; tel: 2525464. Convenient for Delhi main station and a firm favourite with British travellers, perhaps because of its colonial style as well as its superb value for money, with even standard rooms having a separate sitting room. It is one of the oldest hotels in India, and was the centre of Delhi's social life during the days of the British Raj. It was *the* place to stay then, and there is a story about two young ladies who were guests there when their funds ran out. They telegraphed their father in England: "Please Send Money Fast Or Can No Longer Stay Maidens."

Oberoi, Dr Zakir Hussain Marg, Delhi: tel: 363030. India's first modern luxury hotel when it was opened in 1965. It is given warmth and soul by the butlers who attend guests in every room, an innovation that confused me at first as I wondered what a butler did. Mine organised my photocopying and shopping as well as polished my shoes. When I mentioned this book he gave me tips on which trains to try.

BOMBAY

For the rail traveller, Bombay is an exciting introduction to India: the city's stations have all the rail glamour you could want, as well as trains that go to most major destinations. The booking and information system works well, if you're patient, for it isn't that simple. There is the added attraction of Bombay itself – an exciting and bustling metropolis.

If you arrive by air, there is a railway enquiry desk and reservations centre at Bombay's international airport, open from 2300 to 0700, to coincide with flight arrivals. If your itinerary is complicated, though, wait until you get to the foreign tourist desk at Bombay TV station. As with New Delhi, I recommend a day to settle in before trying to sort out your onward rail travel.

Your first problem will be to find out whether your train leaves from Bombay VT or Bombay Central or even from Dadar, an

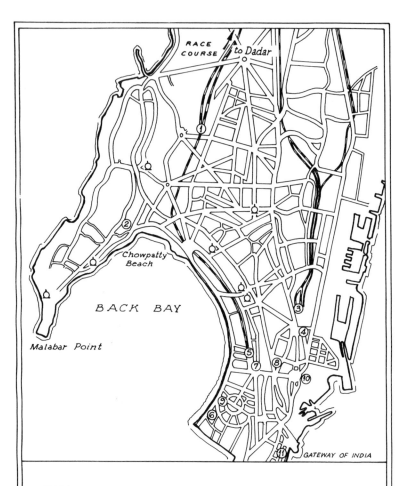

RACE COURSE

to Dadar

Chowpatty Beach

BACK BAY

Malabar Point

GATEWAY OF INDIA

KEY

① BOMBAY CENTRAL RAILWAY STATION
② KAMALA NEHRU PARK
③ VICTORIA TERMINUS RAILWAY STATION
④ POST OFFICE
⑤ CHURCHGATE RAILWAY STATION
⑥ OBEROI HOTEL

⑦ TOURIST OFFICE
⑧ AMERICAN EXPRESS & THOMAS COOK
⑨ AIR INDIA & INDIAN AIRLINES
⑩ TOWN HALL
⑪ TAJ MAHAL HOTEL
Ω TEMPLE

BOMBAY

0   1
km

N

important subsidiary station. The confusion is compounded by there being two railways in Bombay: Central and Western.

Central Railway (CR) does not operate trains from Central station but from Bombay Victoria Terminus. This is traditionally known as Bombay VT although it now has an Indian name: Mumbai Chhatrapati Shivaji Terminus. Trains from Bombay Central station are operated by Western Railway (WR). It takes time to unscramble, especially if you try to make a reservation on a WR train which should be done at a third station, Churchgate, which is not a main line station but a suburban one.

Bombay VT

At first sight it seems unbelievable that this Victorian Gothic pile, with its stained-glass windows, cathedral arches and stone animals leaping from its walls like gargoyles, is a railway station. It is regarded as one of the finest station buildings in the world, from the architectural point of view. In May 1988 it was 100 years old.

Entry to the station is not actually through the portals of this glorious façade but around the back to the side of it. What you see when you stand and stare in amazement at the front of it is the administration building, for VT is the headquarters of Central Railway. The entrance gate is guarded by two massive stone animals, a lion and tiger, representing the United Kingdom and India.

Originally the Great Indian Peninsula Railway Company, CR has grown into one of the country's major railway systems. With 6,486 route kilometres, it traverses six states: Maharashtra, Madhya Pradesh, Uttar Pradesh, Haryana, Karnataka and Rajasthan. Within its jurisdiction are some famous tourists spots, including the Taj Mahal at Agra, Ajanta near Jalgaon and Khajuraho (which has no rail station) near Satna (which has).

The VT complex has reached saturation point having expanded as much as possible during its century of existence. As well as its suburban services, it handles more than 55 trains a day from platforms 8 to 13. The suburban platforms 1 to 7 are across the road from the station and handle over 1,000 EMUs – the local suburban commuter trains – a day. A new terminal is planned at Kurla, north of Dadar, its other overflow station.

For line enthusiasts, these notes are by Samit Roychoudhury:

- Kurla Terminus, some distance from the local station, is just like a shed; a few trains terminate there, such as the *Kurla–Howrah Express.*
- EMU services from VT on the main line bifurcate at Kalyan (on the Pune line, up to Karjat) and at Bhusaval (on the Howrah line up to Kasara).
- Central Railway also has services on the harbour line up to

Andheri (WR), which joins the WR line at Bandra. An offshoot of the harbour line from Kurla goes to Vashi/Belapur in New Bombay and eventually joins the Konkan Railway. There is an EMU up to Khandeshwar.

At Bombay VT station, there is a non-veg restaurant (open 0630–2130) on the second floor which serves the usual range of railway food. Its attraction is the Victorian furniture: umbrella stands, dressers and a wooden and mottled glass screen concealing the kitchen. Also on the second floor is an attractive fast-food self-service snack bar (1100–1900, closed Sundays), and a vegetarian restaurant at the other end of the corridor.

The retiring rooms are located upstairs in the main station building, with tall, polished wooden doors and huge brass bolts, and there are two dormitories with six beds in each. Waiting rooms here are large and peaceful.

In the station concourse there are electronic indicators, coach guidance systems and train time indicators. It has all the amenities and ambience of a major station with plenty of thrills, tearful farewells and the last-minute panic associated with train departures.

Adjoining the station is the CRS building, built in 1987 to fit in with the Gothic grandeur of the station. It houses a computer reservations system like the one in New Delhi, with a telex room linking it with other stations. There are counters (numbers 21 and 22) for foreign tourists on the ground floor. Start with the tourist guide at counter 22; he will check your reservation requisition chit, your date of entry into India in your passport, and your IRP. If you intend to buy a single-journey ticket, you can only do so here with UK pounds or US dollars, or with rupees accompanied by a photocopy (which he will keep) of your foreign currency encashment certificate. The guide will stamp authorisation on the reservation chit and pass it to his colleague who will issue the computer reservation coupon. Reservations from the foreign tourist quota are available only one day in advance, except for IRP holders. The IRP can be bought here.

Because of lack of space, you'll have to stand in a queue, although there are some chairs beside the guide's desk on which you might be invited to sit. The counter is open 0800 to 1630 (lunch 1330 to 1400), closed Sundays; the computer is manned daily until 2000 hours, including Sundays.

Services from this station go east and south and some northwards, serving among others Bangalore, Bhusaval, Chhapra, Cochin, Delhi, Faizabad, Firozpur, Gorakhpur, Guwahati, Howrah, Hyderabad, Itarsi, Jabalpur, Jhansi, Kanniya Kumari (via Trivandrum), Kolhapur, Lucknow, Madras, Mangalore, Miraj (for Goa), Nagpur, Pune, Secunderabad, Sholapur and Varanasi.

A new service introduced in June 1996 has greatly added to the prestige of VT station: the 2027/2028 *Shatabdi Express* between Bombay and Pune. This leaves VT at 1625, arriving in Pune at 1945. It reaches VT at 1105 after leaving Pune at 0745.

The suburban services almost overwhelm VT station. The suburban booking office is on the right of the main concourse; gaze up at the ceiling and you'll feel you're in church. Suburban trains are operated from here, carrying passengers in chaotic, crowded conditions which have become notorious. The trains are fast and frequent and during offpeak hours are a pleasant way to traverse the city; they have 1st class and ladies only carriages.

Tickets can be bought at any counter in the booking hall. There are no waiting rooms on the platforms served by EMU trains and the free toilets are busy because the EMU trains don't have any. Electronic displays indicate train departures, platform and destination.

CR publish a small booklet containing details of all the suburban services from Bombay VT, heading northwards to Dadar and beyond.

Dadar station

A small terminal was provided at Dadar in 1968 to cope with increasing demand by passengers. It is the only Bombay station served by trains of both Central and Western Railways. It is used as a transfer station by passengers on Bombay VT bound trains who want to change to a train bound for Bombay Central or Churchgate, and vice versa.

WR's main line trains both outward and inward stop here and it is a main stop on WR's suburban service. Dadar is 8.85km from Bombay VT, 4.48km from Bombay Central, and 10.17km from Churchgate.

Some main line expresses which originate and terminate at Dadar are the 1057 to Amritsar, the 1027 to Gorakhpur, the 1161 *Lashkar Express* to Agra Cantt, the 1439 Sewagram to Nagpur, and the 6063 Chennai to Madras.

Churchgate station

This station, under the control of Western Railway, was built for suburban services. The station is in Bombay's central business area and is of interest to foreign tourists because of its proximity (across the road from its eastern exit) to WR's reservation office and a Government of India Tourist Office.

The tourist office is open from 0830–1800 Monday to Friday; 0830–1400, Saturday and holidays; closed on Sundays. It is staffed by charming ladies who hope you're not going to ask about train times since the rail office is next door. They will supply information or pamphlets on most places in India.

The Western Railway's reservation office is open 0800–1400 and 1415–2000 Monday to Saturday, and on Sunday 00800–1400. The place for foreign tourists is the desk at the far end of the office (which is on the mezzanine floor). The guide I met there in 1996, Kamal Singh, is a remarkable character with train information in his head and an abiding concern for the welfare and travel arrangements of foreign travellers. He is at his desk from 0930 to 1630 and, on Saturday, 0930 to 1430. He explains all the reservation details and directs tourists to counter 28 for actual ticket purchase. The Indrail Pass is also sold there. Don't go to Churchgate for reservations to Goa, that's done at VT station, but Churchgate does have computer ability for making reservations on the Delhi and Madras terminals.

When I asked why, in the age of computers, a tourist can't make a reservation from the foreign tourist quota at Central station, instead of having to come to Churchgate, I was told that any problems can be resolved immediately at Churchgate since it is the HQ of Western Railway. As with the other foreign tourist bureaux, remember a photocopy of a rupee encashment certificate if you plan to purchase a ticket with rupees.

Kamal Singh explained to an anxious tourist that berth numbers are not entered on the reservation coupon since the allocation of berths is only done on the day of departure of the train. However, if a lower berth, or a coupé, is requested at the time of booking, that information is entered on the computer and, while it cannot be guaranteed, foreigners get preference over everyone except government VIPs, so requests are usually granted.

As the suburban terminal for WR, Churchgate station has about 100 trains arriving during the three-hour peak period in the morning, with each EMU train discharging nearly 3,500 commuters.

The traffic is unidirectional which makes it a concentrated flow from the north into Bombay in the morning and from south to north in the evening, like a human assembly line. Bombay's suburban services are the most intensively utilised in the country, carrying 70 to 75% of India's commuter traffic.

There are 28 stations in the WR suburban network, extending 59.82km from Churchgate to Virar. In 1993, electrified suburban services to Bombay completed 65 years. While WR is proud of its 95% punctuality rate, delays are often caused when pedestrians use the tracks as a passage between built-up areas.

Tourists find the suburban system an excellent way to travel across the city, but not in rush hours. One family told me: "It's clean, fast, safe, cheap and well signposted. The only problem is when you arrive at a station there are no signs to show which end of the platform has the exit you want. One is the main exit and the other leads to the back, but how do you know which one?" You don't.

Bombay Central station

This station can be reached by the suburban line from Churchgate on one of the EMUs. The journey takes ten minutes. There is no direct suburban line link from Bombay VT to Bombay Central. So if you arrive at one station to leave from another, the best method is by taxi which is unlikely to take less than 30 minutes.

The entrance to Central station is surprisingly rural, a small building with a driveway. It has been landscaped with place of honour in a park given to an NG loco (563K) of the old BB&CI Railway, formerly on the Bilimora and Waghai section. There is a tiled lobby with local and long-distance platforms and the usual station facilities including a pharmacy.

There are ten retiring rooms on the top floor with wooden doors and western movie-style swing shutters. The waiting rooms are on the first floor overlooking the passenger hall and a notice advises passengers to leave luggage in the "clock" room where, in fact, a list of the times it is open is on display.

The computer reservations office has no facilities for foreign tourists, who should go to Churchgate.

The non-veg restaurant is somewhat lavatorial, the vegetarian one with blue tiles is larger and brighter with a self-service counter and payment at the end according to what you take, a good way of trying some of the exotic snacks on display when you don't know what to ask for.

The Western Railway zone reaches up to Agra Fort and New Delhi, embracing Rajasthan (Jaipur and Ajmer) as well as the whole of Gujarat. It also has services branching eastwards across country to Jalgaon and Bhopal, destinations it shares with Central Railway.

The most important trains from Bombay Central are the *Rajdhani Expresses*. The 2951 leaves at 1655 every day, except Monday, for New Delhi via Vadodara, and the 2953 *Rajdhani* leaves at 1741 for Hazrat Nizamuddin, also via Vadodara, every day except Wednesday. There is a *Shatabdi Express* every day except Friday from Bombay Central to Ahmedabad via Surat and Vadodara.

Day trips from Bombay Central

From Bombay Central station there are two short rail trips which lead to a different slice of Indian life. A train to Borivli station (a journey of 30km) starts the adventure. When you get to Borivli take an auto-rickshaw to the Gorai Creek where you can catch a ferry to Esselworld. This is an amusement park spread over 64 acres. Popular are the Rainbow, Zyclone and Rock 'n' Roll rides, or you can swim or take a boat trip. The park is open daily, 1100 to 1900; entry is Rs150.

The Western Railway's commuter trains to Bandra (about 10km, 30 minutes) transport you to another world; the traditional lifestyle

THE DABBAWALLAS

The *dabbawalla* is a familiar character at Bombay's railway stations. He is a food runner, a participant in the courier network which ensures that the tiffin (lunch) cooked by a man's wife or mother at his home in the suburbs reaches his desk in the city in time for lunch.

A *dabbawalla*'s working day begins with cycling to the homes in his area to collect the *dabbas* (tiffin boxes), all of which look alike, apart from the markings which only he and his colleagues understand. The *dabbas* are put into long, shallow crates which can hold 36 to 40 tiffin boxes when full. These crates are loaded into the luggage compartments of suburban trains for the journey to the city.

At Churchgate station, the trays seem to bob along by themselves among a sea of heads as passengers descend from the train and surge up the platform. The *dabbawallas* move carefully, their straight backs and jogging gait keeping the trays balanced on their heads.

Hundreds of them arrive at Churchgate station every working day. More of them assemble on platform 1 at VT station, adding their bit to the clamour and chaos of the city.

How the *dabbas* get to their various destinations in the city without getting mixed up is baffling. First the trays are assembled on the pavement where they are sorted according to the marks painted on them in yellow, blue, green, red and black. A typical lid I saw outside Churchgate station bore the markings IB25 CH ABUK VLI.

"This will go only to your table, not to my table," a passer-by told me with a laugh at my bewilderment. "This is the most beautiful courier system. It never messes up."

When the tiffin boxes are sorted they are repacked in different crates, ready for delivery. While one man stands with a wedge of cloth on his head to ease the weight, two others lift the tray up and ease it on to the prepared head. Before long the *dabbawalla* is jogging off into the traffic, competing with cyclists, motorbikes, cars and double-decker buses for a space on the road, while balancing the tray, weighing at least 40kg, on his head.

Thousands of lunches are delivered by train and *dabbawalla* every day. Thanks to them, chaotic Bombay survives without losing a single tiffin.

of a mainly Christian village, Chimbai, in the northern suburb of Bandra. According to a report: "The atmosphere is like Goa: fat fisherwomen squat in narrow winding lanes, while the aroma of freshly baked bread wafts from tiny bakeries." You'll need an auto rickshaw from Bandra station to this warren of small cottage and village shrines.

Where to stay

The nostalgic head like homing pigeons for the **Taj Majal Hotel** with its **Intercontinental Hotel** appendage in Apollo Bunder (tel: 2023366). **The Bombay Oberoi** is also part of a pair as it is joined to the **Oberoi Towers**, a short taxi ride from Bombay VT station (Nariman Point; tel: 2025757, room price includes butler.) The management are proud of this hotel and it shows in everything, even down to the brightly polished buttons on the liftboys' spotless white uniforms. It's quite a wrench to get back on a train.

CALCUTTA

Calcutta is fun; a sophisticated city despite the teeming millions, but it is not the best city in which to begin a rail journey. If you do arrive at Dum Dum Airport wanting to catch a train, there is a good rail booking office there with quotas for same-day travel on some main trains but your best bet would be to wait until you get to the Fairlie Place reservations office.

Calcutta is served by two main line stations, Howrah and Sealdah, and two railways: Eastern (ER) and South Eastern (SER). Both railways have their headquarters in Calcutta although SER doesn't actually have a station to itself; it rents platforms at Howrah and Sealdah from Eastern Railway. There is also a circular railway run by ER, and India's first underground railway, the Calcutta Metro.

The Eastern Railway network fans out westwards with Bangladesh to its east and the mouths of the Ganga to its south. It serves the states of West Bengal, Bihar, eastern Madhya Pradesh and part of Uttar Pradesh. It covers 4,290 route kilometres and 730 stations.

ER boasts of handling 561.11 million passengers in the year ending June 1996, 2.23 million more than the year before. Throughout the zone 154 mail and express trains, 369 other passenger trains and 941 suburban trains run every day.

However, it is mainly a freight carrying railway, serving the major coalfields at Asansol, Jharia, Karanpura and Singrauli. Many of the tourist sites within the ER zone are religious, such as the footprint of Lord Vishnu at Gaya and the Buddhist temples at Bodhgaya and Sarnath.

South Eastern Railway celebrated its centenary in 1987 as the direct descendant of the BNR. It serves stations in six states: West Bengal, Orissa, Andhra Pradesh, Bihar, Madhya Pradesh and Maharashtra. It deals with two lakhs of passengers a day at Howrah alone.

Despite carrying nearly 195 million passengers in a year, SER is primarily a freight-carrying railway serving an area rich in basic materials such as coal, iron and manganese ore, limestone and

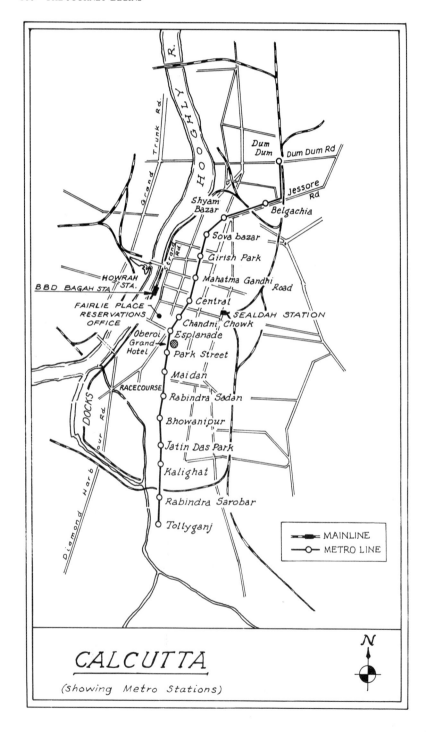

CALCUTTA

(showing Metro Stations)

bauxite. The raw materials of seven major steel plants are carried by SER which also serves three major coalfields and two aluminium complexes.

Another side of this industrial railway is seen in SER's afforestation programme. In five years from 1981 to 1986, 74.6 lakhs (a lakh is 100,000) of saplings were planted by SER; with a survival rate of 80%, that's a lot of trees. In its zone are the picturesque wilds of Saranda, the greens of Chhotanagpur and the foliaged heart of Madhya Pradesh.

Reservations

Eastern Railways is proud of its computerised reservation system (CRS) which enables "an intending passenger to obtain a reservation for any train (ER or SER) in any class on any date within the advanced reservation period from any of the computerised reservation counters in Calcutta".

Yet for the foreigner there is only one place where reservations can be obtained from the foreign tourist quota, that is Fairlie Place, which is not even near a mainline station. It is close to the BBD Bagh station which is on ER's circular railway but it is easier to get there from Howrah station by ferry. The terminal for the Chandpal Ghat Ferry is at the end of the road that splits Howrah station in two. The ferry operates at 15-minute intervals from 0815 to 2000 daily, except Sundays. Once across the river, you walk across the railway line and Strand Road, then into the thorough-fare opposite, where the Fairlie Place building is on the right, at number 6.

This ancient building used to belong to the army. A sign saying Computerized Railway Reservation Office hangs over the doorway, with working hours given as 0800–2000 on weekdays, 0800–1400 on Sundays and the three national holidays (January 26, August 15 and October 12). Another sign says Computerized Foreign Tourist Bureau. Outside on the pavement are shoe cleaners and wayside kitchens; inside on the ground floor is all the chaos of general reservations: any counter for any train to any destination.

Upstairs on the right of the entrance is the foreign tourist bureau (working hours 0900–1600, lunch 1300–1330; 0900–1400 on Sunday). The atmosphere is pleasant and friendly. The office is air-conditioned and box-like with chairs for waiting passengers, a counter with chairs in front of it and, when I visited in 1996, only two computer monitors. There is a railway guide to help plot itineraries and a very helpful staff, although their ability to deal with lots of tourists is limited by lack of computers. In the season, there can be as many as 100 tourists a day trying to make bookings, so start early in the day.

Applications for reservations are made on the usual requisition slips and can be made here for all mainline trains. Payment for tickets must be in foreign currency; if you only have rupees, you'll have to buy your ticket downstairs.

Indrail Passes can also be purchased at Fairlie Place and, when possible, the staff try to accommodate passengers who want to begin travelling that very day. Reservations can be made for Darjeeling if the line is open.

Howrah station

The distinctive brick-coloured station on the opposite bank of the river to the Fairlie Place office was built in 1905. A few years ago there was an attempt to paint it lemon yellow but public protest kept it brick red. A road (vehicles, except taxis, are allowed for a toll) divides the station into north and south sections, and provides access to platforms 8 and 9.

The north side opens on to the non-ticket area running alongside the entrance to platform 1. It also links up with a subway entrance with shopping kiosks on both sides. The 2nd class booking office is here and also lots of fresh fruit stalls.

The north section has a first-aid post with a doctor available for a few hours every day from 1000 and there is a medical hall (chemist) in the centre of the concourse. Bridging the road is a large mural over the platforms. The main entrance is flanked by ornamental wood panelling which used to front the old booking office. At this side of the station are three restaurants: a coffee corner serving non-vegetarian meals (I had a very good Western-style lunch there), and, from 1400 to 2100 hours, Chinese meals. Adjoining this is a vegetarian self-service restaurant, with waiters in attendance at meal times, and next door a non-vegetarian restaurant with lurid green tables. Both are open 0600 to 2200.

In the main concourse is Wheelers book kiosk, and a delight is the Globe Nursery, a florist. Behind this is the entrance to the retiring rooms which, by 1996, had been reduced to four. A grand staircase, close to the computerised train enquiries office, leads to the various classes of waiting rooms which are rather airless, although there is a view of the river and the traffic-clogged Howrah Bridge from the terrace. Next to the staircase is a war memorial with a brass crest of the old East Indian Railway. Other features of this station include a "public grievance redressal booth" in red and yellow stripes, a West Bengal State Tourist Office and, on the right of the wood panelled entrance, a barber shop. Another relic of the past are the hand-pulled rickshaws which can be hired outside the station. Turn right at the exit to walk the 200m to Howrah South station.

Opened in 1992, this building is a paler version (pink instead of rust) of the formidable main station, a graceful reproduction with towers, arches and balconies like its neighbour, senior by 85 years. There is no platform-to-platform link so for platforms 18 to 21, served by the new station complex, you have to come out of the main station and walk around to your right, passing the open-air barber's on your right, and the main entrance to the Rail Yatri Niwas.

The station entrance is narrow with an alcove on its right with an emergency desk and booking hall for that day's departures. The 2nd class sleeper waiting room is upstairs. Also upstairs, on the first floor, is the computer reservations complex, open 0800–2000, Sunday 0800–1400, where there is no special counter (yet) for foreign tourists. There were ten terminals when the complex opened, but space for 24.

A cafeteria is on the mezzanine floor with a gallery where passengers can sit and watch trains arriving. Electronic indicators show departures and arrivals. Up another floor are the waiting rooms for upper class passengers, the gents room glorying in planters' chairs with reclining backs and long arms.

The platforms can accommodate trains 22 coaches in length and the new station, which cost 10 crores to build, is easing the pressure on the old one.

Unfortunately, not even the regional timetables indicate from which platform (and thus which of the two stations) trains leaving Howrah depart, so either enquire by telephone first or be prepared for a walk from one station to the other. Three *Rajdhani Express* trains serve Howrah. These are 2301 from Howrah via Dhanbad to new Delhi (not on Thursdays and Sundays), 2305 from Howrah (on Thursdays and Sundays) via Patna and New Delhi, and, once a week, 2422 from Howrah to Bhubaneswar which becomes 2421 on its way from Bhubaneswar via Howrah to New Delhi.

There are two *Shatabdi Express* trains from Howrah. Daily except Sunday, 2019 leaves Howrah at 0620 for Asansol, Dhanbad and Bokaro. Also never on Sundays is the 2021 from Howrah at 0650 to Tata Nagar and Rourkela. Major expresses link Howarth with Madras, Bombay, Bangalore, Hyderabad, Secunderabad and other important stations, including Pune. There are also EMU services up to Burdwan (Barddhaman) and a spur up to Tarakeshwar.

Sealdah station

The first thing to learn about this station is how to pronounce it. The locals say Sheldah. It deals mainly with suburban and local trains and is used by about a million passengers a day. The main station building, the north block, was built in the 1970s and has ten platforms. The computerised reservation counters on the first floor are open 0900–2000 and 0900–1400 on Sunday and holidays. In special cases, foreign tourists can make reservations here though there is no special counter, or even signs, for them. Better to head for Fairlie Place.

Sealdah station is in the heart of the city of Calcutta, on the eastern bank. Mainly serving commuter traffic, most mainline trains leave from platform 8 which is on the right as you wander into the station. Vehicles have access to this platform. Electronic signs indicate from which platform the trains leave, but you'll have to decipher the code of abbreviations. The computerised reservations complex on the first floor is usually very crowded. Also on the first floor is the V and NV restaurant, a haven – but a dull one – from the chaos in the booking hall below.

The retiring rooms are on the second floor. All four of them are non air-conditioned; rooms 2 and 3 are bright, with windows that open on to a view of the forecourt below. The dormitory is very basic. The waiting rooms are spartan with stone benches. The SS here has two offices, one on the first floor and the other off the booking hall where he can be found during important train arrivals and departures.

Platform 8 is for VIP trains and has a VIP waiting room. There is a passenger guide on duty with his own desk and a "May I Help You" booth open for important trains. There is a bookstall and a first-aid post as well as kiosks selling soft drinks.

Perhaps the most popular departure from Sealdah is the 3143 *Darjeeling Mail* which actually doesn't go to Darjeeling at all but overnight to New Jalpaiguri, arriving there in time to connect with the 0900 departure of the NG passenger train on the Darjeeling–Himalayan Railway. There are also departures from Sealdah for Delhi, Mugalsarai, Jammu Tawi and Gorakhpur.

Shalimar station

Under construction and supposed to open before the end of the century (although it probably won't), Shalimar station will be run by South Eastern Railways. Completion is linked with that of the second Hooghly Bridge. It will handle mainline and suburban trains. The goods terminal there is being shifted to Sankrail.

Suburban services

A circular railway system is run by ER operating a stretch of 10.5km between Prinsep Ghat and Ultadanga Road stations to Dum Dum Jn. You can try this line from BBD Bagh station (the initials stand for Benoy Badal Dinesh) to Prinsep Ghat.

Trams

The tram, looking more like an attempt to fashion a vehicle out of flattened tin cans and a Meccano kit than a passenger conveyance, ground slowly to a halt. The conductor had already given up and got off.

We were stuck in one of Calcutta's chaotic traffic jams, a spectacular display of motorists' impatience as they gunned their engines, leaned on horns and shouted abuse at each other. The only vehicle which wasn't on the wrong side of the road was our tram, locked to its track and blocked by oncoming cars.

Exhaust fumes drifted into the open windows, adding a grainy, toxic fog to the dank, tropic night. The tram's headlights picked out the conductor walking in the haze ahead, waving at cars to get out of our way. Until we moved, there wasn't a hope of clearing the intersection where eight lanes of traffic converged in a hopeless tangle.

The conductor spotted a space. With the help of some passengers he lifted the back of a stalled van off the track. The bell jangled vigorously and we jerked forward. We moved sluggishly (four miles an hour is average) through the evening traffic, accompanied by the clang of the motorman's bell whenever we pulled off from a halt. Despite its battered appearance, the tram was not old. Over 50% of the trams in operation were built in West Bengal after 1986.

Now the service is being reduced and will probably disappear completely before long. The irony, as one newspaper pointed out, is that since trams were banished from Bombay on the advice of an expert, "the peak hours speed in Bombay is still less than that of the trams." The same could easily happen in Calcutta. There have been trams here since 1880 when a metre gauge track for horse-drawn trams was laid. Later, steam locomotives ran for two years but, by 1908, the whole system was electrified and the tracks reconstructed to standard gauge. In 1943, Howrah station, reached by the new bridge over the Hooghly river, was linked up to the network. The length in double track of the entire system never exceeded 69km. Now it has shrunk and you can no longer catch a tram from outside Howrah station.

Trams may be slow and losing passengers to Calcutta's zippy new Metro, which takes only 20 minutes from Esplanade to Tollygunge, but a ride on them yields a fascinating view of the city and its moods. When the last tram has left for Tollygunge more than just an Edwardian form of transport will be lost; an integral part of Calcutta will have vanished too.

The Metro

The idea for building an underground railway in Calcutta was conceived in 1949 but it was 20 years before the project was studied and a plan for a Mass Rapid Transit system prepared. The foundation stone was laid in 1972. That it was able to open at all amazed observers but in 1984 the first part was inaugurated. Now it is fully operational running 16.43km under the city from Tollygunge to Dum Dum via Esplanade and Belgachchia. Trains run during peak hours at intervals of ten minutes.

Every day close to two million transit trippers are estimated to use the Metro. The journey from one end to the other takes just over 30 minutes. Trains consist of eight coaches, each one capable of carrying 278 standing and 48 sitting.

A ride begins by buying a printed ticket, issued by a machine, from the ticket counter. Fares start at Rs2 depending on destination, defined by zones. Two people travelling together can buy a ticket for two. Return tickets are available and tickets can also be bought in carnets of 12 for the cost of 11. Entrance is through turnstiles where ticket checkers are on duty. Passengers should keep their tickets while travelling in case of on-board checks, but there is no checking at the exit.

The timetable says "Do not squat, vend, eat, smoke or drink in Metro train or premises" and the cleanliness of the station owes much to the pride with which its users regard it. Potted plants grow undisturbed on platforms and the station walls are free of graffiti. Each station has a wide island platform with trains entering on either side. Murals adorn the entrances and walls of some stations and the customary CCTV plays full blast.

Replicas from the Calcutta Museum are on display in showcases at some stations. A cute idea at Esplanade Station is a noticeboard for personal advertisements. It adds a bit of charm to the strictly functional lines of the station. Off peak, many lights are dimmed to save electricity, but no one turns down the CCTV.

Users are so proud of the Metro, they reprimand those who don't show proper respect of it. I queried the reason for the sign that says "Photography Prohibited" and was told the reason was "security". And when the Metro's own staff photographer took a picture of Esplanade Station he was curtly told off by a passenger for not obeying regulations.

As soon as a train has pulled in, its doors open automatically. There is no time to dawdle as they snap shut within seconds, but only after a recorded announcement in Hindi, Bengali and English, and a bell, has warned that they are about to close. Slogans and jingles are broadcast after the door has closed but the progress of the train is so noisy you can't hear what they are about.

The seats are metal benches running the length of the coaches, which have the familiar appearance of mainline carriages, having been built at the same factory in Madras. They are fully vestibuled with no doors dividing them. Some of the carriages are very noisy because of air-blowers which keep them cool. These drown out the recorded announcements, in three languages, made on the approach to each station, giving the station's name, and whether the platform is on the left or right.

Where to stay

There are several hotels of character in Calcutta, as befits the former capital of British India with its ornate Victorian architecture. The old tradition of gracious living is preserved at the **Oberoi Grand** which dates back to the 1870s. The style of the hotel is grand but not snooty. It is in Chowringhee which is practically equidistant from Howrah and Sealdah stations, in case you need an excuse to justify the enjoyable extravagance of staying there.

At Howrah station is the **Rail Yatri Niwas** (see *Chapter Seven*).

A collector's item for those who adore old hotels of character, the kind that are bound to vanish in time, is the **Fairlawn Hotel** (13A Sudder Street, Calcutta 7000/16; tel: 2441835). It is a few blocks behind the Oberoi Grand and years behind the rest of Calcutta in style. With green painted galleries and a jungle of plants as its front garden, it is furnished with the chintz of a grandparent's drawing room. Dining there is to experience British home cooking with a touch of the Raj, at a fraction of the price of fashionable establishments depending on ersatz nostalgia for atmosphere.

MADRAS

Madras may not at first seem an obvious place from which to begin your rail journey but it has a lot of advantages. The atmosphere is right: hustling isn't brazen, people are polite and there seems to be a feeling that rushing around isn't really worthwhile. Madras is a gentle introduction to India.

There are now direct flights to Madras from Europe and there is a rail booking-cum-reservation counter at the international airport. This is open 1000 to 1700 hours daily, and there is a rail facility at the domestic air terminal too.

The major advantage of starting a rail journey in Madras is that it is the HQ of the best railway in India: Southern Railway (SR). It's not my view alone; ask Indians themselves. The trains are cleaner, the service friendlier, the food better and the entire journey on an SR train seems more enjoyable.

The railway was founded in 1951 by the integration of the erstwhile Madras and Southern Maharatta Railway, South Indian Railway and Mysore State Railway. It traverses 6,729 route kilometres serving over a thousand stations. It covers about 10% of India's land area with a passenger catchment of 14% of the country's population.

SR links the southern states of Tamil Nadu, Kerala, the major portion of Karnataka, a small part of Andhra Pradesh and the Union Territory of Pondicherry with the rest of India. It is an area of great variety for the tourist, with beaches, hill resorts, forests and animal parks, monuments, temples and ancient traditions, and a welcoming people.

"It's the people that make Southern Railway better than the others," a passenger told me. "Better staff and better passengers." There are better public relations, too, with "May I Help You"

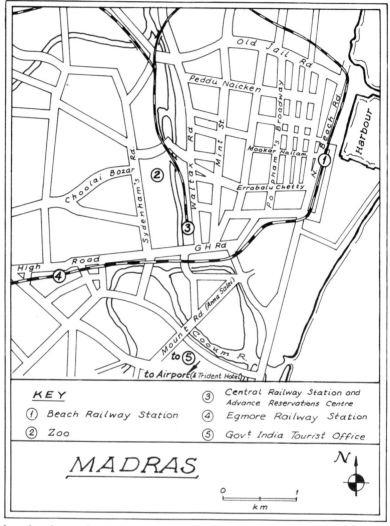

KEY

① Beach Railway Station
② Zoo
③ Central Railway Station and Advance Reservations Centre
④ Egmore Railway Station
⑤ Gov.t India Tourist Office

MADRAS

N

0 ——————— 1
km

booths located at important stations to attend to passengers' problems.

A train conductor suggested that SR is better because the competition from road transport is greater in the south than the north so, to keep business, Southern Railway must offer a better service. Another theory is that the nature of people in the south is placid so that they do not misuse the railway.

Reservations

At one side of Madras Central station is a new building looking like a modern hotel; this is the advance reservations centre and is part of the suburban station complex. The office is open 0800–1300 and 1330–2000 daily, and 0800–1300 on Sunday. The best time to make reservations is early morning, 0700 to 1000. Bed rolls can be reserved from the same counter where reservations are made. There is a separate counter for ladies.

Foreign tourists should go to the first floor where there is a special office and computer just for them, so the process of booking and getting confirmation is streamlined. Even if there is no foreign tourist quota on the train you want to go on, the staff make a special effort to find space.

There are three main stations in Madras: Central, Egmore and Beach. A rail minibus service links Central with Egmore station, meeting important trains.

Madras Central station

This is a distinctive rust-pink building with white-trimmed arches, but inside it is less romantic, overwhelmed by passengers and with a patina of grime. At night, when energy-saving yellow sodium lights are switched on, it looks Dickensian.

At this station the SS has his name in lights. His office is on the right of the entrance to the booking hall which leads from the forecourt. Opposite his office are counters for platform tickets and current reservations.

Before the barrier leading to the platform, on the right, there is a Tamil Nadu Tourist Office (open 0715–1900 every day). Twin flights of stairs lead up to a first floor where there are upper class waiting rooms and a restaurant (open 0600–1430 and 1530–2130). Both have wide balconies overlooking the station forecourt.

The waiting rooms (one is for ladies) have bathrooms with showers and toilets and mirrors. A table on the balcony of the restaurant is good for a meal with a view of the city; the staff will sometimes cook something special if you ask.

Activity on the passenger concourse can be watched from the landing in front of the restaurant. Down a passage to the left is a corridor leading to the retiring rooms. These are airless and depressing with king-size rats, and they reverberate with the noise of CCTV. (At this station, children who are separated from their travelling companions and found by station staff are shown on the CCTV screen for them to be claimed.)

Downstairs, the entrance to the concourse is on the left of the lobby with a large Higginbothams bookstall (open 0630–2130) just inside on the left. There is also an India Tourism Development Corp counter for tour bookings and a kiosk selling air pillows with handwoven pillowcases.

The cloakroom for left luggage is down a passage on the left with separate counters for deposit and collection. Boards with the reservation lists for 2nd class are in the central waiting area; upper class reservation lists are in the main entrance hall.

The vegetarian refreshment room is a grubby, standing-only outlet with a self-service counter containing bins from which various snack items can be removed with tongs. Paper plates are charged extra; a public cup is chained to the water cooler. A medical shop is next door (open 0600–2200). There is also a cafeteria with various kinds of fried cakes and a coffee counter before the ticket barrier.

At the other side of the concourse, beyond the mass of people sprawled on the ground and in plastic chairs in the fan-cooled general waiting area, are more refreshment kiosks.

Outside is a taxi park with auto-rickshaws parked on the right and children asleep on the pavement. Taxi drivers have an agreeable approach and even the begging is restrained. One man asked me politely for the train fare home, saying he'd lost his ticket. I steered him towards the office of the SS, just in case he was genuine.

A new *Rajdhani Express* serves Madras once a week from Hazrat Nizamuddin and there is another which also stops on its way, once a week, between Trivandrum and Nizamuddin station. *Shatabdi Expresses* have also been introduced with the 2007 from Madras every day except Tuesday to Bangalore and Mysore. Another *Shatabdi*, number 2023, serves Coimbatore via Salem, daily except Wednesdays.

There are two expresses a day to New Delhi, the 2615 *Grand Trunk* and the faster, by four hours, 2621 *Tamil Nadu Express*.

To Bombay VT is a daily departure by the 6010 *Bombay Mail* which takes just over 30 hours, while to Dadar there is a daily morning departure by the *Dadar Express*, arriving 24 hours later. The daily 2842 *Coromandel Express* takes 28 hours to reach Calcutta/Howrah and the 6004 *Howrah Mail* also makes the trip daily but takes two nights to do it. Expresses pass through Madras from Trivandrum, Cochin and Bangalore on their way to Calcutta and/or Guwahati on different days of the week.

Madras Egmore station

If the minibus isn't available from Madras Central to Egmore station, a taxi takes about five minutes. Egmore station still has metre gauge, serving the southern part of India. The station is a sedate, Victorian (1880s) style, brick-red building with a canopy covered entrance off its courtyard. The station now has a splendidly ornate (red walls and cement scrollwork) new annexe in keeping with the flourish of the original station, with a computer reservations complex. Any train anywhere in India, not just MG from Madras, can now be booked here, but there is no special provision for foreign tourists.

There are three mainline platforms at Egmore and two suburban ones. The 15 retiring rooms are on the first floor with a view from the gallery of the lively action in the street. Waiting rooms are also on this floor.

Madras Beach station

This is the main suburban line station located behind Burma Market, a street of kiosks selling luxury imported (smuggled?) goods that runs parallel to the platforms. There are six platforms in the station, and a vegetarian restaurant.

Where to stay

Madras has some very good budget hotels, especially around Egmore station. A hotel re-opened in late 1989 directly opposite Egmore station is the **Hotel Impala Continental** (12, Gandhi Irwin Road, Madras 60008) with low-budget prices for suite-style rooms. Only Indian cash is accepted. The hotel also operates the grandly named Impala Vegetarian Heart Queen Cleopatra Pleasure Palace – a snack bar.

At the airport, there is an orange courtesy coach which meets all flights to take passengers to the nearby **Trident Hotel**. A useful feature of this garden hotel, opened in 1988, is its special 12-hour rate. This is not the same as a day rate since it applies for any 12 hours, even overnight such as 0200 to 1400. It works out at 40% less than the rack rate. Ideal if you just want to recover from a flight before taking an overnight train.

Traditional, converted from a grand colonial mansion at the end of the 19th century, is the **Taj Connemara**. This is not named after Lord Connemara, governor of Madras from 1886 to 1890, but after his wife. The good lady is said to have stormed out of Government House to become a permanent guest in the hotel in protest at her husband's philandering with, according to a contemporary account, "very young girls".

The hotel's unique open-air restaurant, The Raintree, specialises in Chettinad dishes, hot and darkly pungent with fresh ground masalas and sun-dried and salted vegetables. It is an institution worth catching a train for.

TRIVANDRUM

One of the pleasantest places to arrive to begin a rail journey is Trivandrum, capital of Kerala, in India's deep south. The airport is small and leisurely with none of the frenzy of India's major airports; it is only 6km from Trivandrum central station and served by seasonal charter flights from Europe as well as by scheduled flights from Colombo, the Maldives and the Gulf States, and by domestic flights. The new name of Trivandrum is Thiruvananthapuraam.

The station building is Victorian, extending the length of its main platform. 1st and AC class tickets for current trains are sold from a counter on the right of the main entrance where timetables and platform tickets are also sold. The entrance lobby itself is small; steps lead from it upstairs to the SS's office and a porticoed gallery where the nine excellent retiring rooms are located. There is also a dormitory with eight beds.

The computerised reservations office is in a building adjoining the station. Downstairs are the counters selling 2nd class tickets for same-day trains. Up the stairs at the side is the long room where advance reservations are made at counters marked by destination. The office is open 0800–2030, lunch 1300–1300; only current reservations, enquiries and cancellations on Sunday.

The enquiry desk is at counter 1 and credit cards (but only local ones) are accepted for payment at counter 13. A notice states, somewhat obtusely, "ladies seeking reservations for themselves and handicapped persons are not required to join the general queue and can come separately in the same counter for getting reservations".

There is no smoking inside the reservations office, in keeping with the sentiments expressed in another sign: "Railway Cleanliness Drive. Railways versus Dust. The fight is on. Whose side are you on?"

Indrail Passes can be bought here. The chief reservation supervisor (CRS) has his office at the head of the stairs and foreign tourist should go in and see him. "They can stand in a queue at one of the counters if they like," a CRS once told me, "but we don't insist."

Trivandrum Central has all the atmosphere of a major station with none of the hassles. There are three platforms, number 1 having the usual offices, restaurants and waiting rooms. The deputy station superintendent's office is near the entrance and that's where to apply for a retiring room by filling in a requisition slip.

The lobby of kiosks includes a milk counter, a fruit stall, a nut vendor (cashews are locally grown), a bookstall and an apple-juice bar. A notice at the station entrance that warned "Beware of pickpockets, jewel snatchers and baggage lifters" has been replaced by another that reflects a greater risk to Indian Railway passengers. I have retained the spelling. "Please keep in touch with the Station Manager or Deputy Station Manager or platform inspector in case of any harrashment by licensed porter." (The porter charges here are given as Rs7 for a load of 40kg and Rs11 for a trolley load.)

Although it is so far south, Trivandrum Central is a gateway to all parts of India with daily direct trains for New Delhi (3,054km), Bombay (2,061km), Madras (907km), Mangalore (635km), and Bangalore (851km).

There are also trains daily to Shoranur, Ernakulam Jn, Cannanore and Kanniya Kumari (express and passenger). Weekly, or bi-weekly, there are direct trains to Guwahati (3,625km) and to Rajkot via Ahmedabad (2,734km).

As part of the progressive development of Indian Railways, with the spread throughout its network of good standard trains with superior accommodation, a *Rajdhani Express* now serves Trivandrum. It is only once a week and, alas, is not up to the standard of the classic *Rajdhanis*, but it does provide AC 1st class cabins, an essential for the long (two night: 44hr 30min) journey to Delhi. Food is charged extra; although it is cooked on the train you might still prefer to bring your own.

Popular destinations from Trivandrum are Quilon (65km) which can be reached by northbound expresses or slower passenger trains, and Coimbatore (for Ooty) on the main line to Madras. To go to Cochin from Trivandrum, take a northbound train to Ernakulam Jn.

Where to stay

The beach resort of Kovalam is 16km away. Its somewhat lacklustre **Kovalam Ashok Beach Resort** is the foremost hotel in the area.

The **Rockholm** at Vizhinjam, Kovalam, is close to the lively beach, built on a sandy cove. It looks good and is recommended by many; economy.

If you want to stay "up market" in Trivandrum itself, there are no international chain hotels, but the **Hotel Lucia** tries hard. It has 100 air-conditioned rooms, all with TV, and even a business centre. For me the delight is the welcome by doormen, porters and broadly smiling receptionists. A good bar and restaurant add to its appeal. Rates are under US$40 a double. Hotel Lucia is at East Fort, Trivandrum; tel: 463443; fax: 463347.

TIRUCHCHIRAPPALLI

Tiruchchirappali, mercifully shortened by everyone to Trichy, has an international airport 15 minutes from the main station, Tiruchchirappali Junction. The airport, served by international flights (from Colombo), is a frustrating experiencé due to the slow processing of passengers. Trichy Jn station, however, is well run and good for starting a journey, especially through the south Indian countryside.

Trichy is a town of nearly 400,000 inhabitants, dozens of exotic temple towers and no less than six railway stations. It is situated on the banks of the Cauvery River and is a blend of history and tradition as well as a pilgrim centre and a thriving commercial city. Built in 1935, the station has been selected for transformation into a model one.

To the left of the spacious forecourt a new building houses the computerised reservations centre. It has the atmosphere and facilities of an efficient system, with a bright waiting area, CCTV, fans, a refreshment stall, a pay toilet, and a suggestion box. My suggestion was that there should be a sign indicating which counter attends to foreign tourists. Counter number 2 deals with enquiries, and foreign tourists should start there. Surprisingly, since Trichy is an international gateway into India, the IRP is not on sale but holders can begin their journey at this station.

The station has a good Tamil Nadu tourist information office on the right of its entrance. Steps lead up to refurbished retiring rooms (14 doubles, two with air-conditioning) and dormitories for 24. Room service is available. There is a non-vegetarian refreshment room and a reception desk for the retiring rooms, presided over by a matron. Passengers staying in the rooms are lulled to sleep, or jerked awake, by the sound of trains shunting throughout the night. The rooms are fronted by a wide veranda with a view over the station forecourt where local buses wait for major trains.

The platforms are linked by a tunnel. Platform facilities include vegetarian and non-vegetarian restaurants, a book-shop and book trolleys that meet all important trains. One of these is the fast 2605 *Pallavan Express* running daily between Trichy and Madras Egmore. It is all chair car with a pantry car, and is painted an eye-catching silver grey and white.

Some MG trains also stop at Tiruchchirappalli Town, a new (1988) temple-like station at the end of a pot-holed village street. The reservation and booking counter there is open 0700–1130, 1430–1730, and there are pleasant waiting rooms with toilets and showers. The station handles mainly commuters although it is an ideal halt to see the nearby Rock Fort.

Srirangam station (10km from Trichy Jn) is another new building designed to fit in with its surroundings. It is popular with pilgrims who come to visit the Vaishnavite temple with its 21 towers built in the 13th century AD. The upstairs of the station has two twin-bed retiring rooms with writing desks and dorm beds. Trichy's other MG station is Golden Rock. Two other BG stations are Palakkarai and Trichy Fort.

Where to stay

Possibly the best value accommodation in Trichy is Room 8 at Trichy Jn station. This air-conditioned twin-bedded room is as big as a hotel suite with wallpaper, wall-to-wall carpet, dressing table, settee and armchairs, lots of lights, fans and a dining-cum-work table. A dressing room leads to a large bathroom with Western style toilet, and loo paper, and a hot water shower. There is even a private balcony with a view over the platform roof of the sunrise. However, this is railwayland so don't expect "star class".

For that, go to **Jenney's Residence** (formerly Rajali Hotel), 3/14 McDonalds Rd, Trichy, a luxury hotel with economy rates per

24hrs – any period of 24hrs, not just from check-in to noon – only minutes' walk from the station. It has 78 bedrooms and suites and a renowned restaurant. There's a friendly atmosphere, especially in the Soaring High bar by the swimming pool (the only one in Trichy and open to non-residents).

LEAVE THESE BEHIND
WHEN YOU BOARD
THE TRAIN...

Or else a small mistake on your part may lead to a fire in the train with disastrous results.

THEREFORE:

• Do not smoke in trains. It is prohibited.
• Do not carry inflammable articles or dangerous goods like explosives, acids, kerosene, petrol in compartments.
• Don't throw lighted match sticks or cigarette ends in the coaches.
• Never use stoves or sigris in trains.

Carrying explosives, inflammables, acids is prohibited and punishable under Indian Railways Act.

WESTERN RAILWAY
Concerned for your safety
1995 - Year of the Rail Users

Sai-WR-1

WESTERN RAILWAY

T 524 F

Requisition for Reservation / Cancellation / Return Journey

IF YOU ARE A DOCTOR PLEASE TICK(v) IN BOX YOU COULD BE OF HELP IN AN EMERGENCY.

Dr.

Train No...................................... Train Name...................................

Journey Date..................... Class............ No. of Seats / Berths................

Station From............................ Station To.................................

Boarding at..

Sr. No.	Name in Block Letters	Sex	Age	Choice, if any
1.				
2.				
3.				
4.				
5.				
6.				

Onward Journey Message Details

Train No............. Train Name.................... Journey Date...........

Class............ Station from............... Station to.......................

Name...

Address...

Signature

....

Telephone No.......................... Date.................... Time...............

TO BE FILLED IN BY STAFF

PNR No........................... Tkt. No................. Status..................

Note :-1. **Maximum permissible passengers 4 per party and 6 per family**

   2. Only one requisition slip will be accepted from one person at a time.

   3. Please check your ticket and balance amount before leaving the counter.

   4. Forms not properly filled in, or illegible forms shall not be entertained.

WRP, MX. 51/06/105/3; 1-95; 2,15,00,000.

Chapter Nine

Around India by Rail

DESTINATIONS

A list of the most popular destinations for foreign rail travellers, after the cities of Delhi (the top favourite), Bombay, Calcutta and Madras, has been compiled by studying the travel patterns of foreign tourists from bookings made at the ITB (see *Chapter Two*). Rail tourists tend to follow itineraries of their own devising, to the chagrin of the planners at ITB who have prepared itineraries which rail travellers ignore.

For many trail travellers, part of the fun is poring over timetables to draw up one's own itinerary. The *Trains at a Glance* timetable is the best for that. Zonal timetables are useful for local passenger trains and for discovering through-carriages attached to different trains so you can reach your destination without changing.

Some of the places popular with tourists are listed here, together with their closest station. Where a distance is shown, this is from the closest railway station.

Location	Station
Srinagar	Jammu Tawi
Mount Abu	Abu Road
Khajuaraho	Jhansi (172km) is best; also Harpalpur (94km); Mahoba (65km); Satna (117km)
Pushkar	Ajmer
Kodaikanal	Kodaikanal Road (or Madurai)
Yercaud	Salem

Buddhist tour

Location	Station
Bodhgaya	Gaya, via Varanasi
Sarnath	Varanasi (10km)
Kushinagar	Gorakhpur (54km)
Sravasti	Balrampur via Gorakhpur
Lumbini	Naugarh via Gorakhpur
Kapilavastu	Naugarh

National parks

Location	Station
Dachigam	Jammu (200km)
Keibul Lamjao (Manipur)	Dimapur
Corbett	Ramnagar (51km)
Sultanpur Sanctuary	Gurgaon (15km)
Keoladeo Ghana (Rajasthan)	Bharatpur (2km)
Sariska Tiger Reserve	Alwar (36km)
Desert (Rajasthan)	Jaisalmer (32km)
Gir (Gujarat)	Sasan (1km)
Tarboa	Chandrapur (45km)
Bandhavgarh	Umaria (35km) Satna (112km)
Chilika Sanctuary	Balugaon
Kaziranga	Jorhat (95km)
Manas Tiger Reserve	Barpetta Road (41km)
Sunderbans Tiger Reserve	Canning (105km)
Nagarjunasagar Srisailam Sanctuary	Machesla (13km)
Nagarhole Sanctuary	Mysore (96km)
Bandipur	Nanjungud (20km)
Mudumalai Sanctuary	Udagamandalam (Ooty) (64km)
Periyar	Kottayam (114km)

Indian Railways has a directorate of rail tourist guides who are professional itinerary planners. The directorate can be contacted in advance if help is required. (Directorate of Tourism, Railway Board, Government of India, Rail Bhavan, New Delhi. 110001). Another source of help would be the chief public relations officer (CPRO) of each zonal railway.

Other popular destinations

Popular destinations are listed below with gateway stations, although not all linking trains run daily, and not all intermediate stations are mentioned.

With the broad gauging of many metre gauge lines underway, some rail links might be temporarily closed. Although inconvenient now, when work is completed those stations will be linked by broad gauge to the rest of the Indian Railways network.

Agra Cantt from Ahmedabad (to Agra Fort via Ajmer and Jaipur), Amritsar, Bangalore, Barmer, Bhopal, Bilaspur, Bombay, Calcutta, New Delhi, H. Nizamuddin (Delhi), Firozpur, Gwalior, Hyderabad/ Secunderabad, Indore, Jabalpur, Jaipur (to Agra Fort), Jammu Tawi, Kanniya Kumari, Kathgodam (to Agra Fort), Lucknow (to Agra Fort), Madras, Pune, Puri, Ratlam, Trivandrum, Varanasi, Vasco da Gama.

Aurangabad from Bombay, Kacheguda (via Secunderabad), Manmad, Nanded, Nizamabad.

Bangalore City from Ahmedabad, Bombay, Calcutta, New Delhi, Guwahati, Hyderabad, Madras, Manglore, Miraj, Mysore, Nagercoil, Simoga Town, Solapur, Talguppa, Tiruchcirappalli, Trivandrum, Vasco da Gama.

Bhubaneswar from Bangalore, Calcutta, Cochin, H Nizamuddin, New Delhi, Guwahati, Hyderabad, Madras, Puri, Secunderabad, Trivandrum.

Gorakhpur from Ahmedabad, Allahabad City, Barauni, Bombay, Calcutta, Chhapra, Cochin, New Delhi, Guwahati, Gwalior, Hatia, Hyderabad, Kanpur, Jammu Tawi, Lucknow, Muzaffarpur; also daily passenger trains from Nautanwa or Naugarh (from Nepal).

Jaipur from Agra Fort, Ahmedabad, Ajmer, Barmer, Bikaner, Delhi, Jodhpur, Lucknow, Sawai Madhopur, Udaipur.

Jaisalmer from Jodhpur.

Jalgaon from Ahmedabad, Amritsar, Bangalore, Bombay, Calcutta, Cochin, Firozpur, Gorakhpur, Itarsi, Jammu Tawi, Kolkapur, Madras, Nagpur, Pune, Varanasi, Vasco da Gama.

Jammu Tawi from Ahmedabad, Bombay, Calcutta, Delhi, Kanniya Kumari, Madras, Pune, Vasco da Gama, Trivandrum.

Jhansi from Ahmedabad, Allahabad, Bangalore, Bilaspur, Bhopal, Bombay, Chhapra, Cochin, Delhi, Firozpur, Gorakhpur, Gwalior, Hyderabad, Indore, Jabalpur, Jammu, Kanniya Kumari, Lucknow, Madras, Pune, Puri, Secunderabad, Trivandrum, Ujain, Varanasi

Madurai from Coimbatore, Madras, Rameswaram, Quilon, Tiruchchirappalli, Tirunelveli, Tirupati, Tuticorin.

New Jalpaiguri (for Darjeeling) from Bangalore, Bombay, Calcutta, Cochin, Delhi, Guwahati, Trivandrum.

Puri from Bhubaneswar, Calcutta, Delhi.

Quilon from Bangalore, Bombay, Cannanore, Delhi, Ernakulam, Guwahati, Jammu, Kanniya Kumari, Madras, Mangalore, Shoranur, Tiruchchirappalli, Trivandrum,

Rameswaram from Coimbatore, Madras. (The ferry service from Rameswaram to Sri Lanka is suspended.)

Shimla from Bhiwani (to Kalka), Calcutta (to Kalka), Delhi (to Kalka); Kalka, and other connections via Ambala to Kalka.

Udagamandalam (Ooty) from Coimbatore and from Madras to Mettupalaiyam; Coonoor, Mettupalaiyam, and trains from Trivandrum, Bombay, Madras and Delhi to Coimbatore.

Varanasi from Agra, Ahmedabad, Allahabad, Amritsar, Bombay, Calcutta, Dehra Dun, Delhi, Dhanbad, Gorakhpur, Gwalioer, Jammu, Ludhiana, Lucknow, Madras, Puri, Sonpur.

Vasco da Gama from Bangalore, Bombay and Delhi (change at Miraj); Miraj, Mysore, and from Agra via Miraj.

ITINERARIES

It is obviously impossible to reproduce here all the combinations of trains that could make a superb rail trip through India. However, when you are at home and don't have an Indian Railways timetable, such as *Trains at a Glance*, to hand, what do you do?

My solution is to decide where I want to go and then to send the list of places to Dr Dandapani and his son at their office in London (see page 53). They are ever willing to work out an itinerary. Alternatively, you could ask them to let you have some of their prepared standard itineraries. They even have journeys worked out at a price that includes hotels as well as the rail fare (and air fare, too, if you like). And you don't have to live in the UK to utilise their service as they airmail tickets to anywhere in the world.

New Delhi/Agra/New Delhi

If you only have time for one rail trip in India, it will probably be this: to Agra to see the Taj Mahal. There are two good trains from New Delhi which allow enough time to see the sights and return in the evening, but it means an early start.

The following are suggestions. Creative study of the timetable will yield other trains since the route is the main one from Bombay and from the south.

From	To	Train	Depart	Arrive
New Delhi Hazrat	Agra Cannt	2002 *Shatabdi Express*	0615	0810
Nizamuddin	Agra Cannt	2180 *Taj Express*	0715	0945
Agra Cannt	Hazrat Nizamuddin	2179 *Taj Express*	1845	2145
Agra Cannt	New Delhi	2001 *Shatabdi Express*	2018	2225

Delhi/Jaipur/Delhi

Jaipur is another must on every visitor's list. Now that the line between New Delhi and Jaipur is broad gauge, it is possible to make a visit in one day, if that's all you have to spare, or to return early the next morning.

From	To	Train	Depart	Arrive
New Delhi	Jaipur	2015 *Shatabdi Express*	0615	1030
Delhi	Jaipur	9760 *Intercity Express*	1700	2215

SCENES OF INDIA

Above: *Bombay Victoria Terminus (VT) station* (GA)

Below: *Nuns travelling by camel, Jaisalmer* (GA)

INDIAN LIFE
Above left: *Phoning from New Delhi station* (GA)
Above right: *Cigarette vendor, Madras Central station* (GA)
Below: *Bhang shop, Jaisalmer* (GA)

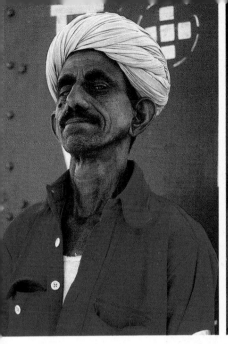

Above: *Porter at Jodhpur and detail of his badge* (GA)

Below: *The gleaming interior of the* Desert Queen *locomotive driver's cab* (GA)

The Deserted City, Fatehpur Sikri, Uttar Pradesh (PB)

| Jaipur | Delhi | 9759 *Intercity Express* | 0605 | 1110 |
| Jaipur | New Delhi | 2016 *Shatabdi Express* | 1800 | 2215 |

Indrail Pass itineraries

Indian Railways has several set itineraries for Indrail Pass holders for which reserved train accommodation can be guaranteed as long as arrangements are made at least 90 days in advance. A selection of the itineraries is included here although I don't think the trains they recommend are very practical.

For instance, there are many timings like this:

Day 3   Arr: Varanasi 0200   Dep: Varanasi 2350

That makes a long day without sleep. So I am not quoting the suggested trains, only the stations as a guide to the best sequence of travelling.

Seven-day tours

Buddhist tour   New Delhi/Gaya/Varanasi/Gorakhpur/Naugarh (for Lumbini in Nepal by road)/Lucknow/New Delhi

Rajasthan tour   Delhi/Jodhpur/Jaisalmer/Udaipur/Jaipur/Agra/New Delhi

Temple tour   New Delhi/Agra/Jhansi (for Khajuraho by road)/Varanasi/New Delhi

To Goa   Delhi/Jaipur/Agra/Jalgaon/Bombay/Vasco da Gama

City and cave   New Delhi/Jalgaon (by road to) Aurangabad/Secunderabad (by road to) Hyderabad/Madras/Bombay

City and cave   Bombay (Dadar)/Madras/Bangalore/Lonavla/Bombay

Temple and hill   Calcutta (Howrah)/Varanasi (by bus to) Mughalsarai/New Jalpaiguri/Darjeeling/New Jalpaiguri/Calcutta (Sealdah)

Temple tour   Calcutta (Howrah)/Nalanda/Rajgir/Gaya/Varanasi/Gorakhpur/Agra/New Delhi

15-day tours

Temple and beach   Bombay/Jalgaon (by road to) Aurangabad/Secunderabad/Madras (change at Kurda Road) Puri (for Konark). Varanasi/Agra/Jaipur/Delhi

Desert and cave   Dehli/Jaipur/Jodhpur/Jaisalmer/Udaipur/Khandwa/Jalgaon (by road to) Aurangabad/Secunderabad/Agra/New Delhi

North to south   New Delhi/Madras/Madurai/Kanniya Kumari/

Trivandrum/Cochin/Ooty (by road to) Mysore/Bangalore/
Hyderabad/Bombay

Religion and wildlife   Delhi/Jaipur/Bharatpur/Agra/Jhansi (for
Khajuraho by road)/Varanasi/Haridwar/Dehra Dun/Delhi

City tour   New Delhi/Bombay/Madras/Bangalore/Bhubaneswar/
Calcutta/Varanasi/Amritsar/Delhi

South tour   Madras/Bangalore/Mysore (by road to) Ooty/Cochin/
Trivandrum/Kanniya Kumari/Madurai/Trichy/Thanjavur/
Villupuram/Pondicherry/Villupuram/Madras

21-day tours
Miscellany
New Delhi/Sawai Madhopur (wildlife)/Jaipur/Agra/Varanasi/
Calcutta/Puri/Madras/Bangalore/Vasco da Gama/Lonavla/Bombay

New Delhi/Jammu Tawi (by road to Srinagar and back)/Varanasi/
Gaya/Calcutta/Madras/Bangalore/Secunderabad/Agra/New Delhi

Calcutta/Puri/Madras/Bangalore/Secunderabad/Bombay/
Aurangabad (by road to) Jalgaon/Agra/New Delhi/Varanasi/
Calcutta

30-day tours
Madras/Puri/Calcutta/Darjeeling/Varanasi/Haridwar/Delhi/Agra/
Jaipur/Udaipur/Chittaurgarh/Indore (by road to) Mhow/Jalgaon/
Bombay/Miraj/Vasco da Gama/Miraj/Bangalore/Trichy/Madras.

Circular tours
The zonal railways have devised their own circular tours for which a
circular journey ticket (CJT) can be purchased at the station of
origin, with reservations made at the same time. Details appear in
the zonal timetables.

Tour group itineraries
There are few travel agencies which specialise exclusively in
organised tours by rail in India, although many tour operators do
feature some rail travel in their package holidays to India.

All India Rail Tours are run by J A Butterfield, Burton Fleming,
Driffield, Yorkshire YO24 0PQ. Tel: 01262 87230. (See *Chapter
Eleven, Great Trips*).

Special trains
Special luxurious trains have been introduced recently by the
railways, following the success of the *Palace on Wheels* train which
made its first run in 1981.

The itineraries of trains already operating, or still waiting to see the light at the end of the tunnel, are given here. Reservations can be made through S D Enterprises Ltd, 103 Wembley Park Drive, Wembley, Middlesex, England HA9 8HG; tel: 0181 903 3411; fax: 0181 903 0392.

Palace on Wheels in Rajasthan: Delhi–Jaipur–Jodhpur–Jaisalmer–Sawai Madhopur–Bharatpur–Agra–Delhi. Distance 2,753km. Departures every Wednesday, September to April. Capacity 104 tourists. Broad gauge. (Manager, *Palace on Wheels*, Bikaner House, New Delhi; tel: 3381884; fax: 011 3382823)

Royal Orient in Gujarat: Delhi–Chittaurgarh–Udaipur–Ahmedabad–Junnagadh–Veraval–Sasan Gir–Delwada–Palitana–Sarkhej–Ahmedabad–Jaipur–Delhi. Distance 3,044km. Departures every Wednesday, September to April. Metre gauge. (Central Reservations, Tourism Corp of Gujarat Ltd, A-6 State Emporia Building, Baba Kharak SIngh Marg, New Delhi 110 001; tel: 3734915; fax: 011 3732482)

Royal Indian (Southern): Bangalore–Mysore–Madras–Kodaikanal Road–Kanniya Kumari–Trivandrum–Cochin–Mettupalayam (Ooty)–Bangalore. Distance 2,118km. (Foreign collaboration with Sterling Holiday Resorts is provided by Royal Scotsman of UK, according to the Railway Board)

Royal Indian (Northern): Delhi–Jaipur–Agra–Gwalior–Jhansi (Khajuraho)–Varanasi–Lucknow–Delhi. Distance 2,330km.

Western Region: Bombay–Aurangabad (Ajanto/Ellora)–Nanded–Secunderabad–Hyderabad–Pune–Bombay. Distance 1,876km.

Southern Circuit: Bangalore–Mysore–Madras–Kodaikanal Road–Kanniya Kumari–Trivandrum–Cochin–Mettupalayam (Ooty)–Bangalore. Distance 2,118km.

Coastal Circuit: Goa (Madgaon)–Mangalore–Mysore (Belur/Halebid)–Hospet (Hampi)–Bangalore–Goa (Madgoan). Distance 3,312km.

Rail weekenders

Tours organised by Indian Railways include rail reservation, boarding and lodging and sightseeing, commencing from the originating station on a Friday evening, returning on Monday morning. One ticket covers everything. Itineraries so far introduced include the following:

Pilgrim's Progress	from Delhi to Jammu
Sabarmati Revisited	from Bombay/Delhi/Jaipur to Ahmedabad
Shrine and Sarovar	from Delhi/Ahmedabad/Indore to Ajmer
East–West Tour	from Madras to Coimbatore–Ooty–Mudumalal

Pandyan Tour	from Madras Egmore to Madurai–Kodalkanal–Palan
Sakthi Tour	from Madras Egmore to Trichy–Thanjavur
Yercaud Servocayan Tour	from Madras to Salem–Yercaud–Iloganekkal
Sethu Yatra	from Madras Egmore to Rameshwaram–Tiruppulani–Devipattinam–Mandapam
also	from Madras Central to Kanniya Kumari
	from Calcutta to Bhubaneswar
	from Calcutta to Puri
	from Calcutta to Balasore

Enquiries about Rail Weekenders should be made to the originating station's computerised reservations office.

1. THIS IS YOUR OFFICE PLEASE HELP US TO CLEAN IT.
2. PLEASE DO NOT PUT YOUR LUGGAGE ON THE SOFA AND CHAIRS PLEASE DONOT SLEEP IN THE OFFICE THANKS.

M.N. PUROHIT
INTERNATIONAL TOURIST BUREAU

Chapter Ten

Some Popular Rail Destinations

AGRA

Agra has seven stations but only two of them, Agra Fort and Agra Cantt, are frequented by tourists. **Agra Fort** station was built in 1891 as a halt for colonials on picnic expeditions to the Red Fort and Taj Mahal. It is a Western Railway station with MG trains to Rajasthan and Gujarat. There are also BG trains to Lucknow, and it is a stop for the *Toofan Express* linking Delhi with Howrah.

Walls of the Red Fort tower over the station and the Taj Mahal is a short auto-rickshaw ride away. There is a fine view of the Red Fort from the terrace in front of the six-bed dormitory and the retiring rooms. The railway offices and waiting rooms are off platform 1 but the cloakroom is on platform 4. In the main lobby, the reservation office is on the left and the booking office on the right. First class reservations on all trains can be made at the counter by the enquiry office.

This enquiry office is a separate kiosk where foreign tourists can obtain help. A useful feature of Agra Fort station (which could be copied by other stations with lots of foreign passengers) is a sign which states: "In case of difficulty, the Indrail Pass holders should approach CRS." Although it doesn't explain what CRS means, it's nice to know foreigners are being thought of.

The auto-rickshaw drivers and their touts lurking to prey on tourists in the small forecourt are rapacious. Be firm, though, and they will soon lower their prices. The fare to Agra Cannt station drops after stern bargaining and it is an exotic ride through bazaars and pot-holed roads.

At **Agra Cannt** (it means cantonment) station, the taxis and rickshaws are organised by their own unions and have printed tariff cards which they show to passengers as they come off the train. Taxis and tour buses park on the right of the forecourt with auto-rickshaws gathered around the circular gardens and cycle rickshaws

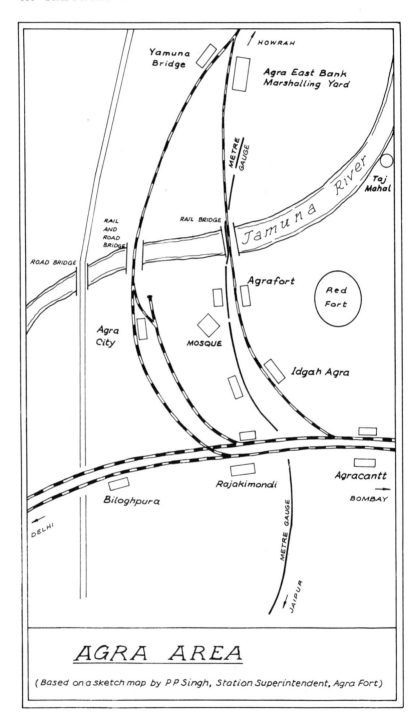

AGRA AREA

(Based on a sketch map by P P Singh, Station Superintendent, Agra Fort)

and tongas on the left. The tour buses are run by the Uttar Pradesh Tourism Department and the UP Transport Department and link with the arrival/departure of major trains. Tour tickets (taking in the major sights) are sold on board the trains, and from a booth on platform 1. There is a very helpful Uttar Pradesh tourist bureau (0800 to 1500) in the station lobby. If you are wait-listed for the return journey to New Delhi, check at the counters on the right of the booking hall; number 3 is for upper class reservations, number 6 for the *Taj Express* and number 7 for the *Shatabdi Express*. They all function at different hours with "bookings for counter number 7 between 1400–1700 being done on counter number 6". There is no counter dedicated to foreign tourists, which is puzzling since so many foreigners use the station and the Indrail Pass can be bought there (at the upper class counter, but there's no sign saying so). There is a 2nd class booking hall for local trains in an annexe to the station.

The present station was constructed in 1960 and has retiring rooms: six non air-conditioned double rooms and two air-conditioned and a large dormitory with ten beds. Bottled mineral water can be bought at this station, as well as a variety of nasty plastic models of the Taj Mahal. There is a post office at the end of platform 1.

AHMEDABAD

The delights of Ahmedabad station are many which is fortunate since, as the junction for trains to and from Rajasthan, Gujarat and Bombay, it handles nearly 200 trains and serves over 105,000 passengers a day, many of them being tourists stuck there while they await a connection. But if you want to phone home you can since there is a streamlined, modern telephone complex on the right of the lobby where faxes and telexes can be sent, and a "Home Country Service" where collect calls (to USA, Japan, UK, Spain, Netherlands, Italy and Singapore) can be made at the press of a button.

The station has 12 platforms, of which 1 to 4 are BG, 5 and 6 both BG and MG according to demand (thanks to a unique dual track which has three rails) and 7 to 12 for MG. There is another exit from the station by platform 12 but don't use it since all the action, and efficiency, is at the BG side, the main exit to the town.

The waiting rooms are large and some have wooden beds. The retiring rooms are on the first floor, with three dormitories offering 32 beds and other rooms for singles, doubles and triples. The best, number 23, has a fridge as well as a TV, four air-conditioning units and an Indian-style toilet.

The floor overlooks the booking hall and on the opposite side there is a V and NV restaurant. Vegetarian food is practically obligatory in Gujarat and the variety is much greater from the platform mobile food vendors. Recently opened in the station is the Mandarin restaurant which Samit Roychoudhury reports "is an extremely reasonable stand-and-eat Chinese restaurant with homely tasting food". There is also a "Medicell" (medical shop) and some bookstalls with counters both on the lobby and platform sides. The tourist office in the lobby is open only occasionally.

At the left luggage office a sign advises passengers not to keep "eatable items in luggage to avoid damage of your articles by rats". Worth remembering in the retiring rooms of most stations too. The office closes for 30 minutes three times in 24 hours. Current bookings can be done in the lobby where there is also a helpful enquiry office.

Ahmedabad has its own *Shatabdi Express* connection with Bombay Central, number 2010 which leaves every day, except Friday, at 1425. It stops on the way at Nadiad, Vadodara, Bharuch and Surat before reaching Bombay Central at 2115. As number 2009, it leaves Bombay Central at 0625 to reach Ahmedabad at 1315.

As well as the many expresses and mail trains that originate in Ahmedabad, there is a weekly train, number 8403/8404, known as a *Janseva Express*, fully unreserved, that goes across India to Puri. Quite a trip.

For advance reservations, Ahmedabad has a computerised reservations building to the left of the station. This is better than many in other major cities, being clean (no food vendors inside) and air-conditioned for passengers, not just for the computers. It is open 0800–2000, Sunday 0800–1400, and handles about 12,000 reservations a day. Foreign tourists should head for the supervisor's counter, number 12, where the physically handicapped, senior citizens, grievances and Freedom Fighters are also dealt with "on personal appearance".

Gujarat being a dry state need not deter you. Ask a taxi to take you the 6km drive to the Cama Hotel where a very trendy-looking liquor shop provides a permit "to possess and use foreign liquor for personal consumption" and permission to buy one unit (equivalent to one bottle of spirits or ten bottles of beer) a week. The chit cost me Rs35.

ALLAHABAD

There are two sides to Allahabad station: the residential side and the city side. A bridge links all nine platforms whereas previously passengers had to use two. The bridge is a boon for passengers since reservations are done on one side and tickets purchased on the other. Close by there is another station, Allahabad City.

The main booking counter for 2nd class reservation and tickets is in the lobby. None of the counter signs are in English but there is an enquiry office (with its sign in English) where directions can be obtained. At the side of this complex is a counter for buying upper class tickets, but not for making reservations which has to be done across the bridge.

The retiring rooms at Allahabad are on the second floor, city side, with access by steps from the 2nd class waiting hall. There are 13 rooms and two dormitories. The upper class and ladies' waiting rooms are on the first floor. There is a restaurant (open 0730 to 2300) off platform 1 with ancient, grouchy waiters. It has a separate section specialising in "South Indian dishes". There are lots of snack bars and book stalls: Allahabad is the headquarters of the A H Wheeler chain of station bookstalls.

Notices on the platform say "Alight here for Sangam Pilgrimage". Located at the confluence of the Ganga, Yamuna and the invisible Saraswati rivers, Allahabad, the City of God, is one of the important ancient cities of India. As a sacred centre, it attracts thousands of rail passengers every day.

Allahabad is on the main line from Calcutta to New Delhi. Delhi is 627km distant, Howrah 814km. There are lots of trains from Allahabad to Satna where there is a road link to Kharjuraho.

ALLEPPEY

This station, opened in 1989 as the temporary terminus of the new BG line from Ernakulam Jn, has become popular on the tourist circuit as it gives access to the inland waterways from Cochin. It is a stop on the way to Trivandrum. It has a vegetarian snack counter, two spacious retiring rooms and a small dormitory. The sole platform can take 34 carriages at one time, and land is available for station expansion.

There are booking counters at one side of the bright lobby with counter 1 handling advance reservations. The quotas have been inherited from the Alleppey out agency which used to be near the boat jetty and is now closed. A huge, locally made coir mat hangs like a tapestry above the booking office with a vivid design of the Kerala boat races.

With the opening of the station, Alleppey has become the ideal railhead for a backwaters boat trip. The jetty is 3km from the station with occasional buses available. The boat journey to Quilon is overnight so pointless if you want to see the scenery; better is the shorter (2½hr) trip to Kottayam (qv). Boats leave Alleppey throughout the day with a seat costing a few rupees, tickets available on board. In 1990 with some friends I chartered a "pilot" (read "pirate") boat to Kottayam. It was a memorable trip by canals and lakes alongside waterlogged paddy-fields and coconut groves.

AMBALA CANNT

Ambala is a major transit station in the Northern Railway network where passengers from Shimla connect with Lucknow and Jammu Tawi trains. It can be a pleasant place to wait. Just outside the station are some open-air restaurants with comfortable seating and brick ovens for cooking chapatis. There is also an English wine shop open all day selling Indian spirits and chilled beer. The NV restaurant at the station has some magnificent pieces of antique furniture, almirahs, dressers, a hat-stand and screens, all in daily use. There is no special counter for foreign tourists but there is a helpful reservations counter open 0930 to 1630 daily.

AMRITSAR

If Amritsar is on your itinerary, there are several trains to get you there, including a *Shatabdi Express* 2013, which arrives at 2215 after leaving New Delhi at 1630. As 2014 it leaves for New Delhi at 0510, arriving there at 1050. There is also a fully unreserved train, 5209/ 5210, running bi-weekly between Amritsar and Barauni. Rob Dobson reports that people at the station are geared up to taking you to the Golden Temple by bicycle rickshaw and then putting you back on a train again.

There is a service to Lahore, the 4607 *Indo-Pakistan Express*. This is scheduled to leave Amritsar at 0930, arriving Atari at 1010, departing from there at 1245 to arrive Lahore at 1335. The return is by 4608 *Indo-Pakistan Express* with departure from Lahore at 1130, arrival at Atari at 1220 and departure at 1420, reaching Amritsar at 1500. From Atari a minibus service is also available into Pakistan.

AURANGABAD

Aurangabad, a popular place to stay while exploring the caves at Ellora (30km distant) and Ajanta (106km) is now linked by BG line to Manmad with a direct Bombay–Aurangabad express.

Some travellers prefer to go to Jalgaon instead for access to the Ajanta Caves (59km distant), since many trains stop at Jalgaon as it is on a broad gauge line linking it with Bombay and other main stations (see *Chapter Nine* for connections).

BANGALORE

Bangalore is expanding so fast as an industrial and business centre, its beauty as a garden city has been obscured. Infrastructure is struggling to keep up but the railway recognised the boom and, in 1981, made it a fully fledged division of Southern Railway. Bangalore is about to become the fourth major metropolis of India, overtaking the position held by Madras. In 1988, a new railway administration building was opened, next to the City station, and it has been crowned with the nose of a metre gauge steam engine as an authentic replica of the Indian Railways emblem.

At **Bangalore City** station, the high-ceilinged lobby has a booth for the Karnataka State Tourism Development Corporation, promoting its tours. The bus station is opposite the railway forecourt and tourist agencies line the road to the right. Also in the entrance-lobby is a police information kiosk where a notice warns passengers about unauthorised "ticket nippers". The chemist (open 0600–2200) sells bottled mineral water and the bookshop (0900–1300, 1400–1700) has lots of locally produced guides about India.

Tickets for same-day departures can be bought in an annex to the lobby. For advance reservations go to the new building on the right of the station forecourt where there is a special Indrail Pass counter where foreign tourists can buy tickets and make reservations. This counter (number 14) can be busy as it is for foreign tourists, Freedom Fighters, concession holders and handicapped and senior citizens, so allow plenty of time.

Thee is a veg restaurant off platform 1 with mechanised food mixers and fast-food boilers. A non-veg restaurant is on the upper floor, beside the gallery overlooking the booking lobby. Waiting rooms are also there. The 23 retiring rooms are much in demand: double rooms all have twin beds, fans, settee and armchairs, a writing desk, dressing room and bathroom with hot water and towel. There are dormitory beds in a ward-like atmosphere.

In keeping with its new image as the city of the future, Bangalore has an extensive system of direct rail links with the rest of India. There is also a *Shatabdi* service, with 2008 (from Mysore) leaving Bangalore at 1630, arriving Madras at 2115, daily except Tuesday. An *Intercity Express*, number 2725, leaves Bangalore daily at 1500 for Hubli, via Davangere. It arrives back the next day at 1420.

The once a week *Rajdhani Express* leaves Bangalore on Mondays at 0645 bound, via Secunderabad, for Hazrat Nizamuddin (New Delhi). It arrives back on Sundays at 2000, providing a good link from Secunderabad as well as from New Delhi. To Madras, there are morning, afternoon and evening departures taking between six and seven hours for the 362km journey.

Bangalore Cantonment station is more rural with light blue tiles lining the platform walls and an odd cluster of arches opposite platform 1. No trains originate here; it is a halt for those going to and from Bangalore City station. It has a bank to facilitate customers clearing freight from the goods yard that adjoins it. Bangalore is an inland port linked with Madras for imports and exports. In one shed in the yard I saw hundreds of drums of aspirin being loaded into a rail container for direct shipment to the UK.

Not far from both stations is the Welcomgroup's Windsor Manor

Sheraton hotel (25 Sankey Road, Bangalore), an Indian architect's interpretation of an English stately home. Although constructed in 1983, it blends in perfectly with Bangalore's genuine historic buildings. The hotel is popular with local and foreign tourists and business people both to visit (the Royal Derby bar reeks of British nostalgia) and to stay. The city's newest hotel is the opulent Oberoi.

BERHAMPUR

A small station with fantastic connections. You can get here any day from Howrah or Bhubanswar by superfast trains, and also from Madras (on the *Coromandel Express* or *Howrah Mail*) or from Hyderabad by the *East Coast Express*, and from Tirupati too. At least once a week, expresses stop from Trivandrum, Guwahati and Cochin.

You go to Berhampur to get to Gopalpur-on-Sea, a beach resort on the Bay of Bengal. It is also the station closest to the huge (70km by 15km) freshwater Chilka Lake, which the railway runs beside. There are dormitory beds at the station and doubles.

Buses and taxis go to Gopalpur-on-Sea, 18km distant. This town still seems undiscovered by most foreign visitors. It has a backwaters fishing village, retaining a tranquillity that's a joy to discover after the relentless throb and beat of rail travel. There are old-style comforts at the Oberoi Palm Beach Hotel which match the irresistible charm of this delightfully Indian seaside resort.

BHUBANESWAR

There are plans to make Bhubaneswar into a model railway station with a new building opposite the existing station to house a computer reservations facility and other offices. The station, built in 1965, is on the Calcutta–Madras main line with the railway tracks separating the new town from the old. Bhubaneswar is famed as the temple city of India and taxi drivers pester passengers with offers of city temple tours as soon as they arrive.

A staircase off the booking hall leads to the retiring rooms, of which the best are the air-conditioned rooms at a rate which includes tea and newspaper. I didn't fancy the dormitory, nor the gloomy waiting rooms. On the same floor are doors marked "Veg" and "Non-Veg" which open into the same restaurant. The 2nd class waiting hall is downstairs at platform level. As well as the Wheeler's bookstall there is a Sarvodaya stall with locally produced guidebooks among the religious tracts.

A good way to Bhubaneswar by train is by the once a week *Rajdhani Express*, number 2422, which leaves New Delhi at 1700 on Friday and arrives, after a 20-minute break in Howrah, at 1830 the next day. It leaves Bhubaneswar, as train 2421, on Sunday at 0850, reaching New Delhi at 1000 the next day.

Bhubaneswar's attractions are historical as it is part of ancient India, although its proximity to the coast resort of Puri (reached by train) and to the Sun Temple at Konark (reached by bus) draws visitors. Rob Dodson recommends a modest but comfortable, central hotel near the station with good views of the city gardens: Hotel Keshari, 113 Station Square – economy rate. There is a hotel (the Oberoi) at Bhubaneswar built in 1985 that has become an attraction in itself because it has been conceived along temple lines with an outer sanctum leading to another and on to the inner heart of the hotel, in this case a pool and garden surrounded by rooms. At this hotel, before serving my beer, the barman asked "Are you German or English, sir?" When I said English he tilted the glass and poured the beer frothless and to perfection.

CANNANORE

Not many foreign tourists find their way to Cannanore but it has a vast beach (no beach life or package hotels though) and is a friendly, middle class town. The pleasure begins at the station where the five retiring rooms (above the police post) are well managed, each one with a comments book on which the SM takes action. Room number 5 overlooks the tiny station garden. Both the VRR (veg refreshment room) and the NVRR serve good food, the NVRR in a charming small restaurant, the VRR in a dining room. A station door marked "Hindi Class" does not refer to a class of passenger but to lessons for railway staff. There is an information counter off the large entrance lobby where the advance reservations desk deals very effectively with foreigners, open 0900–1300; 1400–1700.

There is a forlorn, colonial style hotel, the Savoy, 1km from the station. On a cliff overlooking the sea, the economy rate choice Seaside Hotel, once a tea planters' retreat, is an amazing find which guests like to keep secret, so only go there if you're good company.

CHANDIGARH

A modern-looking station with very clean waiting rooms, on the line from Delhi to Kalka (for Shimla). There are two retiring rooms, both at the end of the office block on the sole platform. The reservation office says it's open 24 hours but it is actually closed between 0130–0200, 0630–0900 and 1800–1830. Chandigarh is the capital of Punjab and Haryana states and the station is 8km from the centre of the city planned by Le Corbusier.

Chandigarh is blessed with not just one but two *Shatabdi Express* services to New Delhi. Numbers 2006 and 2012 leave for New Delhi at 0641 and 1240 respectively; the journey takes three hours. As

2005 and 2011 they arrive in Chandigarh from New Delhi at 2012 and 1035. There is also a link by *Shatabdi* with Kalka, departing Chandigarh at 2018 every day, and returning at 0631 daily, on its way to New Delhi.

CHITTAURGARH

Set in the plains of Rajasthan, Chittaurgarh station is on the MG line. It has a long tree-lined platform which doubles as 1 and 2, with retiring rooms, refreshment room and separate ladies' and gents' with upper class waiting rooms beside it. The station is basic in appearance with a lobby that leads to a combined enquiry and reservation kiosk (open 1000–1700), with signs in English. A booking office for general tickets is on the left and a waiting hall on the right. The station is 6km from the impressive fort ruin which is what visitors come to see.

COCHIN (KOCHI)

The full name for this station on India's southwestern coast is Cochin Harbour Terminus and it is built on Willingdon Island in a natural harbour famous for its maritime history. Access to Cochin is also via Ernakulam Jn (qv). It has recently been renamed Kochi. The station is simple and small (one island platform) compared with its importance with direct services to Rajkot, Bangalore, Bilaspur, Bombay, Coimbatore, Gorakhpur, Guwahati, Howrah, Hyderabad, Indore, Madras, Patna, Trichy and Varanasi. A reminder of the train called the *Tea Garden Express* exists in the old 1st and 2nd class sleeper coach and the general unreserved coach attached to the nightly Cochin to Trichy Express (6366) for Ooty-bound passengers. At Coimbatore (qv) the two coaches are shunted into a siding for four hours then attached to the *Nilagiri Express* (6105) for the ride to Mettupalaiyam (change for Ooty). On the return journey the coaches enable through-the-night travel to Cochin without changing at Coimbatore.

To cater for passengers, a restaurant was opened opposite the station in the 1950s to which were added three bedrooms to qualify for a liquor licence. It was given a flashy name, Casino, to attract customers. Now it has grown to a hotel of five-star luxury. Several readers share my opinion that Cochin's Casino Hotel rivals India's top hostelries for comfort, service and good food, and all within low, standard rates. Arrangements (including permit) are handled here for a fascinating side trip, a flying visit to the only island in the **Lakshadweep** group open to foreigners. The Casino Hotel runs the Bangaram Island Resort; it's in the luxury rate category but a wonderful way to relax after too much rail. (Casino Hotel, Willingdon Island, Cochin)

COIMBATORE

This station, perhaps because it's newish (1987), is one of the cleanest on Indian Railways. It isn't particularly pretty – they call Coimbatore the Manchester of south India because of its industry – but it is neat, tiled, bright and well-run. You can judge a station's efficiency by the number and appearance of the mobile vendors on its platforms. Coimbatore excels: they are many and they are smart. You change trains here on the way to Mettupalaiyam for Ooty (see *Udagamandalam* in this chapter), unless you are coming from Madras on the 6105 *Nilagiri Express* which stops in transit for 30 minutes. The station is served by a dozen major trains daily, and by a score more on a weekly or bi-weekly basis.

A boon to rail travellers is the new *Shatabdi* service between Coimbatore and Madras, reducing the journey to under seven hours (494km), and adding comfort. The 2024 *Shatabdi* departs from Coimbatore every day at 0615. As 2023, it gets back in the evening at 2200.

The spacious lobby has an expanse of granite floor tiles and natural light from its many windows. On the left on entering from the forecourt is the cloakroom and a tourist information centre (0700–1900, except holidays: 1000–1730). A tunnel leads to each of the station's six platforms, numbers 5 and 6 being MG.

Unreserved tickets are sold at the counters to the right of the lobby, while computerised reservations are made in a separate hall upstairs. There are no foreign tourist quota berths available but an enquiry to the CRS or SS (his office is on the ground floor) will bring instant and friendly help. On the first floor, on the other side of the gallery overlooking the lobby, are the retiring rooms with non air-conditioned double rooms and an air-conditioned apartment.

DEHRA DUN

This station is the rail gateway for Mussoorie, 22km away by bus or taxi. Mussoorie is a picturesque hill resort commanding views of Himalayan snow ranges to the northeast, and of the Doon Valley and Haridwar to the south. There are retiring rooms at the station, with the usual rates for a double room being increased during the May and October peak season. The station is served by the daily *Dehra Dun Express* direct from Bombay via Delhi, a 1,701km journey covered in 42 hours. From Delhi (320km away) the trip takes ten hours overnight by the *Mussoorie Express*, or nine hours during the day by the *Dehra Dun Express*. The *Doon Express* terminates in Dehra Dun at the end of its 36 hour (1,524km) run from Howrah via Lucknow. There is also an express from Varanasi. By train to Shimla or Jammu Tawi is via Laksar and Ambala Cantt.

Every day except Wednesday there is a *Shatabdi Express* number 2018, leaving Dehra Dun at 1620, arriving New Delhi at 2205. It arrives in Dehra Dun, from New Delhi, at 1225.

ERNAKULAM JN

This is Cochin, although trains bound for Cochin terminate at the Harbour Station on Willingdon Island. If yours doesn't go there, alight here for the 8km ride by bus or taxi, unless you are staying on the mainland. There are no special facilities for foreign tourists at Ernakulam Junction although the station does have an information counter. There is a computerised reservations office. Stairs from the lobby lead to the three double retiring rooms and a new dormitory. The station is served by direct expresses from Bangalore, Delhi, Madras and Trivandrum, while other trains stop at Ernakulum Town. A rail link to Alleppey (qv) was opened in 1989.

ERNAKULAM TOWN

This is a halt station for incoming trains that bypass Cochin HT, and could be the station you go to by mistake when you should be catching your train from Ernakulam Jn. If you alight here, buses go to Junction station, Cochin or the ferry jetty. There are no retiring rooms but several tourist hotels are opposite the station.

ERODE

More people pass through this station than join trains here, which is not surprising since the station entrance with booking hall is 100m down a tunnel (under the goods yard) from the platform. Five retiring rooms overlook the goods yard and are reached by dual staircases with 1920s iron bannisters. Food vendors patrol the platform throughout the night when nearly 30 BG trains stop for a breather.

GAYA

This Eastern Railway station teems with begging children, shoe cleaners and vendors of *gram* which people spit into your face as they talk with mouths full. Yet this is the station from which to travel (15km by bus or taxi) to the great pilgrim centre for Buddhists, Bodhgaya. Gaya itself is a centre for Hindu pilgrims. The station has four retiring rooms with two beds in each and two with air-conditioning. It is well served by mainline trains and can be reached by direct expresses from Delhi (984km in 18 hours, approximately), Howrah (458km/8 hr), Bombay (1,715km/30½ hr), Jammu Tawi, via Lucknow and Varanasi (1,509km/36 hr), Puri via Bhubaneswar (589km/17–18 hr), Patna (92km/2 hr) and Ranchi (337km/8½ hr).

GORAKHPUR

Gorkahpur is the headquarters of the North Eastern Railway. Its attraction to foreigners is as a transit station to Nepal or for a visit to Kushinagar where Lord Buddha died. It is a spacious station with its upper class facilities centred around the main entrance, under a clock tower. Reservations are computerised. Train timetables are in Hindi although there is an illuminated sign in English giving current departures and platform numbers. A left luggage office is on the right, with the sign in Hindi.

The lobby leads to the platforms where there is a bookstall (open 0430–0130 daily) and a combined vegetarian and non-vegetarian restaurant (0630–2130) with an all-night refreshment stall outside it. Waiting and retiring rooms, some with air-conditioning, are upstairs. The one I stayed in actually had toilet paper to go with its Western toilet. There is a deluxe double with TV, fridge and two cold drinks. There are 25 beds in three dormitories; plans are in hand to construct a 35-bedroom railway hotel at the station.

An Uttar Pradesh tourist bureau is on platform 1 where an excellent set of leaflets is available, including one about Buddhist pilgrimages in the area. There are also police assistance, tourist help and grievance redressal booths on the platform. People in a hurry who have a complaint can collect a stamped lettergram to complete at their leisure and mail back to the station. Buses meet the main trains and from the nearby bus station buses leave on the hour for the 54km journey to Kushinagar. Kushinagar can also be reached by bus (35km) from Deoria Sadar Station, 45 minutes by train from Gorakhpur.

There are several ways of reaching **Nepal**. Nautanwa (close to the border) is served by daily MG fast passenger trains; the best one departs from Gorakhpur at 0630 and arrives at Nautanwa two hours later. The train leave Nautanwa at 0910 and arrives back at Gorakhpur at 1110. The closest station in India for Lumbini (Buddha's birthplace in Nepal) is Naugarh. This can be reached via the MG loop line from Gorakhpur, with the passenger train taking 60 minutes to Anandnaga, a junction from where trains go to Naugarh (a further 52 minutes). Another way to Naugarh is by bus from Basti, a station on the main line to Gorakhpur from Delhi and Bombay which has the cleanest dormitory bathroom of any I've seen in India. The journey via Raxaul station involves too many changes to be practical. The final leg over the border is by bus or taxi.

Visas for Nepal are necessary. You'll need a re-entry visa to return to India but this has to be applied for at the time you apply for the original visa to enter India (ask for a double or triple entry then). When you arrive at Gorakhpur from Nautanwa by train, you could be subjected to a casual customs search on the bridge from the MG platform to the station exit; but the customs check at the border is more serious. If you are coming from Kathmandu or Pokhara in Nepal, beware of travel agents there who offer tickets on Indian Railways. A chief travelling ticket inspector (CTTI) on NE Railway told me he has discovered at least 20 cases of foreigners being overcharged. He proved it when we met a young German who had been charged Rs200 more than the correct fare for his ticket to Cochin.

"The foreigner is an innocent, we must help him," the CTTI said. He advises foreigners travelling from Nepal to leave purchasing their Indian Railway tickets for onward journeys from Gorakhpur until they are actually in Gorakhpur. The Indrail Pass is sold there and single-journey tickets are available. If reservations are difficult, the CRS or SS could be asked for help; it's better than being ripped off.

HARIDWAR

Situated at the foot of the Shivalik Hills and on the banks of the Ganga River where it enters the plains from the mountains, Haridwar is one of the holiest of Hindu religious places. It is on the line to Dehra Dun (qv) and is served by the same trains. The holy town of Rishikesh with its hanging bridge over the Ganga is 24km and about an hour away by passenger train. There are several wildlife sanctuaries within a few kilometres drive of Haridwar.

HYDERABAD

Look for Hyderabad – "the City of Love" in *Trains At A Glance* and it says "Please see Secunderabad", but this station is the terminus (and starting point) for several important trains and is the one foreign visitors are likely to use when coming to see the city's best known landmark, the Charminar, four minarets built in 1591 (5km distant). The station has a large courtyard and six platforms and a reservation office in the main building. It is more relaxed than its twin, Secunderabad, and handles about half the number of passengers. There are no retiring rooms. It is 10km from Secunderabad station and through trains generally stop at both.

JAIPUR

Jaipur station was built in 1956 in imitation of the flamboyant buildings which abound in this laid-back city of pink proscenium arches and turreted palaces.

Camels loping through the city's traffic are just one of Jaipur's extraordinary sights. The city has gone over the top with its fondness for pink. Horse-drawn buggies, and some buses, are painted pink and even carrots sold by sidewalk vendors are crimson. You'll see pink-bottomed monkeys gambolling on the rooftop terraces of the one-storey pink-walled shops that add to Jaipur's fascination.

At the station, the coolies (porters) wear red Rajasthan turbans. The city's street people congregate at night to view the 24-hour CCTV in the booking hall and you'll have to pick your way over them to get to the enquiry desk in the lobby.

If you want to make an advance reservation, go to the new computerised reservation building on the right of the station as you leave it. In the centre of the forecourt is a park with an MG steam loco on a plinth. The reservations complex has its entrance at the side furthest from the station. The "any counter, any train, anywhere" rule applies here, with queues at all counters instead of a single queue for all the counters. Foreigners have their own window, 769, but since it's also for "handicapped persons, Freedom Fighters and senior citizens" it is usually as crowded as the other windows. It's open 0800–1400, 1415–2000, Sunday 0800–1400.

There is a real rogues' gallery at Jaipur Station, with framed photographs of what the SS calls "mischief makers" on several of its walls. Off platform 1 is the tourist office with well presented literature about Rajasthan, including an elaborate map which may cost you Rs5 or may be free. The soft drinks counter is not open in winter; there is a restaurant with tables reserved for vegetarians marked with cards.

The retiring rooms are upstairs with a bright reception office (CCTV also here). There are 17 double rooms, three air-conditioned doubles, nine singles and two dormitories, one for women (Four beds) and one for men (12 beds).

Dinner tip: while waiting for a train, I discovered the Handi Restaurant with superb lamb and chicken barbecued at its entrance; you eat in a thatch-covered courtyard. It's near something called the Copper Chimney, about a mile's auto-rickshaw ride from the station. For a drink, try the rundown palace-style villa called the Tourist Hotel operated by the Rajasthan Tourism Development Corporation; great fun in its first-floor bar. The Handi Restaurant in its courtyard is not the one I recommend above.

Jaipur, known as the Pink City and the Gateway, and Jewel, of Rajasthan, is one of he most popular destinations for foreigners and has been extensively covered in guidebooks and colour supplements. It is easy to reach from Delhi and is a convenient day trip. A painless way is by the *Shatabdi Express*, number 2015, which leaves New Delhi at 0615 and arrives in Jaipur at 1100. It departs from Jaipur (having come from Ajmer) at 1735 and arrives in New Delhi at 2215.

It does not operate on Sundays. There is also a new direct link, Jaipur to/from Bombay Central by superfast express 2955/2956.

If you do want to stay, and fancy a night in a former Maharaja's palace, the Rambagh Palace (Bhawani Singh Rd, Jaipur) run by the Taj group, is Jaipur's finest hotel with superb lawns and palatial atmosphere.

JAISALMER

After a day or night run through the desert from Jodhpur (the only way to get there by train) the sight of Jaisalmer station, small though it is, is welcome. Its sand-coloured buildings date from 1967 when the line to Jaisalmer was laid.

Opened in late 1991 was a Northern Railway sponsored office for foreign tourists, offering comfortable seats, occasional folkloric shows and quota tickets on a strict waiting-list basis. It is run by the same amiable character responsible for the Jodhpur office.

Jaisalmer is about 120km from the Pakistan border, which is perhaps why there are signs at the station, in English, proclaiming: "(1) Be Indian. Buy Indian. (2) Kashmir to Kanniya Kumari, India is one. (3) Many religions, one nation. Let us be proud of it. (4) India is our country, let us help make it strong and prosperous." Jaisalmer was left undisturbed by tourists until 1974 when a tourist bungalow was built; now there are over 30,000 tourists a year.

The attraction is the fort settlement, emerging out of a hillock in the desert like a phenomenon of nature until you are inside and see the intricate designs of balconies and doors wrought by skilled craftsmen over centuries. There are jeeps and auto-rickshaws to take rail passengers to the gates of the fort and then it is a fascinating ramble through alleyways and alongside temples watched by hospitable and curious people. Actually many of the traders, street musicians and hangers-on are there for the pickings and don't come from Jaisalmer at all.

Chilled bottled mineral water is to be had at a reasonable price in the town square but for a beer wend your way through the alleys (or ask for directions) to the Hotel Jaisal Castle. It has no sign outside and is fashioned out of the walls of the fort, above the scrub and new buildings of the outer town. A narrow balcony with space for two hangs out over the fort wall and is a heady place on which to drink that ice-cold beer. The hotel is the perfect desert guesthouse: cool, white-washed walls, low-ceilinged rooms with ornate hangings and rustic furniture, and clean, attached bathrooms with showers and Western toilets with loo paper too. Although there is a tiny restaurant, dinner can be served on the roof under the stars. Economy bracket.

JAMMU TAWI

This busy station is the best railhead for Kashmir, abounding in touts to help or confuse the traveller heading for the bus stand for transport to Srinagar. Since the station is on the "new town" side of the Tawi River, you'll have to take a minibus to the bus stand on the other side. There are retiring rooms at the station; doubles and dormitory beds.

It can take between ten and 15 hours to travel the 585km to Jammu from Delhi, depending on which train you choose; all trains are overnight.

The real train nut may want to try the longest haul of all, from the Cape to Kashmir, the 6017/18 *Himsagar Express*. This runs the length of India between Kanniya Kumari and Jammu Tawi, a distance of 3,726km, via Trivandrum, Madras, Agra and New Delhi. The departure days of this once-a-week trip change according to the season, so I dare not quote them, but it means four nights on the train.

However you travel by train, advance reservations are essential, especially in the season (summer) and are best done through your Indrail Pass GSA before going to India, or at the ITB in New Delhi station. For return reservations, make them at Jammu Tawi on your way to Kashmir or contact the railway booking office at Srinagar to avoid having to hang around Jammu while waiting for a berth on the way back.

JAMNAGAR

Jamnagar in Gujarat is not on the usual tourist route. There are two platforms and a modern entrance lobby in the station, built in 1987 far from the town and isolated amidst salt pans that pong a bit. There are two retiring rooms and a six-bed dormitory on the first floor, pleasant enough and ideal for watching the BG locos hauling local trains with their picturesque passengers, especially the oddly garbed milkmen with their churns hanging from the windows. The old station, a splendid rococo affair with a clocktower, stands abandoned downtown.

Catering and other services are limited. You'll get a meat fix at a place popular with the military stationed in Jamnagar: the Hotel Daavat, Bagga Mansion, opposite Amber Talkies, Jamnagar.

JHANSI

You would only want to get out at this station if you're going to see the erotic temples at Khajuraho, 172km (five hours) away by bus. The list of trains that stop at Jhansi is long because of its location at the centre of lines running north, east, south and west. Not many people stay, though, and there is only one, rather nasty, retiring room and a dormitory for six adjoining platform 1. Both are controlled by formidable ladies who lock you in on arrival and only let you out on demand. The restaurant (open 0600–1900) is small and gloomy; behind it is a major, modernised base kitchen with capacity for 3,000 meals a day. The dinner that is served (included in the fare) on the evening run of the *Shatabdi Express* from Bhopal to Gwalior, Agra and New Delhi is prepared here. The *Shatabdi Express* is the best train to take to get to Jhansi, leaving New Delhi at 0615 and arriving at Jhansi, 414km, distant, at 1039, averaging 92km/h (see *Chapter Eleven*).

The station has two tourist bureaux; the one for Madhya Pradesh is very helpful with lots of leaflets; the one for Uttar Pradesh was closed whenever I visited. There is a rash of electronics here: digital clocks in the retiring and waiting rooms, and a display board that flashes when a train comes in. The gents' upper class waiting room has taped music. If you have to stay at Jhansi, escape from the station and try what is called "the oldest western-style hotel of Bundelkhand", the Jhansi Hotel (Shastri Marg, Jhansi, UP), a short auto-rickshaw ride away, where tea is served in silver pots left over from British days and there are some remarkable oil paintings of colonial gents above the bar and in the TV room. There is a full range of accommodation at Khajuraho, which is actually closer (65km) to Mahoba station than to Jhansi, but the train links are impossible for same-day onward travel.

JODHPUR

When I saw the booking counter at Jodhpur station had a notice saying "Foreign" in English above it, I was pleased this small station had a counter dedicated to foreign tourists. I was wrong. On this notice, "foreign" means the counter sells tickets to "foreign" stations, those outside the Northern Railway zone, not to foreigners. However, the station does have more signs in English than most. It also has a rail tourist bureau, an offshoot of the ITB in New Delhi and a sister bureau of the one newly opened in Jaisalmer. This is run by a personable gentleman called M M Purohit, whose enthusiasm for tourists knows no bounds. It is open 0500–2300 daily especially to help foreign tourists with reservations, ticket purchase and information, and it also serves as a waiting room and a temporary left luggage office; it even has a toilet. Run by Northern Railway, it is a facility that other stations frequented by foreigners could copy. Jodhpur has been computerised for making advance reservations.

The city isn't just a transit stop on the way to Jaisalmer but worth a longer visit for its grand palaces, 15th century fort and the bazaar atmosphere of the old town. Another reason for staying is to check into the fabulous Umaid Bhawan Palace, 6km from the station, which is a museum and a Maharaja's home as well as an unusual and very stately hotel, actually built 1929–42. If its hallowed marble halls, filled with Western classical music, are too intimidating, dive down to the basement for a swim in its subterranean pool reminiscent of the pool on the old *Queen Mary* liner and open to non-residents. Room rates are in the luxury bracket. Rob Dobson discovered modest but comfortable accommodation opposite the station at Shanti Bhawan Lodge, economy bracket.

A treat for rail buffs is the sighting of the private railway carriages of the Maharaja of Jodhpur.

KANNIYA KUMARI

You go to Kanniya Kumari (KK), or Cape Cormorin, because it's there – at the tip of India where the Indian Ocean and the Arabian Sea meet the Bay of Bengal – and to see the sun rise. It is the Land's End of India and has probably the only station in the world with a specially built sunrise observation roof, and sunset and sunrise times posted in an information booth. The SS wears green epaulettes with gold stripes on his smart white uniform and proudly shows visitors around the station. There are two single retiring rooms, two doubles and one dormitory with eight beds; all are basic but convenient for the early-morning stint at the viewing platform. Since that faces east, for sunset and simultaneous moon rise on full moon days, head for the seashore, within walking distance. September to January is the best time; March 15 to July 15 is the period of summer vacation when KK, which is really rather seedy, is packed.

Separate counters cater for ladies' and gents' bookings in the station lobby. Not many trains come to KK because it is the absolute terminus, but every afternoon the 1082 *KK Express* completes the 2,149km journey from Bombay. It leaves for the return trip before sunrise and takes almost 48 hours to reach Bombay VT. There are three other daily arrivals/departures, all passenger trains, from/to Nagercoil Jn, or Tirunelveli Jn.

Once a week the 6017/8 *Himsagar Express* comes from Kashmir and returns 13 hours later (see *Jammu Tawi*).

KARJAT

Mainline trains heading south from Bombay stop at Karjat, 100km from Bombay VT station, to have one or two extra locos attached to the rear of the train to push it 28km up through the ghat section to Lonavla where the extra locos are detached and sent back to Karjat to start again. There are suburban EMU trains to Karjat from Bombay VT but none up to Lonavla (qv) because of the steepness of the ghat section. There are 1st class waiting rooms/

toilets on both main platforms. Tourists heading south after a visit to Matheran use this station to connect with mainline trains after taking the suburban service from Neral to Karjat.

KOTTAYAM

On the mainline between Trivandrum and Ernakulam, Kottayam station seethes with pilgrim traffic from November to January: 34 trains a day stop there for a few minutes. There are good V and NV restaurants as well as fruit stalls, and apple juice and milk counters. The exit is up a flight of stairs, where the waiting and five retiring rooms are also located. An information bureau is in the centre of the entrance lobby with advance reservation and current booking offices at the sides.

Auto-rickshaws are available in the forecourt for the 2km ride to the Kottayam boat jetty. Boats leave throughout the day for the 2½hr cruise through the backwaters to Alleppey (qv). The Anjali Hotel (4km from the station) is highly praised and has a smart ground floor restaurant, a rooftop bar and a Chinese restaurant. Run by the same people who own the Casino Hotel in Cochin, modest standard rate. In Kottayam, don't miss a ride through the coconut grove countryside and a taste of toddy, the liquor extracted from the coconut flower.

LONAVLA

Situated 127km out of Bombay on the line to Pune and beyond (to Madras or Goa), Lonavla is a small station you may not notice except when the train stops for the locos that pushed the train from Karjat to be detached. At 625m above sea level, it is a hill resort popular as an escape from Bombay's heat; it gets chilly in winter. You alight here for the 2,000 year-old Buddhist caves at Karla (10km). The station forecourt is small and the station building barely seems to be a station at all. There is a booking office inside but the main platform is the centre island platform, number 2. There are no retiring rooms and few facilities. The 1st class waiting room has a fine dressing table from the British period which looks out of place in its drab surroundings. Foreigners are rare at this station and should seek out the SS (his office is on platform 2) for any special requirements.

Trains from Bombay VT and Dadar stop here and so does the 2123 *Deccan Queen* every evening from VT station, taking just over two hours for the journey. As well as being well served by commuter trains, Lonavla has direct trains from Bangalore City, Hyderabad, Secunderabad, Kanniya Kumari, and Madras. An EMU service at peak times connects Lonavla with Pune, a journey of 90 minutes.

Lonavla has some lively eateries, and is famous for its sweet confection, *chikki*. A tourist information bureau is near the station, and there are several places to stay at economy rates within its vicinity.

LUCKNOW

There are two stations at Lucknow (at Charbagh, 3km from downtown), both in the same compound but otherwise quite different in facilities and atmosphere. The main one is the stone building with dozens of turrets that symbolises Lucknow for the visitor. A stone set into the wall of the station proclaims: "Within this turret wall was laid on the first day of August, 1925, by G.I. Colvin, Esq. CB, CMG, DSO, agent of the East Indian Railway, a casket containing current coin with newspapers of the day to commemorate the successful completion of the foundations of the building".

That is one of the few signs in English. The lobby of the station is hung with signs in Hindi, including one saying enquiry office, so you'll have to ask for it unless you can read Hindi.

On the left of the lobby are counters for upper class same day reservations. There is an Uttar Pradesh tourist bureau (open 0800–2000) with a leaflet on Lucknow which puts Charbagh Railway Station (this station's real name) as the first on its long list of "What To See". It says the station was built in typical Rajasthani style and stands in place of the gardens of the nawabs from where it derives its name – Charbagh means four gardens.

A story told to illustrate the sophistication of Lucknow residents is of the two nawabs who kept on requesting each other to board their train first, until the train puffed out of the station leaving both of them behind.

Lucknow station, which in 1988 won my award for the filthiest platforms, has cleaned up its act. Step out of the booking hall and you see a spacious square where taxis and rickshaws are prevented from blocking the access road. On the right is the new (1991) reservations complex built in the flamboyant style of the old station. Computerised reservations to any station (by BG or MG) can be made here. There are two counters (601/602) for foreign tourists and various other categories, so they are usually busy. Better to dedicate one counter exclusively for foreigners. The office is open 0800–2000, Sunday until 1400. No luggage is permitted inside the complex, but there is a free luggage room opposite the entrance.

In the station there is an assistance booth on platform 1 and an enquiry office (with a large sign in English). The Tarana self-service restaurant (open 0600–2200) has a wall of 1930s mirrors; it also has a private dining room furnished like an Indian stereotype with couches, hookah water-pipe and fringed lamp shades.

Upstairs (there's a lift) on the first floor are various waiting rooms which have retained their original ornate green wall tiles. There are seven retiring rooms, two with air conditioning and one deluxe which has three beds and is reached through the dormitory where there are 16 beds. The booking office for these rooms is on platform 1.

Lucknow's other station, run by North Eastern railway, is called **Lucknow Jn** and used to be exclusively MG; now three platforms are BG. It is situated on the left of the forecourt of the main station and has had a facelift, with false turrets added to make it a scaled-down version of its neighbour. It is compact and neat, and is being upgraded to a model station.

There are two air-conditioned and four non air-conditioned rooms plus two dormitories (on the noisy side of the station) with nine beds in each. Downstairs, on the left of the station concourse, is the V and NV restaurant, called Apporna, which could have a bright view of the platform but for the curtains. There is a fast-food counter in front of it. Potted plants have been placed on the platforms and in the forecourt to give the station a pleasing appearance.

The station superintendent here is proud of his "pictogram" signs. By no means easy to understand, the one that seems to depict a dustbin with an open lid is actually a book and pen and indicates where complaints can be made.

There is also a station called **Lucknow City**, about 6km away. No trains originate there and only some halt there on the way to and from the main Lucknow stations. Since it is served by trains of Northern and North Eastern Railways, Lucknow has many direct connections with northern India. It is on the line from New Delhi (507km) and trains stop here on the way to/from Gorakhpur (276km), New Jalpaiguri (1,118km) and Guwahati (1,541km). The fastest from New Delhi is the *Shatabdi Express*, which leaves ND at 0620 and arrives at 1245. From Bombay VT there is a superfast express which takes 26 hours for the 1,414km trip via Bhopal and Jhansi.

MADGAON (GOA)

Madgaon is the official name for this station but people refer to it as Margao. It used to be recommended as the railhead for Goa's capital, Panaji, but now that its bus station has been moved 5km from the station, it is best to stay on the train to Vasco da Gama (qv) and get a bus there. You're near the tourist area at Madgaon station, obvious from its signs warning passengers "not to entertain touts".

MADURAI

With the abolition of steam and the broad gauging of metre gauge lines, the station at Madurai has had a facelift. This includes improvements to the retiring rooms which are reached by a flight of stairs from platform 1. (There are four platforms.) Ten double rooms, air-conditioned room, two family rooms and two dormitories are here. The rooms open on to a long gallery overlooking the station forecourt, with the bathrooms (Western style) backing on to the station roof.

Station facilities include a large 2nd class waiting hall, a vegetarian restaurant with a "Tiffin and Coffee Section" (open 0430–1000, 1700–2130) and a "Meals Section" (open 1830–2130). The booking hall has drawings of trains above the reservation charts so that passengers can identify their carriages. There is also a diagram of the station showing its facilities. Madurai itself, for all its bustle, has a certain raffish charm. It is dominated by the Meenakshi Temple complex with its orange and black vertical striped walls around which traffic swirls. It is a determined shopper's haven, as well as a focal point for pilgrims.

The hill resort of **Kodaikanal** is 120km by road from Madurai station and a tourist leaflet advises visitors to wear "tweed and flannel" during the day. The closest rail access is Kodaikanal Road, but that's actually 80km from it. There is a rail booking office at Kodaikanal, run by a licensee.

MAHE

Mahe station is not actually in the Mahe part of the Union State of Pondicherry, but in Kerala: not surprising since Mahe is only $3km^2$ in area, embracing the River Mahe and containing 30 bars and 32 wholesale liquor shops (it's cheaper here than in Kerala) and countless coconut trees. There are about 30,000 inhabitants too.

The station is delightfully rural, a short rickshaw ride from Government House or the liquor shops that constitute downtown. Nowhere much to stay unless you try the upstairs Green Tourist guesthouse opposite the Roman Catholic church. Hotel Coolland on the Mahe side of the river is an inexpensive eatery. There is a fruit and tea stall at the station and the 1st class waiting room has a beautiful umbrella stand and antique chairs, and a table embossed with SIR (South Indian Railway). Sixteen trains a day stop at Mahe at convenient times in the morning to give you a chance to stock up with booze and leave in the afternoon.

MALDA TOWN

Clinging to the edge of West Bengal, above Bangladesh, Malda Town is the last major station in the Eastern Railway zone before the Northeast Frontier zone station of New Jaipalguri. Its attraction is that it is small and friendly with ticket collectors who wear ties and uniform jackets and smile, and a passenger information centre that actually helps instead of staff merely repeating train times by rote.

My regard for Malda Town began when, having sent a message ahead for soda water, I was met at the carriage door by the SS and his traffic inspector who both apologised for there being none available. At another station, my message would probably have been ignored. Since I was feeling pretty rotten, I decided to stay.

The station was built in the 1960s and is in the process of being modernised. On the first floor there are two non air-conditioned retiring rooms with two beds, one air-conditioned room and two dormitories of four beds in each. The roof of the station at the end of the corridor has been converted to a terraced garden with a forest of plants in pots. Access to the rooms is by stairs alongside the passenger information counter and the reservations office. Since my stay at Malda Town was unscheduled, unannounced and on impulse, and it was a Sunday night, I was very impressed by the help I received.

My colleague in India, Samit Roychoudhury, has another view. He says there have been reports of passengers at the station buying a delicacy which consists of dried mango in layers, only to find that the inner layers were pieces of rubber slippers. Thefts have been reported too.

The reservation office is on the right of the small entrance lobby. The 2nd class waiting hall, not very comfortable, is on the left; the 1st class waiting room shows its need for modernisation. There are signs in English as well as Hindi and Bengali for the various facilities. The station is 2km from downtown where there is the Malda Tourist Lodge (Malda, West Bengal), operated by West Bengal Tourist Development Corporation. A sign in reception says "Lunch/dinner compulsory".

The town is also called English Bazaar, a name derived from Englezabad; it dates from 1680. The station is on the line between Calcutta and New Jalpaiguri, and between Delhi and Guwahati as well as Howrah and Guwahati. On a gruesome note, look down out of the window as the train approaches the next station of New Farakka and you'll see the bloated bodies of the dead bobbing against the sluice gates where the railway bridge spans the holy Ganga river.

MANGALORE

There are three retiring rooms at Mangalore, on the first floor gallery overlooking the booking hall. The rooms are compact and clean with twin beds, a Western-style bathroom and hot shower. There are also eight beds in a large, well ventilated room. The station has lots of reading matter on its notice boards with one advising on "Guidelines for passenger grievances". The booking office is open 0200–2200, with separate queues for ladies and gents. There is no special desk for foreigners but instructions are that they should have priority; if no berths are available efforts are made to accommodate them through the emergency quota.

Sara Keen, confined to the Manjuran Hotel, of the Taj Group, during riots in Mangalore, found it "a wonderful haven" at US$44 a night.

The station is the terminus for both broad gauge and metre gauge. The BG line follows the Malabar coast northwards from Shoranur (see *Chapter Eleven*) and is linked with Madras by the daily 6027/28 *West Coast Express* and the 6001/02 *Madras Mail*. The MG line, sometimes closed through landslides, provides a spectacular ride through the western ghats to Hassan. Access to the town at Mangalore station is easier from the end of platform 2 or 3 than from the main entrance/exit.

MATHERAN

There is a garden refreshment room attached to this fairytale station, run by a Matheran personality, J Y "Baba" Diwadkar, who also operates the Divadkar Hotel (sic) opposite the station (it has a full bar and economy rate rooms). Tickets for the downhill journey are sold 45 minutes before a train's departure. The free baggage allowance is 7.5kg in 1st class and 5kg in 2nd, with penalties for excess, but don't worry.

Across the line from the station, on a plinth, is a gaily painted engine with the inscription: "Here rests the steam locomotive which moved up and down in the service of the people of Matheran for over 77 years, manufactured in 1902, rendered service since 1905, year of opening of section." Photos of the two pioneers whose efforts brought about the opening of the railway, Sir Adamjee Peerbhoy and Abdul Hussein Adamjee Peerbhoy, known as Matheran Railwaywala, hang above the booking counters.

Within walking distance of the station along a red carpet (of mud) is Lord's Central Hotel, an amalgamation of buildings that were previously a Christian bakery, a Jewish photographers and a Muslim bungalow. This hotel is unique in the "hill station" tradition with country house hospitality from its owners, Mr and Mrs "Jimmy" Lord. One British guest I met there said he had found heaven and the Lord's name is Jimmy.

MIRAJ

The signs at Miraj station give an idea of the place: "This way to the Railway Police Station", "Do not exhibit your valuables and ornaments while sleeping or sitting near the window", and "To be safe from pickpockets, take care of your luggage". There is a disturbing atmosphere about the place. If you want something else to look at, there are some attractive ceramic tiles fronting the counter selling soft drinks. There are retiring rooms here but the less said about them the better.

MUGHAL SARAI

You'll probably stop at this north Indian version of Crewe without knowing it. A major junction for trains running between Calcutta, Bombay and Delhi, 80 trains a day pause here, mostly in the dead of night. You'll not miss much although the cafeteria on platform 2 (standing room only, no seats) has a menu which offers Chilly Chicken and Egg Chowmein takeaways.

The station entrance is modern and if you come here by road to catch a train (which is what you'll have to do if connections from Varanasi aren't convenient), be warned you'll have a long walk from the booking hall up steps and over a bridge to the platforms.

The enquiries booth (where you should ask for your train's departure platform before trekking in search of it) is on the left of the booking hall, as is the left-luggage cloakroom. Up the steps on the left with its entrance marked by a mosaic mural are the functional retiring rooms, six non air-conditioned, two air-conditioned and a dormitory.

In a desperate effort to add some charm, potted plants have been suspended from the ceiling of the bridge. There is lots to read, with signs in Hindi and English, such as "Remember all the garbage which you do not like to touch and you are disposing of on the platform has to be cleared by another human being just like you". And "Spitting at open places is injurious to health".

MYSORE

From the outside it is difficult to know that Mysore station really is a station. Built during the days of the maharajas, it is on palatial lines with a domed clocktower and wide verandas on its first floor. A road used to run on to the main platform to allow the maharaja to drive right up to his private carriage. The main lobby has the booking office (open 0400–2300) and a pay toilet. A separate lobby leads to the advance reservation counters (0800–1330, 1400–2000) with an enquiry desk where the needs of foreign travellers are attended to promptly. A display cabinet shows photos of the stunning western ghat rail journey – the Emerald Route – from Hassan to Mangalore.

The main platform is wide and clean with Victorian cast-iron pillars (down the inside of which the rain runs) supporting the roof and adding to its period appearance. Zinc-topped tea counters do a brisk business alongside the V and NV restaurants which are only open during train departures. A wheelchair and self-help trolleys are available, and there is a bathing cubicle on the island platform. A dormitory of ten beds, each with its own locker (bring your own padlock) is at platform level.

The retiring rooms are on the first floor and used to be rated the best in the Southern Railway zone. They have high ceilings and a walk-around veranda with a view of the pretty station forecourt on one side and trains shunting on the other. Number 1 has been air-conditioned yet it was built with high arched doors and windows that, pre-air-conditioning, could be opened to catch the breeze from different directions.

Mysore is renowned as a leisurely city, famous for its jasmine, maharaja's palace, zoo, and government sandalwood oil and silk factories. The Brindavian Gardens and Krishnarajasagar Dam are 19km distant by road. The main way to get to Mysore by rail is via Bangalore (139km) from where there are daily expresses. Now the line to Mysore from Bangalore is broad gauged, a fast way to travel is by *Shatabdi Express*. This leaves Bangalore (after arriving from Madras) at 1055 every day, except Tuesdays, and arrives at Mysore at 1255. *Shatabdi* leaves Mysore at 1420, arrives Bangalore at 1615 and Madras at 2115. Other routes are from Bangalore (qv) via Hassan or from Arsikere (also via Hassan).

Rail Museum
Walk to the end of the platform at Mysore station, cross the track to the Krishnarajasagar Road and follow the curve of the road northwards for about 100m and you will find the entrance on your right to the Regional Rail Museum (KRS Road, Mysore 570001). Admission tickets are sold from a guard's brake van that came from an old goods train; you must also pay for a permit if you have any kind of camera. The museum was set up in 1980 as the first (so far there no others) regional display of India's railway heritage. It is small and seems somewhat neglected although its gardens are well maintained and it is a fascinating place to visit. A guide booklet is available.

The Chamundi Gallery houses a series of paintings and photographs about the history of the railways. The adjacent Sriranga Pavilion is home to two coaches which formed part of the royal train of the Maharaja of Mysore; the Maharani's saloon, built in 1899, and the kitchen/dining car, built in 1914. (The Maharaja's saloon is at the Rail Museum in Delhi.) These coaches are adjustable to BG or MG track. The saloon is complete with platform and brass railings, bedroom, bath and lavatory, luggage room and servants quarters. Rail bygones in the gallery include a Theobold's Block instrument used before 1929 between Dodjala and Devanahalli stations on the NG line, and a Mysore State Railway clock, made in New York in 1889. Wooden pillars, doors and balustrades from the old Srirangapatna railway station were used in the construction of the gallery itself.

In the grounds are various MG and NG steam engines and a coach, built in 1927, from the Bangalore to Bangarapet NG line with bench type seating facing the sides, not forwards, and its special dog box. The oddity is an Austin motor car, adapted to run on rails as an inspection vehicle. A battery operated electric mini-train, built at the Mysore Railway Workshop mostly out of scrap metal, runs on a small circular track to provide a joy ride for children.

NAGPUR

If you have to waste time waiting for a connection, there can be few pleasanter stations to linger at than Nagpur, although it can get very hot at summer's peak. Trains between Calcutta and Bombay, or Delhi and Madras, pause here for about 20 minutes while meals are put on from the (very clean) base kitchen and the train is watered. In the season you can buy oranges here as it is the orange city of India and few travellers can resist a few, or even a sack.

I liked Nagpur station when I discovered a retiring room with a modern, tiled bathroom with one of those odd loos that have a commode with a seat that enables it to be used either for standing or sitting on, and with a view of the sole narrow gauge line in Nagpur. Alas, it is no longer steam but you can watch, from the bathroom, the diesel loco hauling wooden rolling stock, built 30 years ago, in and out of the station.

Seventy-two trains a day pause a while at Nagpur. If you have to make a reservation here, there are no special facilities for foreigners but the SS will help. There is a magazine library (deposit Rs10) where you can get something to read while you wait your turn in the queue. If you are wait-listed, there are booths on platform 1 where you can check seat/berth availability before boarding your train. Another feature that makes Nagpur a better station than many others is the auto-rickshaw funnel at its exit. You give your name and destination to the despatcher and get assigned the first auto to pop out of the funnel. It's metered too.

NERAL

This station serves as a link between Central Railway's BG trains (main and suburban) from Bombay VT and the NG railway to Matheran. There are two BG platforms with the booking office at the courtyard entrance to the station. The office of the SS is on platform 2 which is platform 3 on its other side where it serves the

NG line. There are four NG platforms with the booking office for Matheran on the island platform between BG and NG. Although a railcar service is promised in the notice, this is reserved for railwaymen only. (You'll see the car in the shed from the left side of the train as it pulls out of the station.)

The 1st class lounge, opened on demand, contains some sturdy ancient wooden dressers of great value, as well as modern ones already collapsing. The hot potato cakes sold by the NV counter are delicious and sell as fast as proverbial ones.

PATNA

The original station was built in the 19th century but the current ugly building dates from 1939 with extensions added in the 1960s and the computerised reservations complex opened in 1992. As a junction, its importance stems from the meeting of the Patna–Gaya branch line with the main and chord lines of Eastern Railway; trains both terminate and transit here. It has seven platforms and a combined vegetarian/non-vegetarian restaurant with a base kitchen that can prepare 1,000 casserole meals a day.

The retiring rooms are upstairs from platform 1. They are small, airless cells, some with air-conditioning. Two dormitories have ten beds in each. A notice, which you can disbelieve, says 'Check out is at 1200 am''. A roof garden is opposite rooms 1 to 7 with the 2nd class waiting hall (like an underground car park for human bodies) below. There is a Bihar Department of Tourism kiosk in the station with useful maps of Patna and information on the town's sights. The 7.5km road bridge, opened in 1983 linking north with south Bihar over the Ganga, is one of them.

Buses to Raxaul, 4km from the Nepal border, cross this bridge at the start of their six-hour journey from Patna.

Patna is on the main New Delhi to Calcutta line and is served by some trains linking those cities. It is 992km from Delhi (about 15 hours train time) and 545km from Calcutta (about nine hours).

PONDICHERRY

The Union Territory of Pondicherry comprises four enclaves in three South Indian states: the seaside towns of Pondicherry and Karaikal in Tamil Nadu, Yanam in Andhra Pradesh and Mahe (qv) in Kerala. From 1814 the territory was French, merging with the rest of independent India in 1954. The new town of Auroville is 10km from Pondicherry station.

The station, with its tall portico, was remodelled in 1987. There are three retiring rooms in a separate building on the sole platform, which sees only four passenger trains a day, from Villupuram. In the high-ceilinged lobby there is a booking-cum-reservations counter open 0900–1200; 1500–1800.

As Villupuram has rail links with towns in the south which are worth visiting (such as Trichy and Madurai) it would be possible to make a side trip to Pondicherry when you pass through Villupuram on the way to Madras Egmore, instead of from it.

The best French food in India, according to its fans, is to be had at the (licensed) Club Restaurant of Pondy's Alliance Française, open to non-members. For real crusty French bread, seek out the bakery Selvan.

PUNE

The approach to Pune by rail with its shanties close to the track doesn't prepare you for the spacious sweep of the station building, extravagantly designed and built in 1925. The black, marble-faced columns of the entrance lobby sparkle in the sodium lights at night. The station has won the Central Railway shield for General Appearance, Cleanliness and Tidiness nine times since it was first awarded in 1946. A statue of the unmistakable figure of Gandhi seen from the rear greets the traveller emerging from the station. Buses to the city and suburbs are available a few minutes' walk to the right of the forecourt.

The waiting rooms, with showers, are on the first floor. The non-vegetarian restaurant has cowboy-movie style swing doors, and antique wood and glass-fronted almirahs serving as crockery cupboards. There is a dormitory ("Janata Room") on the same floor with hot water showers and eight beds. Included in the cost of a twin-bed room are afternoon tea, shoe-shine and morning paper.

Pune (don't pronounce it to rhyme with prune; it's Poona still) is an agreeable town at 549m above sea level. There is a tourist information centre at the station. Express and computer passenger trains link it with Bombay VT. Fast trains such as the superb *Deccan Queen* (see *Chapter Eleven*) do the 192km journey in 3½ hours, others like the *Singhagad* or the *Deccan Expresses* take over four hours. A separate service of EMU trains runs between Pune and Lonavla and there is also a Pune/Daund shuttle service. The *Jhelum Express* from Jammu Tawi (qv) terminates here.

Introduced in June 1996 was a *Shatabdi* service linking Pune with Bombay. Train number 2028 leaves Pune at 0745 and arrives at Bombay VT at 1105. Train number 2027 leaves Bombay VT at 1625 and reaches Pune at 1945. A railway note says that there are no commercial stoppages, only operational ones.

PURI

Puri is known for its annual chariot festival and as a seaside temple city lapped by the waters of the Bay of Bengal. Peak periods are during the winter months, and the summer and autumn vacations. The South Eastern Railway Hotel (Chakratirtha Rd, Puri. Tel: 2063) was established in 1925 and its traditional style has its admirers. Rob Dodson reports that modestly priced places to stay front the beach; a former royal home if now a little decadent is the Z Hotel with its own garden and friendly staff.

There are retiring rooms at the station, doubles and dorm beds. The sun temple at Konark is 28km from the station, reached by road.

Reservations are computerised. Trains originating and terminating at Puri include the 2815/16 superfast *Puri/New Delhi Express*, the 8475/76 *Neelachal Express* and the daily 8477/8 *Kalinga Utkal Express* to H Nizamuddin (2,142km). There are daily expresses from/to Howrah. Connections to Madras are made at Bhubaneswar.

QUILON

People go to Quilon to get away from it, either by backwaters boat to Alleppey or by train to Madurai and Trichy. (The boat trip departs at 1030 to Alleppey, takes eight hours and makes about 70 stops. More fun perhaps is to make your river cruise instead to Kottayam from Alleppey, now that Alleppey has its own rail station.)

Quilon has a long main platform; there are unattractive refreshment rooms. There are five single and two double retiring rooms and a six-bed dorm; some rooms have balconies overlooking the pleasant forecourt. An advance reservations block is on the left of the forecourt; current bookings off the station lobby.

Quilon is a compulsory stop for BG expresses to/from Trivandrum and the beginning of the line that cuts inland to Sengottai.

RAJKOT

At this quiet station, the retiring rooms are on the first floor but the sign at the foot of the stairs is in Hindi so you'll have to ask. You could ask at the enquiry counter but that sign is in Hindi too. The rooms, one air-conditioned, two non air-conditioned, one dormitory with four beds, are among the neatest and cleanest I've seen. The waiting rooms are off the main platform where there is a cosy vegetarian restaurant; being Gujarat, there is no NV one.

RAMESWARAM

Although this station on an island at the tip of India was remodelled in 1986, the sea air, sand, dust and pilgrim traffic have given it a sad appearance. There are 12 retiring rooms built in a block alongside the station and, according to the SS, they are the only rooms for tourists in Rameswaram which have water 24 hours a day. There is a waiting room for ladies on the station, kept locked and opened on request, and a large room for upper class passengers. A combined fruit and NV stall sells quick meal packets and there is also a vegetarian refreshment room.

There are four reservation counters (0700–1300, 1330–1800) on the right of the entrance lobby and a notice saying the Indrail Pass is on sale. When the ferry brought passengers from Sri Lanka, the SS sold 150 passes a year. There is a tourist office here with details of trips around Rameswaram. A devout Hindu who visits Benares (Varanasi) is expected to visit Rameswaram also for the culmination of his quest for salvation, hence its popularity with pilgrims. Buses are available from the railway station to various places on the island. Until the road bridge opened (and it is a magnificent sight from the rail crossing), train or boat were the only means of getting to Rameswaram.

RANCHI

Ranchi station, originally exclusively narrow gauge, had BG added in 1961 and is now subject to a "modelisation" programme.

You can see the Highline Transhipment system of transferring freight from NG to BG. NG wagons loaded with bauxite are shunted up a ramp and on to a track built over a BG line. The BG wagons are shunted underneath, then the floors of the NG wagons are opened and the bauxite falls into the BG wagons below. Hatia station (7km away) is the main depot for Ranchi's BG trains.

There are direct services to Ranchi from Madras which takes nearly 37 hours for the approximately 1,670km journey northwards, and from Howrah. There are also trains from Patna, and from Gorakhpur.

At Ranchi station there is a noticeboard with a list of places of interest in and around Ranchi, mostly hills, lakes and falls, and the tourist literature describes Ranchi as a "popular hill station". Whatever it may have been in the past, it is hardly that now. It has become an industrial centre without much charm, the change being wrought by bauxite and iron ore.

However, the hill station atmosphere (it's 629m above sea level) is retained in the South Eastern railway Hotel (Station Road, Ranchi, Bihar), one of only two railway hotels in India (the other is at Puri). It is reached by crossing the NG line and strolling through a garden of healthy lawns and shade trees to its bungalow verandah entrance. Cottage units with red-tiled roofs and wide galleries, built in 1915, have 22 rooms in all. There are coal fires in the public rooms in winter. The bearers have resisted change and wear the uniform and brass cap badge of the Bengal and Napur Railway.

SALEM

Salem is the railhead for the quiet hill resort of Yercaud. It is on the main line from Madras to Trivandrum and Mangalore and can be reached in under five hours from Madras. There are three retiring rooms in a house built on the island platform, 1 and 2, with individual steps up to each room from the roof. The station is busy throughout the night so the train noise can be disturbing.

A map in the lobby shows the location of the main bus stand (for buses to Yercaud). The reservations office is off the lobby, the current booking counter with separate queues for ladies and gents on the right.

Salem benefits from the introduction of the 2023/2024 *Shatabdi Express* which calls in every day, except Wednesday, on its way from Madras to Coimbatore (at 1915) and from Coimbatore to Madras (at 0838).

Salem station is 280m above sea level; Yercaud, at 1,515m above sea level, is 32km from the station. The hill road begins 8km from the town. It is an easy drive, despite the 20 hairpin bends, through lush coffee plantations and orange groves, watched by monkeys begging for scraps as vehicles slow down to negotiate the curves. I tasted the renowned Shevaroyan Hills coffee (black with a taste that lingered throughout the morning) at the Hotel Shevaroys close to Yercaud's lake. The hotel has new, marble-appointed cottages complete with bath tubs, fridge and TV, plus forest view.

SECUNDERABAD

Secunderabad is the HQ of the South Central Railway which serves six states: Andhra Pradesh, Maharashtra, Karnataka, Goa, Madhya Pradesh and Tamil Nadu (well, eight route kilometres of it). Its zone stretches from Kakinada in the east to Goa in the west, linking the Bay of Bengal with the Arabian Sea. The HQ building, Rail Nilayam, has a vintage 1905 NG locomotive called *Sir Alec* on display outside it.

Secunderabad station has a tourist office run by the Andhra Pradesh Tourist Development Corporation on its main platform, but most of the tourist attractions are in its twin city of Hyderabad (qv). To get a taxi at Secunderabad station for a tour, you must ask a traffic cop (they wear white shirts and khaki pants) since they are parked around a corner from the station entrance. An even more frustrating feature of this station is the location of its reservation office. From the station you turn right, walk to the bus station, then turn right again and enter a yard to find the building is close to the station platform, but there's no short cut. Don't try it with heavy luggage. However, once there, the token system cuts down queuing and computers process reservations speedily. Current bookings are made in the lobby of the station.

From the lobby a wooden staircase leads up to the first floor where there is the Kohinoor Restaurant, opened in 1978. It has fans and meals served on plates, not *thalis* or casseroles, but its atmosphere is gloomy and it seems a fancy name for a station restaurant. Adjacent are the retiring rooms off a flower-bedecked balcony. There is one air-conditioned suite, 13 double rooms and one single.

There are dozens of direct trains to Secunderabad from all parts of India, including Ahmedabad, Ajmer, Bhubaneswar, Cochin, Tirupati and Visakhapatnam. From Bombay the distance is 800km, from New Delhi 1,665km, from Madras 784km and from Howrah 1,581km.

There is a once a week service from New Delhi's Nizamuddin station by *Rajdhani Express*, number 2430/2429. It arrives in Secunderabad at 0755 on Sunday mornings after leaving Nizamuddin at 0930 the day before. Then it goes on to Bangalore where it arrives at 2000. It returns to Secunderabad (leaving Bangalore at 0645) on Monday at 1830 on its way to Nizamuddin, where it arrives at 1630 on Tuesday.

SHIMLA

Shimla station is located at 2,075m above sea level and has a charm to match its breathtakingly beautiful setting. As well as the fascination of getting there (see *Chapter Eleven*), Shimla is a welcome destination after the hectic heat of Delhi. Citizens and visitors stroll through the town for the sheer pleasure of it, watched by monkeys who think they own the place, and by residents gazing from the balcony outside of the Amateur Dramatic Club's Victorian theatre. With snow-capped mountains of the Himalayas in the background and lush green valleys below, the town is not only spectacular but rich in a magical atmosphere. In his wonderful *Guide to Simla* (obtainable from his own Maria Brothers bookshop, straight out of *Kim*, on the town's Mall), Mr O C Sud, the author, speculates that the town's name, really pronounced Shimla despite its occasional spelling of Simla, comes from *Shamla*, meaning "Blue Female" another name for the goddess Kali.

Shimla has almost 150 hotels and guesthouses but there is only one which captures its essence (and one of the few with a bar): the Oberoi Clarke's Hotel (The Mall, Shimla). The rooms have the comfortable feel of the 1930s with views of the forest-clad hills and the town. Rates are standard bracket including all meals, which are superb. Since cars are not allowed, you will have to walk from the lift that takes you from the lower part of the town, near the station, to the Mall. The long-missed Oberoi Cecil was due to re-open in

1997; a perfect complement to the charm of the rail journey from Kalka to Shimla. The air always seems clean here despite the concentration of houses and people. The main season is April to June, September to October, and Christmas. But foreigners, drawn by Shimla's spell, visit year round.

As well as from New Delhi, it is also possible to reach Shimla from Jammu Tawi and from Howrah, via Ambala (qv) and Kalka.

UDAGAMANDALAM

This station will always be known as Ooty, short for Ootacamund, by its fans. A summer resort since the days of the Raj and "Queen of the Hill Stations", the town nestling in the Nilagiris, or Blue Mountains, may have lost its dignity (there are video games at the lake) but it is still relaxed and rural. You sense it on arrival at the station (for the journey there see *Chapter Eleven*).

Although, at 2,203m above sea level, the station is at the end of the line, its loco shed is only for stabling engines and carriages, the main yard being at Coonoor on the way up. Any reservation requirements should be discussed with the affable SS. The station has quotas to Madras, Cochin, New Delhi, Bilaspur and Ahmedabad. If you intend travelling to Cochin or Trivandrum (the most popular destinations for foreign tourists from Ooty) try to get your reservations in advance before reaching Ooty, since the station has no quotas. Ooty is 2,833km, via Coimbatore, from New Delhi, 1,924km from Bombay VT, 394km from Trichy and 578km from Trivandrum.

In the office of the SS there used to be a photo of the very British Bob Hill, stationmaster from 1909 to 1930. His clear blue eyes stared down sternly on the modern world, his handlebar moustache waxed to fearsome points. I hope he has survived the station remodelling.

The town, bus station (for Mysore/Bangalore/Coimbatore) and racetrack are close to the station. Out of Ooty is better than in it, and what remains of the woods and downs can be enjoyed best by a stay (or at least a visit) to the venerable Fernhill Palace Hotel, now taken over by the Taj group.

UDAIPUR

The Udaipur City station building is nothing special to look at, especially when compared with the lavish beauty of the marble and crystal palaces of the city. It was built in 1963 but its drab exterior gives way to a station that's well run and a pleasure to visit. The large booking hall has counters well labelled in English with an enquiry window open daily, and a reservation window beside it, giving reservations on that day's trains until 1230. Since no trains are scheduled in the afternoon, the station staff usually succumb to a siesta then.

There is an embankment of steps up from platform 1 to the exit and the booking office. Steps lead from the lobby to the retiring rooms. The dormitory has wooden screens around each of the ten beds but its (very clean) bathroom is next door. The sole twin-bedded room has attached bathroom and a terrace. Next to the rooms is a vegetarian restaurant like an English tea room; it specialises in breakfast. Downstairs on platform 1 are snack bars which sell bottles of chilled mineral water.

The friendliness of Udaipur City station gives way to a city of magnificent palaces, one of which is an extraordinary hotel. Photos of the Lake Palace Hotel (Pichola Lake, Udaipur) floating like a white marble wedding cake on the clear blue waters of Lake Pichola are instantly identifiable. Built on four acres of rock, in 1628, it was a royal retreat, converted by the Taj group in 1972 into a splendid hotel, reached by a ferry five minutes' drive from the station. It is a maze of courtyards, inlaid ivory and pools. Luxury bracket and worth every rupee, even if it's your last.

This is Rajasthan, so choose your time to visit wisely; October to March is best.

VARANASI

The surprise at Varanasi (formerly Benares) is how it has changed since I wrote about its indifference in the first edition of this book. A foreign tourist bureau (linked to ITB in New Delhi) has been opened to solve the travel problems of the many foreigners who use Varanasi. The bureau is on the left as soon as you enter the station.

Upper class reservations can be made at the counter on the right of the booking office. There is an enquiry office (sign in English) in the hall and also a telecom bureau and a Uttar Pradesh tourist bureau. A sign warns "Please be cautious to your luggage. Do not leave it unattended. Do not trust the strangers".

I was given a station tour by the most helpful CRS I've ever encountered, Mr R K Mishra. The main platform is an island one, number 2 and 3, where the ladies' waiting room has an exquisitely tiled pink and green fireplace (not used).

There are six retiring rooms and a dormitory of 53 beds; the booking office for them is on the first floor. The air-conditioned cafeteria there is gloomy, preserving an obvious dislike of customers. People and dogs sleep unchallenged in areas reserved for ticket holders, and cows wander at will through the booking hall and along platforms.

The real joy of the station is in its exterior. Go outside and gaze up at it, or view it from platform 6. It is art deco, Indian style, and a contrast to the frenzy of the city. In the lobby is a model of a diesel locomotive with the legend: "Home Of Diesel Loco. Builders for the Nation".

If you take a train from Varanasi Jn (or from Varanasi City, the town's station) to Allahabad City, it passes – after Bhulanpur station – through a beautifully landscaped park where at least two lovingly preserved steam engines are mounted on plinths in front of an administration building. This is Varanasi Diesel Locomotive Works (DLW), a factory colony where the general manager is like mayor to a community of 35,000.

The colony has a golf course, an Olympic size swimming pool, playing fields, schools and cinemas. Some 8,400 people work in the plant, manufacturing diesel locos, and spares for the existing fleet of 3,000. It takes 14 weeks from start to finish to produce one of these huge turbo-charged diesels whose generators could provide power for 200,000 people.

The most fascinating aspect of Varanasi is life on the river front at dawn. Hindu pilgrims, inspired by their faith in life after death, flock to the *ghats* (stepped embankments) on the riverbank to perform ablution: a dip in the river and salutations to the sun. Sarnath, the venerated spot where Lord Buddha preached his first sermon after enlightenment, is 10km by road from the station.

VASCO DA GAMA (GOA)

The main railway station from which to reach all parts of Goa is Vasco da Gama, known simply as Vasco and pronounced "Barsco". It's a mean-looking station with few facilities, although its atmosphere is friendly and the SS helpful. Its main neighbouring station is Madgaon (qv).

At Vasco there is a small reservation office with a counter for Indrail Pass holders and foreign tourists, shared with 1st class passengers. Tickets can be paid for in foreign currency and the day's exchange rate is displayed. The general booking office has opening hours of 0800 to 1400 and 1500 to 2300 and closes ten minutes before the departure of a train.

There are clean, if musty, retiring rooms in an annexe to the station, reached by climbing stairs from the end of the platform to a balcony that overlooks the station forecourt. The dormitory has six beds. There is no restaurant at the station, only a tea counter, but since the town abounds in food kiosks, wine shops and restaurants with a Western ambience, meals can easily be obtained.

Panaji is the capital of Goa, 30km from Vasco which is the best station for reaching it since the bus park is opposite the railway station. Limited rail reservations can be made in Panaji at the Railway Out Agency.

Goa's airport is at Dabolim; although there is a station at Dabolim, it is a rural halt with no bus/taxi service so passengers bound for the airport should alight at Vasco. With more international flights going to Goa, Vasco station is a good starting point to begin a rail journey. The Indrail Pass is sold at the station.

Reports that the train is a boring/arduous way of getting to Goa are not to be believed if you enjoy mountain scenery and good company. The atmosphere livens up when the train crosses the Goa border and vendors swarm aboard selling beer and Goa's special tipple, *feni*, a cheesy smelling *eau de vie* made from the fruit of cashew nuts.

Goa is famous for its three fs: fish, football and, say the Goans, the third is left to your imagination. Actually, its *feni*.

Trains going to Goa pass through Londa, and then the *ghats* begin: a range of magnificent green hills through which the train gropes along tunnels, or meanders over bridges with streams plunging below. After Caranajol station, you're in Goa and the hills soar into the distant clouds. Dudshagar has a lookout tower to scan the lush depths of the valley and river below. Then after tunnel number 11, the train emerges into heavy spray as it crosses

THE KONKAN RAILWAY

A joint enterprise of the governments of Maharashtra, Karnataka, Goa, Kerala and the Ministry of Railways, the 760km Konkan Railway, will connect Roha in Maharashtra to Mangalore in Karnataka on the west coast. Its development has involved the construction of 171 major bridges, 1,759 minor bridges and 92 tunnels.

Between Roha and Mangalore, the trains will halt at 53 stations along the route. Fares for passengers will be charged at a 40% inflated distance. Thus, for a distance of 100km, the fare for 140km will be charged; it will be in that proportion for all classes.

When the entire route from Roha to Mangalore becomes operational, these will be among the trains which will run:

- Bombay VT to Madgoan (new overnight express service)
- Kurla–Mangalore–Cochin *Netravati Express* (diverted train)
- Rajkot–Gandhidam–Cochin/Trivandrum (new express train)
- Kurla–Ratnagiri Express cum Madgaon Express (new train)
- Kurla–Ratnagiri and Madgaon–Mangalore (two new trains)

Other trains proposed are:

- Bombay VT–Madgoan Superfast Intercity (new train)
- Kurla–Mangalore (new express)
- New Delhi–Trivandrum *Kerala Express* (diverted train)

The Konkan Railway will reduce the train travel distance between Bombay and Mangalore by 1,200km; between Bombay and Goa by 190km, and between Mangalore and Delhi by 800km.

perilously close to the Dudhsagar waterfalls. The track doubles back on itself giving a heart-wrenching glimpse of the moss-covered railway bridge that spans the rush of the falls and seems so fragile beside the force of the water gushing under it.

The Konkan Railway, writes Samit Roychoudhury, will when completed, probably in 1997, provide a direct link by broad gauge line to Bombay. It joins with the mainline to the south, giving access to such tourist-popular places as Cochin. The line crosses the length of Goa, passing through some breathtaking scenery.

As this is a high-speed line, running at 160km/h should be possible once new rolling stock is ready. The building of the railway and its track alignment

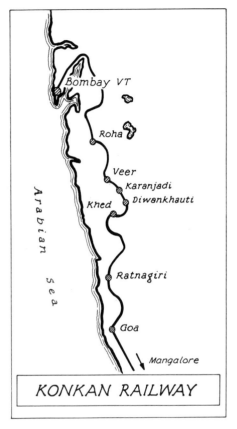

KONKAN RAILWAY

have caused considerable controversy and has been a bone of contention between environmentalists and the authorities. It is claimed that the natural beauty and ecology of the region will be affected by the line. For rail passengers it promises a less arduous journey from Bombay to Goa and the south.

I look forward to reports as soon as any reader has tried it so these can be included in the next edition.

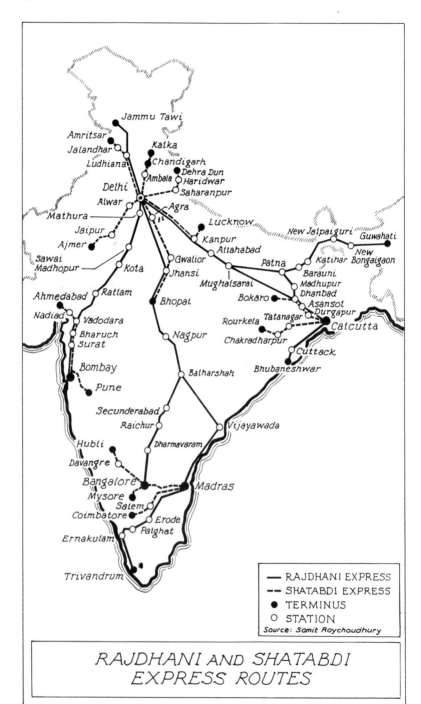

RAJDHANI EXPRESS
SHATABDI EXPRESS
● TERMINUS
○ STATION
Source: Samit Roychoudhury

RAJDHANI AND SHATABDI EXPRESS ROUTES

Chapter Eleven

Great Trips

Great trips by rail in India can be on the country's fastest train, by a maharaja's special, on a crack intercity express, on a trunk route, by a hill railway, in a private coach or on an ordinary 2nd class passenger train chugging through magnificent scenery. Such is the diversity of Indian railways.

SHATABDI EXPRESS

This is India's equivalent of Japan's bullet train. It began service between New Delhi and Jhansi in July 1988 and has a speed potential of 140km an hour, which makes it the fastest train in India. The train's electric loco, designated WAP-3, was made by the Chittaranjan Locomotive Workshop and the coaches by the Integral Coach Factory in Madras. The locomotives are of 4704 horsepower fitted with six traction motors of 784 horsepower each.

My frequent recommendation of the *Shatabdi Express* trains throughout this book is based on my joy that they exist at all. That there are so many new *Shatabdi Express* services is proof that the train is living up to its name: Shatabdi means "century". The idea is that this is the train of the century, perhaps even of the 21st century considering how far advanced it is over other fast trains in India.

It is not just the speed of these trains that makes them attractive; it is the standard of accommodation and the fact that they are daytime trains which means you don't have to travel overnight to their destinations. In other words, they resemble the normal trains of countries where you buy your ticket at the station on the day of travel, find a seat on the train and sit back and relax, gazing occasionally at the scenery dashing past the window.

However, this being India where there are always lots of people wanting to board a train, advance reservation on *Shatabdi Expresses* is essential. With long distances to cover, many of the departures are early in the morning, so it is reassuring to know you have a seat booked and don't have to scramble to find one. And breakfast will be served to the seat as meals are included in the ticket price.

Indrail Pass (1st class) holders travel without extra charge but Sleeper IRP Class holders must pay a supplement as the train is all AC Chair Car accommodation.

These trains also have an executive chair car at double the regular *Shatabdi* fare; the 1st AC class Indrail Pass is valid, but other kinds of IRP attract a supplement.

The *Shatabdis* are prestige trains showing how Indian Railways can transport passengers in speed and comfort.

Promotion about the Howrah/Bokoro *Shatabdi* states unequivocally: "The train in the AC coaches will be pollution free, noise free and tension free. Tea, breakfast and snacks will be served free of cost, by courteous uniformed waiters, on all six days of the train's run." At New Delhi station, the train conductors in tailored light grey suits with blue ties invariably look smarter than their passengers.

The ordinary AC coaches have 69 grey rexine-covered seats which recline by lever control and have lots of leg room. There is a magazine pocket in the back of the seat in front and a table which drops down for meal service. You expect to be told to fasten your seatbelt; instead Indian music comes through the loudspeakers, and continues for the whole of the journey. The Bombay-Ahmedabad *Shatabdi* even has a DJ: a portion of the luggage van contains the DJ and his equipment. He plays an assortment of Indian and Western music over the loudspeakers in every coach.

Each seat is numbered. The layout is 3 x 2, three seats on one side of the aisle and two on the other The aisle links up with the other carriages, but the passage between coaches has an awkward step up and the doors are clumsy to open.

The coaches are air-conditioned, often too cold, and also have fans. Smoking is not permitted. A lighted sign in the coach indicates when the toilets are occupied. These are Western style with fan, toilet paper and liquid soap, but no hand towel or tissues.

There is a galley in each coach, opposite the toilet, equipped with gadgetry for boiling water and keeping food hot. Meals are served to passengers in their seats.

On a trip to Agra, breakfast is included in the fare. Served from a trolley, it is presented on a tray. The foil dish contains an omelette and croquettes, or a potato patty with peas. There is also plastic cutlery, a plastic cup with a tea bag, sachets of sugar and creamer, and of tomato ketchup, salt and pepper, and a roll and butter.

A veg or non-veg dinner, included in the fare, is served from Agra to New Delhi; usually soup and two vegetable curries, dhal, rice and roti, a kind of pancake, with curd, or chicken masala. Snacks between Agra and Jhansi have to be paid for.

Sara and Ron Keen were disappointed to find the train to Agra rather dirty, while their table had a drunken lean, which made handling the (lukewarm) breakfast something of a struggle.

Seating in the executive coach is 2×2 and very comfortable in reclining, cloth-upholstered chairs. Food is supposed to be better in this class but it isn't. Fruit juice is offered about 45 minutes after journey's commencement but neither tea nor coffee are served until after breakfast, so you'll be left gasping if you haven't been able to get a cuppa before boarding at such an early hour.

The windows of the train are darkened so people can't see in and this gives a brownish hue to the outside world as you speed through

Shatabdi Express schedule
(not all transit stations are included)

Train	From	Depart	To	Arrive	Frequency
2001	Agra Cantt	2018	New Delhi	2225	
2010	Ahmedabad	1445	Bombay Central	2140	not Fri
2016	Ajmer	1550	New Delhi	2215	not Sun
2014	Amritsar	0510	New Delhi	1050	
2007	Bangalore	1055	Mysore	1255	not Tue
2008	Bangalore	1620	Madras	2105	not Tue
2001	Bhopal	1440	New Delhi	2225	
2020	Bokaro	1600	Howrah	2115	not Sun
2009	Bombay Cent	0625	Ahmedabad	1320	not Fri
2027	Bombay VT	1625	Pune	1945	
2012	Chandigarh	1240	New Delhi	1540	
2024	Coimbatore	0725	Madras	1410	not Wed
2018	Dehra Dun	1700	New Delhi	2220	not Wed
2019	Howrah	0605	Bokaro	1130	not Sun
2021	Howrah	0600	Rourkela	1215	not Sat
2006	Kalka	0600	New Delhi	0950	
2003	Lucknow	1520	New Delhi	2150	
2007	Madras	0600	Bangalore	1045	not Tue
2007	Madras	0600	Mysore	1255	not Tue
2023	Madras	1510	Coimbatore	2200	not Wed
2008	Mysore	1410	Bangalore	1605	not Tue
2008	Mysore	1410	Madras	2105	not Tue
2002	New Delhi	0615	Bhopal	1400	
2002	New Delhi	0615	Agra Cannt	0810	
2004	New Delhi	0620	Lucknow	1245	
2005	New Delhi	1715	Kalka	2100	
2011	New Delhi	0730	Chandigarh	1030	
2013	New Delhi	1630	Amritsar	2220	
2015	New Delhi	0615	Ajmer	1245	not Sun
2017	New Delhi	0710	Dehra Dun	1225	not Wed
2008	Pune	0745	Bombay VT	1105	
2022	Rourkela	1430	Howrah	2100	not Sat

it. The *Shatabdi Express* is a travel machine, an Indian land plane, clean, fast and comfortable. It's a great trip that will impress you. Pity about the music.

Fares for travelling on the *Shatabdi Express* are priced at a premium over the usual AC chair car fares. The 1st executive class chair car (not found on every *Shatabdi*) is double the usual ACC fare. A half fare applies for children between the ages of five and 12.

PALACE ON WHEELS

The romance of rail travel does still exist, for a price, in a train curiously named *Palace on Wheels*. To quote from *Rail News*, a newsletter for rail passengers published in Bombay: "The erstwhile Palace on Wheels luxury train which was operated by the Railways on the metre gauge section of the railways in Rajasthan and bluffed the foreign tourist into believing that he was the Maharaja of a Princely State of India, is to take a second birth, this time for operation on the broad gauge system."

Actually, the *Palace on Wheels* is in its third creation. The train first took to the rails in 1981 using the reconditioned carriages of the maharajas. They were not too comfortable and failed to live up to the promotion. The whole exercise of touring by train through Rajasthan would have been more aptly called Palaces on Wheels since it involved a series of palaces rather than palatial accommodation. It was, however, a convenient way of touring Rajasthan.

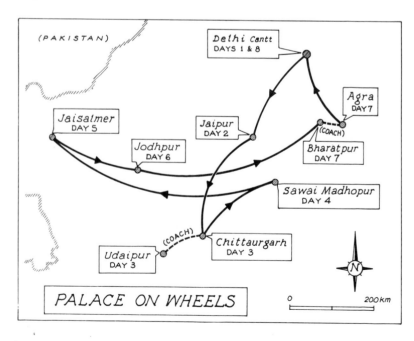

PALACE ON WHEELS

The train was completely rebuilt in 1991 to meet some of the demands of the luxury-seeking rail traveller who did not want too much adventure (and dust from the desert) to intrude on a holiday. But it was meter gauge, so when the metre gauge line from Delhi to Rajasthan was torn up, it looked as though the newly built train had reached the end of the line before it was even paid for. But it was to be reborn as the *Royal Orient Express* (see below).

The *Palace on Wheels* began again in 1995 as a newly constructed broad gauge, air-conditioned 14-coach train. I can do no better, since I have yet to experience this latest reincarnation myself, than to quote word for word from the brochure given to me by the senior manager:

"Each saloons is having four coupes with two beds each with attached bath, shower, channel music, fully carpeted and specially designed furniture. Each saloon has a mini pantry which ensure availability of hot and cold beverages and refreshment throughout the journey. The train has a beautiful lounge attached with well equipped bar car. The train has two restaurants. The Maharaja & Maharani which serves Indian & Continental cuisine."

The tariff for double occupancy up to April 1997 was US$300 per person per night. It includes "cost of travel, full catering, conducted sight-seeing tours in deluxe AC coaches, entrance fee for monuments and palaces, cultural entertainment and boat ride to and from Lake Palace at Udaipur." No, you can't use the Indrail Pass but bookings can be made through the pass agent in London, Dr Dandapani (see page 183).

The *Palace on Wheels*, whose occupants are described by stationmasters en route as *POWs*, actually has 21 coaches. As well as the 14 residential coaches and two restaurant and one bar lounge car, there are two generator cars and two services coaches.

Being broad gauged, it offers not only more space but a more comfortable ride than the previous metre gauge *POW*. Each coupé has attached shower and toilet. Two of them in each coach have twin beds, and two are double-bedded.

In its first season of operation (1995/96), the new *POW* proved a hit with tourists from the USA who provided more passengers (409) than any other nation. The British came next with 198 passengers, followed (perhaps surprisingly) by Indians, many of whom were non-resident Indians, though. In that season passengers represented 41 nationalities.

The journey is a superb introduction to the mysteries and monuments of India and, since so much is included, it seems good value as well as good fun. I know many of the staff, who have been inherited from the metre gauge *POWs* which I've been on twice, so I'm certain passengers on the new *POW* are treated royally.

The journey starts from Delhi Cantt railway station on Wednesday evening, with dinner on board before departure. First stop is at Jaipur for a day, then to Chittaurgarh the next morning. From there a coach takes passengers by road to Udaipur and back to join the train at Chittaurgarh in the evening.

The train travels overnight to Sawai Madhopur with a few hours there before starting the 22-hour journey to Jaisalmer. Jaisalmer is a wonderful experience, not only for exploring the old fort but also because of the evening entertainment. Then it's overnight to Jodhpur to spend a day before travelling on to Bharatpur. A coach takes passengers to Agra to visit the Taj Mahal prior to joining the train for the return to Delhi Cantt.

ROYAL ORIENT EXPRESS

The *Royal Orient Express* would have to be something special to compete with the *Palace on Wheels*, and it is. It is comprised of the same metre gauge coaches that used to be called the *Palace on Wheels*, and added to that is a new itinerary which takes rail travellers in comfort and style to destinations it would take hours of planning and days of hard railroad riding to reach.

The train was specially built in six months at the Integral Coach Factory in Madras, where ordinary Indian Railways coaches are made, but there the connection ends. It is superbly designed and decorated, with each passenger coach consisting of four air-conditioned bedrooms (two beds in each), two bathrooms, a non-air-conditioned saloon (where you can open the windows) and a galley with fridge and toaster. Don't be disappointed that these are not the maharaja's carriages of old; a maharaja himself would love them.

Each cabin is cleverly laid out with lots of little storage cupboards and drawers, and even a dressing table. A bunk, upholstered in velvet, hangs down over one of the beds for a third person, and can be used for luggage or pushed up and recessed out of the way. There are shaver sockets in each cabin and a control to turn off the piped music but then you miss the announcements. Unfortunately, there is no individual air-conditioning control so you have to put up with it as cold or mild, as the coach captain or fellow passengers want.

Breakfast and cold beer can be served in the cabin or in the lounge at the end of each coach, although more than six people in there make it crowded. There is a TV and video player in each saloon/lounge, rather an unnecessary refinement when the train goes through such exciting scenery and the tour itself is packed with so much to do. One passenger told me she had no time even to write her postcards.

Forget the hype and look on the *Royal Orient Express* as a unique and enjoyable and troublefree way of seeing Rajasthan and Gujarat in the manner of a sea cruise. You can even arrange to have your laundry done while travelling. Because of the limited space, service is limited too, but it's fun. Each carriage has a staff of

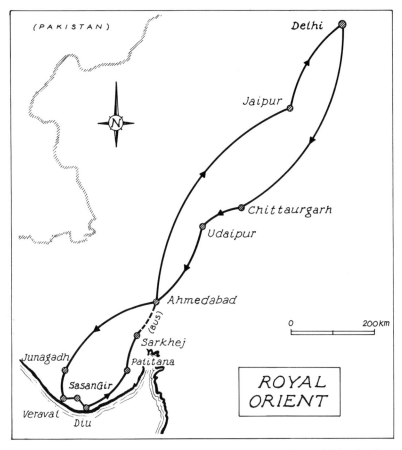

two who somehow manage to live in the small galley which also has a crew toilet/shower. The passenger bathrooms are located in the centre of each coach, between two pairs of cabins; they are not en suite. They both contain a shower.

Although this train has a vestibule that runs its length, the doors between carriages are opened only when meals are served while the train is moving so that passengers can get to the restaurants. There are covers for 40 guests in each coach; adjoining is the non-smoking library and parlour.

The decor throughout the train is opulent, the service obliging, the food – actually cooked on board in two tiny pantries – is pleasant and the tour managers dedicated to seeing their guests (who come from many different countries and cultures) enjoy themselves. No easy task.

Report time for this unusual jaunt through Rajasthan and Gujarat is 1400 hours on Wednesday, September to April, at Delhi Cantt station. The *Desert Queen*, a magnificent steam locomotive, proudly pulls the *Royal Orient Express* for the start of its journey. The first stop is Chittaurgarh with a fort visit before breakfast and then a six-hour run to Udaipur for lunch.

That night's run, via Ahmedabad, is to Junagadh and on to Veraval and temple visits. The train travels overnight to Sasan Gir where passengers visit the Lion Sanctuary. After lunch on board the train arrives at Delwada, which gives a chance to visit the Ahmedpur Beach and see the fort at Diu.

Palitana is visited the following day with chair-slings available for the climb up 3,572 steps to visit 863 temples atop Shatrunajaya Hills. Then the train goes to Sarkhej with a visit to Vishalla Village. Passengers join the train at Ahmedabad and stay overnight, visiting the city the next day before leaving for Jaipur. Next day it's back to Delhi Cantt.

The tariff, including all meals and excursions, was set until April 1997 at US$200 per day per person, sharing a double. Direct reservations could be made through the Central Reservation Office, Tourism Corporation of Gujarat Ltd, A6 State Emporia Building, Kharak Singh Marg, New Delhi 110001; tel: 3734015; fax: 011 3732482.

RAJDHANI EXPRESS

The quickest way of travelling between New Delhi and many of the state capitals is by the almost legendary *Rajdhani Express* trains. The legends have grown since the first *Rajdhani Express* was introduced in March 1969 as a bi-weekly express between Howrah and New Delhi. In 1st AC class on the *Rajdhanis* plying between New Delhi and Bombay and New Delhi and Howrah, the service, and even the food, have been acclaimed for their excellence. Fares are at least 25% higher than on ordinary expresses, so you expect a great trip. But you are mainly paying extra for the speed which, together with the elimination of lots of stops, cuts several hours off the usual journey time.

The train is open only to passengers with reservations and no interlopers are allowed. Accommodation is in three classes of air-conditioned luxury: AC 3 tier, AC 2 tier and AC 1st class. A vestibule runs through the trains so it is possible to visit all the coaches to make friends with passengers in the other classes if you are feeling bored or isolated in your chosen class. You could even inspect the galley if you can stomach the grim conditions under which food is cooked on the train.

While the accommodation on most *Rajdhanis* is the same as in equivalent class in other trains, the Howrah and Bombay trains boast a 1st class of old-style luxury. They have the most luxurious toilets of any long-distance train in India; rubber-tiled floors, real washbasins and liquid soap in a dispenser. There is even toilet paper

in some. For sleeping, there are 18 berths in three cabins of ·
and three of two. During the day, these are converted to sofa-s
seats with woven upholstery. There are flowers in the cabin and a
small washbasin and mirror. At night, the beds are made up with
crisp linen.

Music is piped throughout the train but in 1st class this can be
switched off. There is a stern announcement before departure warning
that it is an offence to drink alcohol on the train and threatening
"detrainment" and prosecution for anyone caught doing so.

When I travelled on the *Rajdhani Express* from Howrah to New
Delhi in 1992, the crew was led by a young train superintendent-
cum-catering inspector in a red blazer and a chief steward clad in a
charcoal grey suit. Both were adept at handling passengers' requests.
A staff of 55 looked after 870 passengers.

Food for 1st AC class passengers is prepared on the train;
passengers in other classes are given meals from base kitchens.

Fellow passengers on 1st AC on the *Rajdhani* are likely to be
fascinating Indians of importance whom you would normally not
expect to meet. I found myself sharing a sofa seat with a Marxist

Rajdhani Express trains
(departure and destination stations)

Train	From	Depart	To	Arrive	Frequency
2429	Bangalore City	0645	Nizamuddin	1630*	Mon
2421	Bhubaneswar	0850	New Delhi	1000*	Sun
2953	Bombay Central	1740	Nizamuddin	1055*	not Wed
2951	Bombay Central	1655	New Delhi	0955*	not Mon
2423	Guwahati	0600	New Delhi	1000*	Mon/Wed/Fri
2305	Howrah	1345	New Delhi	0940*	Thu/Sun
2301	Howrah	1630	New Delhi	0940*	not Thu/Sun
2426	Jammu Tawi	2030	Nizamuddin	0535*	Thu
2633	Madras	1530	Nizamuddin	2105*	Thu
2422	New Delhi	1700	Bhubaneswar	1830*	Fri
2302	New Delhi	1715	Howrah	1045*	not Tue/Fri
2306	New Delhi	1715	Howrah	1250*	Tue/Fri
2952	New Delhi	1600	Bombay Central	0835*	not Tue
2424	New Delhi	1700	Guwahati	2230*	Mon/Wed/Sat
2310	New Delhi	1700	Patna	0800*	Thu/Sun
2954	Nizamuddin	1655	Bombay Central	1015*	not Thu
2425	Nizamuddin	2020	Jammu Tawi	0545*	Wed
2430	Nizamuddin	0930	Bangalore City	1955*	Sat
2432	Nizamuddin	0930	Trivandrum	0630**	Tue
2634	Nizamuddin	1555	Madras	2045*	Sat
2309	Patna	1900	New Delhi	1000*	Tue/Sat
2431	Trivandrum	1955	Nizamuddin	1630**	Fri

*Arrival next day   **Arrival two days later

member of parliament on one side and a war-mongering right wing Indian army colonel on the other. Sparks flew until both men agreed, to my relief, that although their outlooks were opposed, they were both patriots.

A reader commented: "Even though liquor is forbidden on Indian trains, on the *Rajdhani Express* to Bombay, not only were my cabin mates able to order liquor with their meals, they had their choice of several different types of Scotch."

So as not to be disappointed after reading all about the special qualities of *Rajdhani* train travel, be warned that the newly introduced *Rajdhani* trains are not of the same ilk. A *Rajdhani Express* necessarily goes to or from New Delhi as a link between state capitals. The new trains have not followed the tradition of the two original ones (those serving Howrah and Bombay). They are, really, just trains with AC accommodation (including AC 1st class) which are named *Rajdhani*. The service crew on board are from private contractors and have none of the pride in the railways that *Rajdhani* trains epitomise. The food is dreadful and, on top of that, one has to pay for it, instead of it being included in the fare as is the tradition with the Howrah and Bombay *Rajdhani Expresses*.

Yet, between state capitals, the *Rajdhanis* do provide a splendid way to travel and, together with *Shatabdi Express* trains, have made Indian Railways a railway to enjoy, not just endure.

You can travel with your Indrail Pass on the *Rajdhani Expresses* in the designated class, if your pass is valid for seven days or longer.

PANDYAN EXPRESS

The *Pandyan Express* is a crack metre gauge overnight train linking Madras with Madurai. As number 6717, it leaves Madras Egmore nightly at 1805 and arrives in Madurai, 556km distant, at 0640 the next morning. As the 6718 it returns nightly at 1915 and arrives in Madras at 0705.

Apart from the charm of its name, recalling the ancient Pandyan kingdom whose capital over 2,000 years ago was Madurai, the *Pandyan Express* appeals to passengers for its dainty comfort. The track permits speeds of 100km per hour and the train glides along smoothly at 75km/h. It comprises three carriages for 1st class passengers and seven for sleeper class. There are also three unreserved carriages (three-tier berths) and one seat-only carriage as well as a ladies' compartment as part of the guard's coach.

The train is an example of the better accommodation in some metre gauge expresses compared with broad gauge ones. Instead of the 46-berth AC dormitory carriage of a BG train, the *Pandyan Express* offers berths in cabins for two, three or four people. The 1st class AC sleepers are comfortable cabins with a washbasin, and are serviced by attendants who make up the bed and bring tea in the morning.

DARJEELING TOY TRAIN

Considering the time it takes (nearly nine hours from New Jalpaiguri, plus 13½ hours overnight from Calcutta) you might wonder if travelling on the Darjeeling toy train is worth the trouble.

Two guidebooks I consulted had different opinions. One calls the train ride "a superb experience which shouldn't be missed". The other says, almost sacrilegiously for train fans, "I really wonder about all the fuss made over it," and advises travellers to go by bus.

An authority that should know, the Northeast Frontier Railway which runs the train, says in its timetable: "A journey over the Darjeeling Himalayan Railways by 'toy trains' is an unforgettable experience. Starting from New Jalpaiguri or Siliguri Jn in the plains, the railway winds its way along mountains and valleys to reach Darjeeling. On the way, one can break the journey at Kurseong, another hill resort at an altitude of 1,458 metres. The Batasia loop and Tiger Hill on the way are favourite spots."

The Darjeeling Himalayan Railway (DHR) began as a steam tramway in 1880 from Siliguri to Darjeeling following a cart road built by military engineers in 1861. It was the first hill railway to be built in India. The line consists of 82km of narrow gauge (0.610m or 2ft wide) track which climbs to 2,135m in 65km. The gradient in one place is actually 1 in 19 and the ruling gradient is 1 in 25.

To cut down on having to build tunnels, a system of loops and reserves was devised. This has the track circling around and passing over a gradient by means of a bridge, thereby obtaining a higher elevation. The reverse part is when the track runs diagonally upwards for a short distance and later uses a parallel alignment to the original, higher up the mountain. No wonder it takes so long.

The tank engine which pulls the train, with locals strolling beside it as it dawdles alongside the road, offers marvellous photo opportunities and contributes to the fame of this railway. It is unique. It is also frequently closed through bad weather, breakdowns and political problems. If it is operating, the best time to go is September to November, before it gets too cold, or in the spring of mid-April to mid-June.

The conventional way is to take the 3243 *Darjeeling Mail* from Calcutta Sealdah station, daily departure at 1900, which arrives at New Jalpaiguri (NJ) station at 0830 the following morning. This connects with the 1D passenger train (1st and 2nd class coaches) which leaves NJ station at 0900. The train stops at a dozen stations on the way, as well as elsewhere when it pauses for breath. It should arrive at Darjeeling at 1730 but is often late.

The return journey to Calcutta is by either the 4D at 0825, or the 2D at 1000, from Darjeeling, which arrive at NJ station at 1620 and 1745 respectively. The 3144 *Darjeeling Mail* leaves there at 1950 and arrives at Sealdah at 0845 the next day.

There is an earlier departure scheduled from NJ for Darjeeling at 0715 (the 3D). To catch that you will have to arrive at NJ the day before and you could stay at NJ station where there are four double rooms and three dormitory beds.

Check with railway sources before planning to visit Darjeeling by train to avoid disappointment in case the train isn't operating.

MATHERAN HILL RAILWAY

Less than two hours from Bombay there is a great rail trip by another toy train, the one that goes to Matheran. The name means "jungle head" or "forest on the top" and it still applies to this place, discovered in 1850. It is the nearest hill resort to Bombay, 108km away, situated in the western *ghats* at 803m above sea level.

The narrow gauge railway was opened to traffic in 1907 and was, until a few years ago when a road was built, the only way to reach Matheran. Motor traffic does not penetrate beyond the resort's car park from where walking, pony riding or rickshaw is the only means of getting around.

The toy train begins its 21km journey from Neral, pulled by a cute diesel locomotive. Although the climb of 610m is slow (it takes two hours), time passes quickly because of the breathtaking scenery. The ruling gradient is 1 in 20 as the track zigzags upwards, gradually revealing the full beauty of Matheran Hill.

There are usually six coaches, one 1st class, on this narrow gauge train. In 1st class the window seats are numbers 1, 4, 5 and 8; upholstered bench seats facing each other with four places on each bench. The new 2nd class coaches have glass panels to the roof for super views, but wooden seas; sit on the right for the best views going up. The boys travelling on the running board are cheerful vendors of soft drinks; on the way down they help the brakesmen. There are no toilets on this train but Jumma Patti (242m above sea level) and the aptly named Water Pipe (at 484m) are convenient stops. An unnerving sign in the coaches says "Do not crowd on one side of the coach – it is dangerous".

It is possible to visit Matheran on a day trip, but many people (especially Bombayites escaping from the city) stay longer in this lush, traffic-free town. The railway is closed from mid-June during the monsoon season and only opens again at the end of September or early October. There are no retiring rooms at Matheran station, nor at Neral, but the town has lots of places to stay. The fare to Matheran from Neral is calculated on a distance of 126km instead of the 21km actually travelled.

The first train of the day, the 601 passenger, leaves Neral at 0840 and arrives at Matheran at 1040. There are other departures at 1100 (the 603) and 1700 (the 605), with an extra train (the 607) leaving at 1015 in the season of mid-March to mid-June. To connect with these departures the 1007 *Deccan Express* leaves Bombay VT at 0645 and arrives at Neral at 0819 in time for the 601 departure. The 7307 *Koyna Express* leaves VT at 0845 and arrives at Neral at 1032 in time for the 603 departure.

Trains from Matheran are the 602 leaving at 0545, arriving at Neral at 0745; the 604 at 1310 arriving at 1450; the 606 at 1435 arriving at 1620; and the 608 (season time only) at 1620, arriving at 1803. There is no convenient connection back to Bombay unless you try a suburban train on the Karjat to Bombay line, such as the S24 leaving Neral at 1645 and reaching VT at 1850. Another option is to leave Matheran at 0545 so you can catch the *Deccan Express* at 0819 to Lonavla or Pune.

NILAGIRI MOUNTAIN RAILWAY

The broad gauge *Nilagiri Express* from Madras terminates at Mettupalaiyam station. Passengers change over during the 30-minute wait before the fabled *Blue Mountain* train departs for Ooty.

During the wait, vendors pass along the platform selling coffee and breakfast snacks, and the 1920s steam engine shunts into position at the back of the train. The station has the look of a frontier with the modern overnight *Nilagiri Express*, hauled by a huge diesel and with AC sleeper and 3 tier carriages, on one side of the platform, and the old wooden coaches of the metre gauge mountain train on the other.

Although the idea for a railway from Mettupalaiyam to Coonoor, a distance of 27km, was first mooted in 1854, it wasn't in operation until 1899. The problem had been how to get the train up the steep gradients of the mountains and how to stop it running too fast on the way down.

The rack and pinion system was devised. Special rack bars were laid between the track rails where the line slopes to form a kind of elongated ladder. The train pinions itself on to the rack for the climb up, pushed by the engine. The rack section commences just after Kallar and continues up to Coonoor. Maximum speed on that section is 13km/h. The line was extended to Ooty in 1908.

The train is pushed by one of the eight X class steam locos remaining out of seven introduced in 1925 and five put on the line in 1952. One of those eight has recently been retired to the Rail Museum in Delhi.

The train's coaches are as old as the engines. Made of wood, they are painted dark blue and a grubby yellow on the outside and pale blue inside. There are two 1st class cabins at the front of the train, furnished with coconut fibre and foam bench cushions covered in green rexine. Both cabins seat eight passengers, or more, with the best seats on the way up being in the front cabin facing the way the train is going. Since the engine pushes from behind passengers have a glorious view of the jungle, mountains and valleys. Sit on the left side facing the window for the best views.

Second class carriages with wooden bench seats form the rest of the train, with a guards van and luggage box at the rear. Each of the coaches and wagons is crewed by a brakesman who stands on the open gallery at the front of the carriage and independently operates the wheel and rack brakes on whistle codes from the driver.

After the train leaves Mettupalaiyam, its first stop is at Kallar, a phantom station since it is not in the SR timetable, but this is where the rack and pinion system is engaged. The next stop is at the entrance to tunnel number 3, for the engine to take on water. At every tunnel the kids on the train erupt with hoots of excitement as the train passes through it, and look down aghast when the train emerges to cross vast chasms on spindly bridges.

Elephants and rockfalls are hazards on this run. At Hillgrove station where the train stops to take on water again, passengers flock to the refreshment stall. Wild monkeys perform on the station's roof for bananas. There are no toilets on the train but those at Hillgrove are new and good.

Coonoor, a little over half the way to Ooty, is surrounded by mountains and fringed with buildings. Its station was built in 1897 out of granite blocks and is painted bright blue and pale yellow. There are three retiring rooms, a refreshment stall, newly built and clean toilets, a fountain, and a pretty umbrella shaped shelter.

An attraction at Coonoor is the loco shed, the base for all the locomotives on this line. It is close to the station and has a hand-painted scene of a steam engine as its signboard. The engines are maintained and overhauled here with the oldest (number 37384, built in 1920) still in operation. The station bell is an old metal toothed wheel of the pinion system which is hammered with an iron bar to announce the last five minutes before a train's departure. It is possible to break the journey at Coonoor and catch a train later, or another day, up to Ooty.

The military base station at Wellington comes soon after, with an occasional glimpse of soldiers practising on the target range beside the track. At Aravankadu there is a cordite factory opposite the station and the railway retiring room has a view over it. The climb to Ooty broadens as the train chugs gently through forests and hills. On the evening run from Coonoor, skeins of mist hang in the valleys below the track and men wander along the line wrapped in blankets. It is chilly in Ooty in the summer, and cold in winter.

Four kilometres before reaching Ooty is a station named Lovedale, at 2,192m above sea level. It is set in the forest and has a post office for neighbour, so there must be some residents but they are not to be seen. Lovedale lives up to its name; peaceful and romantic. The station, like an English country cottage, has two retiring rooms.

The train crosses 250 bridges on its way to Ooty and passes through 16 tunnels. The ruling gradient is 1 in 24.50 but it is 1 in 12.28 from Kallar to Coonoor. The total length of the line is 45.88km and the journey time is 4hr 25min going up, 3hr 20min coming down.

The line is subject to landslides and is often closed for weeks during the monsoon season. Every day the track is inspected and the train leaves Kallar only when it is safe to proceed. Elephants have attacked station buildings, which is why some have been closed.

"Travel by rail and spend longer among the hills" reads a slogan painted on a retaining wall close to the tea-growing area before Runnymeade, one of the closed stations.

After its arrival at Udagamandalam, as Ooty is now called, the train is shunted over a service trench where an engineer examines it underneath. For its descent, the loco leads (but in reverse) with the brakesman of each coach watching carefully to prevent too fast a run down hill.

The usual itinerary for independent travellers involves taking a bus from Ooty to Mysore since Ooty is the end of the line. It's a shame to do this and miss the descent, which is just as dramatic as the ride up.

The conventional way of getting to Ooty by train is from Madras on the 6005 *Nilagiri Express* which departs nightly at 2105, arriving at Mettupalaiyam at 0720 the next day. This connects with the 562 leaving Mettupalaiyam at 0745, arriving at Coonoor at 1035 and at Ooty at 1215. An additional train (564) operates during periods of extra demand, such as the April/June season. There is also departure from Coonoor for Ooty at 0800.

For the return, the 561 leaves Ooty at 1500 and arrives at

Distances on the Nilagiri Mountain Railway

Station	Remarks	Actual km	Charged km	Elevation in metres
Mettupalaiyam	Rooms	0		326
Kallar		7.46		404
Allderly	Closed	12.27		731
Hillgrove	Snacks	17.26	50	1,092
Runnymeade	Closed	21.97		1,407
Kateri Road	Closed	24.35		1,547
Coonoor	Rooms	27.03	77	1,711
Wellington	Rooms	28.54	80	1,769
Aravankadu	Rooms	31.34	86	1,812
Ketti		37.19	98	2,092
Lovedale	Rooms	41.76	108	2,192
Udagamandalam	Rooms	45.88	116	2,203

Mettupalaiyam at 1835 to connect with the 6006 *Nilagiri Express*, departing at 1925 and arriving in Madras at 0555 the next day. That train gets to Coimbatore at 2000 from where there are many connections to other parts of southern India.

Fares on the Blue Mountain Railway are charged according to a calculated distance rather than actual distance.

KALKA SHIMLA RAILWAY

The best way to appreciate the grandeur of the 96km of 0l.1762m narrow gauge track as it climbs through the foothills of the Himalayas, is by Rail Motor Car. It makes you aware of the extraordinary feats of engineering that created this line with great arched viaducts spanning chasms, and over a hundred tunnels bored through the mountains.

The Rail Motor Car (No 101) leaves Kalka at 0630. It is possible to take an overnight train, the *Howrah/Kalka Mail*, from Delhi station at 2245, and arrive at Kalka at 0500. The Rail Car waits at the end of the platform where the *Kalka Mail* terminates. The sight of it, like a light blue 1920s Ford truck that's escaped from a museum, will make you rub your eyes in disbelief. There are actually four cars in service, built in 1927 and reconditioned in 1982.

The car has space for two next to the driver's cab and behind are four bench seats, all comfortably upholstered, for five passengers each. Upgrading of tickets to ride in this extraordinary vehicle, which has been in operation for over 60 years, is done by a ticket inspector at the empty, marble-topped snack bar counter close to where the car is parked.

The driver engages gear and the car leaps forward for the journey through 103 tunnels (the longest – 1,143.6m – is number 33 at Barog, at a height of 1,144m) and over 869 bridges, climbing from 656m above sea level at Kalka to 2,075m at Shimla. The views are stunning and, seated in the Rail Car, you miss nothing.

The car will stop at any station en route, if the request is made at Kalka or to the driver himself, but usually it sails right through the tiny picturesque stations. There is no toilet in the car but the driver will stop if your need is great and even reverse if he passes your station and you forget to tell him.

A 15-minute halt is made at Barog where the restaurant is one of the nicest of any station in India. It is above the platform with a flower-bedecked veranda, a hillside view, service that is friendly and fast, and food that is freshly prepared. You should order meals in advance through the railway staff before leaving Kalka or Shimla.

Every one of the 18 stations on the journey to Shimla seems an attractive spot to linger, but none has retiring rooms. Above Solan station there is something called a "Relieving Lodge" and Solan

Brewery station is actually in the middle of a heady-sme. brewery. Shimla station has five retiring rooms, with plans for m . The rooms, on the first floor over the station, all have attached bathrooms with hot water. A deluxe room has a TV and fridge.

Shimla station has a magnificent view down the mountains and is kept clean (lots of blue paintwork) and well run. There is no foreign tourist quota for reservations at the station (which seems strange in view of Shimla's popularity with foreign tourists) but the SS and his staff try their best to arrange bookings. Computerisation has taken place. There are two waiting rooms, a tea stall and a restaurant.

The line was built in 1903 on a rising gradient meandering through the Shivalik Range, the steepest one being 1 in 33. The ruling gradient is 1 in 67. About 70% of the track is on curve. The Rail Car is permitted a maximum speed of 29km/h, and the diesel-hauled passenger train is restricted to a maximum of 25km/h.

Nevertheless, Northern Railway has introduced what they call a "superfast express between Kalka and Shimla". An advertisement promoting this new service highlighted these features: "Nonstop journey (4hr 40 min) except stoppage at Barog; free catering at Barog; free newspaper, tea and biscuits at starting station, ie: Kalka and Shimla; wall to wall carpet, curtains and ergonomically designed cushioned chairs; music system in each coach; microphone and alarm bell systems in each coach for communication with the guard and driver respectively; cabin for couples; provision of luggage booking in separate compartment to avoid congestion."

The train, as 201UP, provides a convenient connection with the 2311/2312 *Howrah/Kalka Mail*. It leaves Kalka at 0530 and arrives at Shimla at 1025. From Shimla, as 202DOWN, it leaves at 1745 and reaches Kalka at 2240.

In a report on this astonishing new service ("cabin for couples"?) by Northern Railway, Anu Kapoor informed me that "the Kalka Shimla superfast is a matter of being fast by only a little over the normal service ... the scenery was spectacular and the train made a 20-minute halt at Barog – a charming and quaint station which I believe has not changed even one bit since the days of the Raj. We were given a simple hot breakfast of a masala omelette, bread, tea and a mango drink. All this was part of the fare which was Rs250.

"However, the train did not have an observation deck which is a pity, and the windows were too low to get an unobstructed view. Otherwise it was a lovely ride up and through the 100-odd tunnels."

BUTTERFIELD'S INDIAN RAILWAY TOUR

"I was pretty apprehensive about India and spending so much time on a train with a group of unknowns," wrote Australian Lynne Barraclough to Jane and Ashley Butterfield. "But thanks to you both I would happily return to India for another trip."

Jane and Ashley Butterfield run rail tours in India from September to March by a specially converted railway carriage which is attached to scheduled trains. From their HQ at Burton Fleming, Driffield, East Yorkshire, YO25 0PQ; tel: 01262 470230, they send out fact-filled brochures describing their tours so that potential passengers have a good idea of what's in store. All tours are accompanied either by the Butterfields, or by two experienced and equally enthusiastic guides. The cost (from £845) includes train travel, all meals on board and some hotel accommodation and excursions. Air fares to India are extra.

Their brochure states: "Our carriage accommodates up to 26 people and comprises two large sitting rooms, a small dining room/ library, a pantry, a kitchen, two wash rooms with showers and four Asian style toilets. It is equipped with electric lights and fans ... At night the sitting rooms convert into dormitories, and then you can choose between sleeping on benches, upper berths or camp beds".

A Butterfield's tour begins in Delhi with the "bogie" – the private carriage – being attached to a train to Haridwar. Then it's eastwards to Lucknow and Varanasi, south to Hyderabad, Mysore, Ooty and Cochin, and north to Bombay. Guests can spend an extra week in the south at the end of the tour. There is also a tour of south India starting in Cochin (Kochi), ending in Bombay, which covers the area in depth with nights in hotels and a leisurely pace. The cost (£1,095) includes train travel, meals on full board basis, hotel accommodation and excursions. Air fares to India are extra.

Jane and Ashley Butterfield have written a 50-page booklet called *The Bogiewalla's Guide to Enjoying India – And Helping India Enjoy You!* which can be purchased through their Yorkshire address. Based on the Butterfield's experience during years of touring India with foreigners, the booklet's hints are worth taking seriously, especially since even the most sensitive short-term visitors would not have the time, let alone the patience, to garner such invaluable knowledge for themselves. There are fascinating sections on religion, caste, language and the extended family as well as on behaviour and etiquette. The Butterfields say "it is a fallacy to think that learning follows automatically from being in a new place." Follow their advice and you will indeed learn, as well as avoid causing offence by behaving "normally".

The Butterfields tell passengers: "Although we live together on board, when we stop you are free to be as independent as you please." It is a formula people enjoy, as they can travel safely by rail in convivial company without having to worry about the arrangements, and yet can wander off on their own to explore when they want. Londoner Barry, 25, wrote in the Butterfield comments book: "If I had tried to do India on my own, I suspect that I would still be in Delhi arguing about seat reservations."

Chapter Twelve

Super Trains

India has some trains that really are super: fast, comfortable and with a pantry car and bearer service. Some which were not actually that fast have been downgraded to ordinary expresses and their numbering changed, since 2 as the first digit in a four-digit train number signifies a superfast, and consequently more expensive, express.

Superfast trains do not all share the same standards of accommodation and service, though. Some are exclusively 2nd class and some have no on-board refreshment facility. Express trains are fine if they have decent accommodation. A list of superfast and other trains with 1st AC accommodation is given here. It is not complete due to new trains being introduced occasionally, and some trains changing status or being withdrawn. Not all trains listed here run on a daily basis.

Superfast express and mail trains
A supplementary charge (see *Chapter Three*) is levied for travel on the trains listed here. Not all are daily.

Superfast trains and express mail trains with AC 1st class

Train number	Name	Service between	1st AC
1005/06	*Vidarbha*	Bombay VT–Nagpur	*
1037/38	*Punjab Mail*	Bombay VT–Firozpur	*
2001/02	*Shatabdi*	New Delhi–Bhopal	1ACCC
2003/04	*Shatabdi*	New Delhi–Lucknow	1ACCC
2005/06	*Shatabdi*	New Delhi–Kalka	1ACCC
2007/08	*Shatabdi*	Madras–Mysore	1ACCC
2009/10	*Shatabdi*	Bombay C–Ahmedabad	1ACCC
2011/12	*Shatabdi*	New Delhi–Chandigarh	1ACCC
2013/14	*Shatabdi*	New Delhi–Amritsar	1ACCC

Train number	Name	Service between	1st AC
2015/16	*Shatabdi*	New Delhi–Ajmer	*
2017/18	*Shatabdi*	New Delhi–Dehra Dun	1ACCC
2019/20	*Shatabdi*	Howrah–Borako	ACCC
2021/22	*Shatabdi*	Howrah–Rourkela	ACCC
2023/24	*Shatabdi*	Madras–Coimbatore	ACCC
2027/28	*Shatabdi*	Pune–Bombay VT	ACCC
2179/20	*Taj Express*	Nizamuddin–Gwalior	ACCC
2301/02	*Rajdhani*	New Delhi–Howrah	*
2303/04	*Poorva Express*	Howrah–New Delhi	*
2305/06	*Rajdhani*	New Delhi–Howrah	*
2307/08	Express	Howrah–Jodhpur	*
2309/10	*Rajdhani*	Patna–New Delhi	*
2311/12	*Kalka Mail*	Howrah–Kalka	*
2381/82	*Poorva Express*	Howrah–New Delhi	*
2391/92	*Magadh Vik Express*	Patna–New Delhi	*
2401/02	*Sharamjeevi Express*	New Delhi–Patna	*
2403/04	Express	Delhi–Jammu Tawi	*
2407/08	*Gondwana Express*	Nizamuddin–Nagpur	
2409/10	*Gondwana Express*	Nizamuddin–Jabalpur	
2411/2412	*Gondwana*	Nizamuddin–Jabalpur	
2413/14	Express	Jaipur–Delhi	
2417/18	*Prayag Raj Express*	New Delhi–Allahabad	*
2419/20	*Gomti Express*	New Delhi–Lucknow	*
2421/22	*Rajdhani*	New Delhi–Bhubaneswar	*
2423/24	*Rajdhani*	New Delhi–Guwahati	*
2425/26	*Rajdhani*	New Delhi–Jammu Tawi	*
2429/30	*Rajdhani*	Nizamuddin–Bangalore	*
2431/32	*Rajdhani*	Trivandrum–Nizamuddin	*
2461/62	Express	Delhi–Jodhpur	*
2465/66	Express	Jodhpur–Jaipur	ACCC
2467/68	Express	Bikaner–Jaipur	ACCC
2471/73	*Swaraj Express*	Bombay C–Jammu Tawi	
2473/74	*Sarvodaya Express*	Ahmedabad–Jammu Tawi	
2475/76	Express	Rajkot–Jammu Tawi	
2477/78	Express	Hapa–Jammu Tawi	
2479/60	*Goa Express*	Londa–Nizamuddin	
2497/98	*Shane-Punjab*	New Delhi–Amritsar	*
2553/54	*Vaishali Express*	New Delhi–Gwalior	*
2605/06	*Pallavan MG Express*	Madras Egmore–Trichy	ACCC
2607/08	*Lalbagh Express*	Madras–Bangalore	ACCC
2615/16	*Grand Trunk Express*	Madras–New Delhi	*
2617/18	*Mangala Express*	Nizamuddin–Mangalore	
2621/22	*Tamil Nadu Express*	Madras–New Delhi	*

Train number	Name	Service between	1st AC
2625/26	*Kerala Express*	Trivandrum–New Delhi	
2627/28	*Karnataka Express*	Bangalore–New Delhi	
2633/34	*Rajdhani*	Nizamuddin–Madras	ACCC
2635/36	*Vaigai MG Express*	Madras Egmore–Madurai	ACCC
2639/40	*Brindavan Express*	Madras–Bangalore City	ACCC
2675/76	*Kovai Express*	Madras–Coimbatore	ACCC
2711/12	*Pinakini Express*	Vijayawada–Madras	ACCC
2713/14	*Satvahana Express*	Vijayawada-Secunderabad	ACCC
2723/24	*AP Express*	Secunderabad–New Delhi	*
2725/26	*InterCity*	Hubli–Bangalore	ACCC
2801/02	*Purushottam Express*	Puri–New Delhi	
2815/16	Express	Puri–New Delhi	
2821/22	*Dhauli Express*	Howrah–Bhubaneswar	ACCC
2841/42	*Coromandel Express*	Howrah–Madras	
2859/60	*Gitanjali Express*	Howrah–Bombay	
2903/04	*Golden Temple Mail*	Bombay C–Amritsar	*
2905/06	*Ashram Express*	Ahmedabad–Delhi	*
2907/10	*S N MG Express*	Ahmedabad–Jodhpur	*
2925/26	*Paschim Express*	Bombay C–Amritsar	*
2927/28	Express	Bombay C–Vadodara	*
2933/34	*Karnavati Express*	Bombay C–Ahmedabad	ACCC
2951/52	*Rajdhani Express*	Bombay C–New Delhi	*
2953/54	*A K Rajdhani*	Bombay C–Nizamuddin	*
2955/56	Express	Bombay C–Jaipur	*
2961/62	*Avantika Express*	Bandra T–Indore	
3003/04	Mail	Howrah–Bombay VT	*
3005/06	Mail	Howrah–Amritsar	*
3029/30	*Coal Field Express*	Howrah–Dhanbad	1ACCC
3031/32	Express	Howrah–Danapur	*
3143/44	*Darjeeling Mail*	Sealdah–New Jalpaiguri	*
4033/34	*Jammu Mail*	Delhi–Jammu Tawi	*
4041/42	*Mussoorie Express*	Delhi–Dehra Dun	*
4057/58	*K V Express*	New Delhi–Varanasi	*
4095/96	*Himalayan Queen*	New Delhi–Kalka	1ACCC
4229/30	*Lucknow Mail*	New Delhi–Lucknow	*
4517/18	*Unchahar Express*	Kanpur–Ambala	*
6003/04	Mail	Madras–Howrah	*
6005/06	*Nilagiri Express*	Madras–Mettupalayam	*
6007/08	Mail	Madras–Bangalore City	*
6023/24	Express	Madras–Bangalore	*
6103/04	*Pearl City Express*	Madras Egmore–Madurai	*
6177/78	*Rock Fort MG Express*	Madras–Trichy	*
6319/6320	Mail	Madras–Trivandrum	*

Train number	Name	Service between	1st AC
6347/6348	Express	Trivandrum–Cannanore	*
6717/18	*Pandyan MG Express*	Madras Egmore–Madurai	*
7007/08	*Godavari Express*	Hyderabad–Vishakapatnam	*
7047/48	*Gautami Express*	Secunderabad–Kakinada Port	*
7423/24	*Narayanadri Express*	Secunderabad–Tirupati	*
8001/02	Mail	Howrah–Bombay VT	*
8005/06	Express	Howrah–Sambalpur	*
8007/08	Express	Howrah–Puri	*
8013/14	*Steel Express*	Howrah–Tatanagar	1ACCC
8015/16	Express	Howrah–Hatia	*
9019/20	*Dehra Dun Express*	New Delhi–Kota	*
9055/56	*Sayaj Nagari Express*	Bandra T–Vadodara	*
9101/02	*Gujarat Mail*	Bombay C–Ahmedabad	*
9711/12	*MG Express*	Jaipur–Srigangganar	*
9845/46	*Girnar MG Express*	Veraval–Ahmedabad	*
9901/02	*Delhi MG Mail*	Ahmedabad–Delhi Sara R.	*

*AC 1st Class accommodation available
1ACCC Executive Class 1st Air Conditioned Chair Car
ACCC Air Conditioned Chair Car
MG Metre gauge

Chapter Thirteen

Help

Onboard emergencies

For health and security problems contact the train superintendent or conductor immediately. There are emergency cords in every compartment to stop the train. Trains carry books in which complaints can be made.

At the station

Contact the station superintendent in person or, if the station is too small to have one, the stationmaster, if you experience problems at his station. Many stations have police posts at which reports can be made, and public grievance booths. There are also complaints books available on demand; complaints are taken seriously and investigated. The SS will have a list of doctors who can be called on in an emergency.

Consul

The UK Foreign & Commonwealth Office have a leaflet available called *Consular Assistance Abroad* which contains invaluable advice that applies to travellers of all nationalities. Don't expect your consul to get better treatment for you in hospital (or prison) than is provided for local nationals, or to interfere in local judicial procedures. However, the consul can provide a list of lawyers, interpreters, and doctors, and sometimes arrange for messages to be sent to relatives or friends if you are arrested.

The leaflet recommends that, as soon as you arrive, you jot down the address and telephone number of your local embassy, high commissioner or consul to carry with you; check the local telephone directory for it. Carry your passport with you at all times in India.

Mail/messages

Holders of American Express travellers cheques or credit cards can use the local American Express office as a mail drop. If you have a reservation to stay at a reputable hotel at some stage during your tour of India, have your mail sent there, with your arrival date marked on the envelope. Mail can be sent to stations (see *Chapter Two*) but you might never get it. Telegrams can also be sent to you at stations.

Homesick

If you are feeling homesick, or perhaps simply overwhelmed by India and too much travelling, don't bottle up your misery. Talking to fellow passengers can help. In a town, turn to the telephone directory, or hotel management, or even the SS, for addresses of social organisations or professional associations with which you have some connection at home, such as Lions, Rotary, trade unions, sports clubs, hobby groups.

Foreigners who have an interest shared by Indians are likely to be given a splendid welcome which banishes feelings of loneliness. Some towns have clubs where visitors can become temporary members. If the Club has a Western-style menu, that too can help cure homesickness.

"A customer is the most important visitor on our premises. He is not dependent on us. We are dependent on him. He is not an interruption in our work. He is the purpose of it. He is not an outsider on our business. He is a part of it. We are not doing him a favour by serving him. He is doing us a favour by giving us an opportunity to do so."

—M. K. Gandhi

N.E. Railway

Chapter Fourteen

Endpiece

A summary of how to get the best out of travelling in India by rail:

- Travel on an Indrail Pass, preferably bought from an overseas GSA so he can make your first reservation in advance.

- Go for at least 21 days.

- September to March is the best time.

- Make full use of the facilities for foreigners by booking your subsequent reservations through the ITB at New Delhi station, or through the foreign tourist bureaux at the other main stations.

- If you intend buying rail tickets in India from the foreign tourist quota, have foreign currency or travellers cheques to do this, especially as it saves a trip to the bank to change them.

- Make train reservations well in advance and allow time to do so; if you have problems, ask the CRS or the SS for advice and help.

- It's worth the expense to travel 1st AC class, especially if you can make use of an Indrail Pass. If you hate air-conditioning, you won't like the AC 2 tier so try for non-AC 1st class instead, if it exists.

- Sleeping on trains and in station retiring rooms saves money for memorable nights in classic hotels in Rajasthan and major cities.

- Use *Trains at a Glance* to plot your own itinerary.

- Choose trains which arrive/depart during daylight.

- Avoid tight connections.

- Allow days in your itinerary for doing nothing; you might need spare days in the event of delay.

- Take your full quota of duty-free liquor into India.

- On long-distance trains, let the bearer be your friend since he can be a source of advice and extra comforts.

- Drink lots of liquid, but not station water unless you've purified it yourself.

- Travel light but include a padlock (to secure your luggage to something in the train or waiting room and to lock the retiring room door), a pocket knife/bottle opener, a hand towel, a water bottle and purifying tablets.

- Wear loose cotton clothing and underwear; buy plastic sandals in India to wear in train or station toilets and showers.

- Keep travellers cheques and travel documents on you, never in your luggage; have change handy for purchases from platform vendors.

- Carry photocopies of important documents, including passport and air ticket, separate from the originals in case the originals disappear.

- Do not alight from a train that has not properly stopped but, if you must, then face the way it's going so you don't fall flat on your own face. Always check up and down a track before you cross it.

- Have proper and adequate insurance cover for accident, illness and theft.

- When dealing with railway people, be patient and polite; know what you want and ask for it intelligibly.

THE LAST WORD

Letters from readers of *India By Rail* have been coming in continuously since the first edition appeared in 1989. Many of the tips have been included in this new edition. Here are extracts from a few of the letters, some of which present a different point of view:

From a barrister, Alberta, Canada
"Relying in large measure on your book, my wife and I purchased 60-day green Indrail passes (AC 2 Tier Class). We barely used half of our period of validity before we escaped the Indian Railway system and fled the country. This had been our second trip to India.

"In our opinion your book is misleading and, in many cases, simply false, perhaps due to the passage in time.

"The misleading statements in your book begin with the first sentence of your Acknowledgements. In India we found that railwaymen are far from universally friendly instead behaving like stereotypical, petty bureaucrats, arrogant and unreasoning but ready to be bribed. In fact, the railway system, like the postal system, is used as a work for welfare program giving rise to the expected lack of quality service. This became not only our opinion but is that of many Indians to whom we spoke. Many avoid the railway system.

"I do not recall that you prepare your readers for the violent, lying porters, touts and drivers who inhabit the stations with the tacit approval of the rail bureaucracy. These people are a constant source of unpleasant confrontation for non-Indian travellers. Other countries have controlled the activities of people involved with the tourism industry.

"You repeatedly advise your readers to consult the station superintendent but omit to state that lesser bureaucrats pretend to be that official and shield him from passengers. Perhaps you have too often been accompanied by railwaymen on your travels and no longer share the experience of more typical travellers.

"Additional inconsistencies include, inter alia, the fact that we never found a shower on any of the main trains we took, often trains were without water in the toilets, toilets were filthy, and people were difficult to meet as Indian passengers curtained themselves off and stared at the ceiling or slept the entirety of their journey not even speaking to each other. We surmised that those passengers were seeking rest and privacy not easily found in their lives. Stations and coaches were old and dirty. The only exception to the general description of the trains was the Shatabdi Express which was clean and smooth with good on board service.

"Regardless of our reservations we were often asked to give up our berths so an Indian family who had not bothered to reserve could have the compartment to themselves and sleep together.

"We endeavoured to stay in retiring rooms but only in Mysore were they clean enough to be occupied.

"Lest you believe we are spoiled North American tourists, let me state that we are not. We have backpacked around the world and are budget travellers preferring tents and guest houses to international hotels. I have travelled in Asia on three occasions.

"You may not sell as many books but next time tell it like it is. You will save many people money and disappointment."

From Bruce Webber, Solihull, England
"I took a holiday in India over Christmas which, thanks to your book, went a bit more smoothly than I might otherwise have expected.

"Some points:

Bed rolls: These are readily available in AC 2 tier on all trips without ordering in advance.

Tipping coolies: I think this is a bit of a minefield which Westerners need to be well prepared for. I arrived at Bombay VT from Bangalore in the AC car which was near the back of the train and engaged a coolie to carry my two bags. Near the other end of the platform I was met by a (local) friend who'd brought his own car. As we left the station, I asked him his view with regard to an equitable tip and was told to just sit in the car and wait, so I did that whilst listening to a five minute blazing row.

"It turned out that the accepted rate for locals is about Rs5 for each bag but Westerners are expected to pay five times this plus a bit for 'platform yardage'.

"When my bags were put on the train at Bangalore, which involved a two minute walk from the taxi, I was quite openly requested to pay Rs50 for the privilege. Unfortunately, the train was 30 minutes late in departing so there was quite a long staring competition over that one!

"Taxis: Sometimes the overcharging problem can be eased by avoiding taxis which wait outside good hotels. Walk 100 yards or so and flag one down.

"Nilagiri: With regard to your comment on a bus trip, a good alternative is to hire a private driver to make a trip between Mysore and Ooty. One of the best roads includes 36 hairpin bends to climb the hill from Mudumalai to Ooty: not many buses go that way. This arrangement also gives a good flexibility for visiting the Bandipur and Mudumalai wildlife sanctuaries. A local driver eases the problem of getting punctures fixed – I had four!"

From Mike Booker, Toronto, Canada

"I purchased a 30-day 1st Class/AC 2 tier Indrail Pass from the Indian Railways GSA in Toronto and made some reservations before leaving Canada. Just as you said in your book, all my reservations were 100% confirmed when I arrived at the New Delhi station ITB.

"I was able to make some reservations in India off the foreign tourist/Indrail Pass/VIP quota. The only glitch was in Mathura where I was told that they didn't have a foreign quota of any kind. So I had to go from Mathura to Baroda in Sleeper Class (ie: 2nd Class sleeper) aboard the Janata Express. Not the most comfortable accommodations but I experienced more of the real India than is possible in the AC sleepers. I couldn't lean out of the window and buy tea, samosas, etc. from platform vendors in an AC sleeper.

"Nothing could prepare me for the adventure and the spiritual high (almost as much of a high as the temples and ashrams that I visited) of India's railways. And it is possible to get a good night's sleep aboard the trains. In fact, I slept very well. It felt so nurturing to be gently rocked to sleep by the motion of the train. If was as if Mother India herself was rocking me to sleep!

From Ron and Sara Keen, Dunedin, New Zealand

"Thank you, thank you, thank you, for writing such a wonderful, informative book. My husband Ron, and I travelled from New Delhi to Madras earlier this year (1996), 3,000km of which were by train. We found India both challenging and enormously rewarding. We knew it wouldn't be easy but were determined to make the trip work. (We are in our 50s.) At times, though, the long queues and slow service were a real test of our resolve ... Boarding and leaving trains was a little stressful, particularly at intermediary stations. As we tried to leave the train, the people outside tried to get in, all at the same time ... We'd return to India tomorrow, given the chance."

From Michael Smith, Wem, Shropshire, England

"I only wish I had read your very helpful guide book totally before I arrived at Delhi, because every time I pulled it from my bag someone else would want to look at it ... as a solo traveller I found all the people willing to speak and even met a professor and his wife from Delhi University travelling in the same carriage as me. They shared their breakfast with me because I was asleep when the order was taken and was the only passenger without food. This act of kindness is not unusual to solo travellers and certainly restores your faith in mankind.

"I am also glad I took the trouble to buy an Indrail Pass, even though the conning tourist information office overcharged me by 10%. My own fault, I told them it was my first time in India.

"The Indrail Pass saves a lot of time and effort at railway stations. It got me out of trouble more than once. For example, having been in Darjeeling three days with money running out, I just paid my hotel bills. The bank computers went down and no money could be changed. I caught a bus to Mughal Sarai rail station and without a reservation but because of my Indrail Pass I got on an AC sleeper to Calcutta. A stroke of good luck and wisdom of having a rail pass because I arrived at Calcutta with only Rs6 in my pocket.

"I'm longing to re-visit India, travelling by train using this fantastic book as my main companion."

Appendix

LANGUAGE

Useful phrases in Hindi

Good morning/evening/day/night	*Namaste*
Goodbye/ see you	*Phir milenge*
How are you?	*Aap kaise hain?*
Good	*Acha*
Bad	*Kharaab*
Please	*Kripaya*
Thank you	*Dhanyavad*
Yes	*Han*
No	*Nahi*
What is your name?	*Aap ka naam kya hai*
How much is ...?	*Kitne ka hai?*
Too much	*Bahut zyada hai*
Come here	*Idhar aaiye*
Go away	*Chale jaaiye*
Water	*Paani*
Cold	*Thanda*
Hot	*Garam*
Big	*Bada*
Small	*Chota*
Where is the ...?	*Kahan hai?*
Train	*Rail gdi*

GLOSSARY

Indian Railways bureaucracy is riddled with initials and abbreviations used freely in conversation among railway men as well as in signs intended for foreign tourists. For instance, at Agra Fort there is a sign which tells tourists to contact "the CRS". You'll frequently be asked for your "PNR". Above a door at a station I saw a sign which said VLRRMTP. I pushed it open to find it meant "Vegetarian Light Refreshment Room, Mettupalaiyam".

Terms used in this book are as follows:

AC	Air conditioned
ACC	Air-conditioned class
ACCC	Air-conditioned chair car
BG	Broad gauge
BNR	Bengal and Nagpur Railway
CCTV	Closed circuit television
CR	Central Railway
CRS	Chief reservations supervisor
CRS	Computer reservations system
Crore	100 lakhs, ie: 10,000,000
DHR	Darjeeling Himalayan Railway
Direct	"Without any change of train"
DMU	Diesel Multiple Unit
DRM	Divisional railway manager
EMU	Electric multiple unit
ER	Eastern Railway
ETA	Estimated time of arrival
GRP	Government railway police
GSA	General sales agent (for Indrail Passes)
IRP	Indrail Pass
ITB	International Tourist Bureau
Jn	Junction
Lakh	100,000
MEMU	Mainline Electric Multiple Unit
MG	Metre gauge
ND	New Delhi
NER	North Eastern Railway
NG	Narrow gauge
NJ	New Jalpaiguri station
NR	Northern Railway
NV	Non-vegetarian (restaurant/meal)
PNR	Passenger name record (ie: number on a computer-generated reservation coupon)
R	Refreshments available
RAC	Reservation against cancellation
Rexine	Artificial leather
RPF	Railway Protection Force
RR	Refreshment room
SER	South Eastern Railway
SM	Stationmaster
SR	Southern Railway
SS	Station superintendent
TAG	*Trains at a Glance*
TC	Ticket collector
TS	Train superintendent
TTE	Travelling ticket examiner
V	Vegetarian (restaurant/meal)
VT	Bombay Victoria Terminus station
WL:	Wait-listed
WR	Western Railway

FURTHER READING

Since this book is intended as a guide to India by rail and not as a general guide to India, you will need maps and books that tell you about the places and ways of the country as well. There is no point in travelling by train to, say, Madurai unless you know something about all those temples you'll be gazing at.

Maps

India (Bartholomew) 1:4,000,000
A good general map
Nelles Verlag Maps 1:1,500,000
A series of five regional road maps of the Indian subcontinent, with shaded relief, railways, tourist information, and insets of city plans. The most comprehensive coverage of India at a consistent scale.

Guidebooks

India: a travel survival kit (Lonely Planet).
The book I, and thousands of other visitors to India, depend on. Very comprehensive (over 800 pages).
South Asian Handbook: India (Footprint Handbooks). Updated annually, this hefty book ($\pm 1,500$ pages) also covers six neighbouring countries.

Other guides to India include:
Into India (John Murray)
India (Hildebrand)
The Cadogan Guide to India (Cadogan Books)
India Discovered (Collins)

Local guidebooks are available at bookshops or railway bookstalls in India.

Rail enthusiasts will delight in tracking down these books (try at the Delhi Rail Museum) by a distinguished railwayman, R R Bhandari:

Rail Transport Museum (Railway Board, 1980)
Locomotives in Steam (Railway Board, 1981)
Jodhpur Railway (Northern Railway, 1982)
Kalka–Simla and Kangra Valley Railways (Northern Railway, 1983)
Exotic Indian Mountain Railways (Railway Board, 1984)
Western Railway Metre Gauge System (Western Railway, 1987)
The Blue Chip Railway (South Eastern Railway, 1988)

Highly recommended are *A History of Indian Railways* by G S Khosla (Railway Board, 1988), and *The Bogie-Walla's Guide To Enjoying India - And Helping India Enjoy You!* by Jane and Ashley Butterfield (see page 241).

Bradt Publications
Travel Guides

April 1997

Dear Reader,

With the help of letters from friends and other rail travellers supplementing information gleaned during my own travels in India in 1995 and 1996, I have tried to keep abreast with the changes taking place in Indian Railways.

As much as I would like to spend a few months each year travelling in India by rail, it would take me a long time to ride every train, visit every station, and discover every change. And change is the essence of Indian Railways as it emerges from a period of stagnation to dynamic development with transportation for the next century in mind.

To keep up with the "new" Indian Railways I welcome letters from both visitors and Indians about services, fare increases, station profiles and details of improvements; absolutely anything about Indian Railways that you, the reader, would like to see in the next edition of this book, because it would be helpful to rail travellers like yourself.

So do, please, drop me a line to keep me on track of what's happening in India by rail.

Good training!

Royston Ellis

Royston Ellis

41 Nortoft Road, Chalfont St Peter, Bucks SL9 0LA, England
Tel/fax: 01494 873478

INDEX

Agra, 180, 185
Ahmedabad, 187, 231
Ajanta, 190
alcohol, 34
Allahabad, 188
Alleppey, 189, 204, 215
Ambala Cantt, 190
Amritsar, 190
Anandnaga, 197
Aravankadu, 238
Aurangabad, 190
Auroville, 213

Bandra, 157
Bangalore, 140, 190, 211
Basti, 197
Barog, 240
Batasia Loop, 234
bearers, 109
bedrolls, 20, 36, 89, 103, 251
beer, 34
beggars, 107
Benares (*see* Varanasi), 216, 220
Bengal & Nagpur Railway, 216
Berhampur, 193
BEST, 3
Bhubaneswar, 41, 192
blanket, 103
Bodhgaya, 196
Bombay, 3, 18, 140, 151–9, 235
books, 20
business hours, 32
bus, 117
Butterfield, Jane & Ashley, 241

Calcutta, 18, 159–67
Cannanore, 193
catering, 124
Central Railway, 128, 153
Chandigarh, 193
children, 29, 57, 118
Chittaurgarh, 194, 230, 231
cholera, 22
Churchgate station, 155
circular tours, 182
class, 75–90
climate, 17
clothes, 20
Cochin, 194
Coimbatore, 194
Colombo, 8, 18
coach attendant, 100
communications, 36
complaints, 115
computer coupons, 63
computerisation, 71
conductor, 100
connecting, 16
consul, 247
Coonoor, 130, 237, 238
costs, 25

cushion time, 16
currency, 27
customs, 27

dabbawallas, 158
Dabolim, 221
Dadar, 155
Dandapani Dr S, 53, 71, 140, 180, 183
Darjeeling, 234
Darjeeling-Himalayan Railway, 127, 131, 234
Darjeeling Mail, 164, 235
Deccan Queen, 204, 214
Dehra Dun, 19
delays, 16
Delhi (*see also* New Delhi), 17, 18, 143
Delhi Cantt, 150
Delhi Saria Rohilla, 148
departure, 28
destinations, 177–80
disabled travellers, 30
discounts, 49
distance, 49
Diu, 231
down trains, 95

Eastern Railway, 128, 159
Egmore station, 170
electricity, 32
elephants, 150, 237, 238
Ellora, 190
embassies, 26, 39
emergency, 99, 112, 247
EMU trains, 131
enquiries, 37, 38, 113
Ernakulam, 196
Erode, 196
extras, 47

Fairlie Place, 161
fares, 48, 50
feni, 222
film, 22
first aid, 112
first class, 59
food, 35, 89, 106, 107–9
footwear, 21
foreigners, 2

gauge, 123
gauge conversion, 91
Gaya, 196, 213
Goa, 18, 156, 181, 206, 221, 223
Gopalpur-on-Sea, 192
Gorakhpur, 197
Grand Indian Peninsula Railway, 122–3
groups, 31, 182
Gujarat, 188, 201, 215, 231

Haridwar, 198
Hassan, 209, 210

Hatia, 216
Hazrat Nizammuddin station, 147
health, 22
Hillgrove, 237, 238
Himalayas, 218, 239
Himsagar Express, 201, 203
history, 121
holidays, 31–2, 72
homesick, 247
hotels, 138–41
Howrah, 162–3
Howrah Mail, 5
Hubli, 191
Hyderabad, 198, 217

immigration, 27
Indrail Pass, 51–60
insurance, 24
Intercity Express, 147
ITB, 57, 72–4, 145
itineraries, 180

Jaipur, 147, 180, 198, 230, 231
Jaisalmer, 200
Jalgoan, 190
Jammu Tawi, 200
Jamnagar, 201
Jhansi, 129, 201
Jodhpur, 140, 202
Jumma Pati, 236
Junagadh, 231

Kalka, 218, 239–41
Kallar, 237
Kandy, 8
Kanniya Kumari, 201, 203
Karjat, 203
Karla, 204
Kashmir, 200
Khajuraho, 201–2
Kochi (Cochin), 194
Kodaikanal, 207
Konark, 193
Konkan Railway, 222–3
Kottayam, 204
Kovalam, 173
Kurseong, 127, 234
Kushinagar, 197

Lahore, 190
Lakshadweep, 194
language, 39, 254
liquor, 21, 35
livery, 92
locomotives, 6
Lonavla, 203, 204
Lovedale, 131, 238
Lucknow, 205
luggage, 114
Lumbini, 197

Madgaon (Margao), 206, 221
Madras, 18, 167–71, 234
Madras Beach station, 171

Madurai, 206, 234
Mahe, 207, 213
mail, 36, 247
malaria, 22
Malda Town, 207
Mangalore, 208, 222
maps, 11, 256
Matheran, 203, 209, 212, 235–6
meals, 107–12
meal times, 111
medical aid, 112
MEMU, 131
metre gauge, 90, 91, 148
Metro, 165–6
Mettupalaiyam, 237
Miraj, 209
money, 23, 24
Mughal Sarai, 210
Mumbai (*see also* Bombay), 4, 50
museums, 125, 148–50, 211–12
Mussoorie, 195
Mysore, 191, 210, 239

Nagpur, 212
names, 3, 92
Naugarh, 197
Nautanwa, 197
Neral, 203, 212, 236
Nepal, 18, 19, 25, 187, 198, 213
New Delhi, 140, 145–6
New Farakka, 208
New Jalpaiguri, 234, 235
Nilagiri Express, 236
Nilagiri Mountain Railway, 236
Nizamuddin station, 147–8
Northeast Frontier Railway, 127, 207, 234
North Eastern Railway, 127, 197
Northern Railway, 127, 143
numbers, 93

Ooty, 130, 195, 219, 237–9

Pakistan, 190
Palace on Wheels, 183, 228–30
Panaji, 206, 221
Pandyan Express, 234
passport, 23, 57
Patna, 213
permits, 27
photography, 27
pillow, 103
planning, 15
platform tickets, 44
Pondicherry, 213
prices, 111
Pune, 204, 214
Puri, 139, 193, 214

queuing, 42
Quilon, 215
quota, 63, 70–1

RAC, 65
rail facts, 5

rail museum, 148–50, 211–12
Rail News, 42
Railway Board, 6
rail weekends, 183
Rail Yatri Niwas, 138–9, 146
Rajasthan, 19, 181, 220, 229–31
Rajdhani Express, 57, 63, 64, 146, 147, 173, 191, 192, 218, 232–4
Rajkot, 215
Rameswaram, 18, 179, 215
Ranchi, 139, 216
Raxaul, 197, 213
refunds, 46, 58, 68
reservations, 60–71
restrictions, 47
retiring rooms, 5, 6, 133–8
ring railway, 148
Roha, 222
rolling stock, 92
Royal Indian, 183
Royal Orient Express, 183, 229, 230–1
rules, 99
Runnymeade, 238

safety, 23
Salem, 216
Saran Gir, 231
Sarnath, 221
Sealdah, 163–4
Secunderabad, 60, 198, 217
security, 106
service, 109
Shalimar station, 164
Shatabdi Express, 4, 146, 155, 170, 188, 191, 193, 195, 199, 202, 206, 211, 214, 217, 225–8
Shimla, 218, 239–41
shower, 101, 102, 118, 251
signals, 98
Siliguri Jn, 234
sleeping, 102–5
smoking, 35, 81, 88, 99
snacks, 108
solo travel, 28
South Central Railway, 128, 217
South Eastern Railway, 128, 159
Southern Railway, 128, 167
Sri Lanka, 25, 26
Srinagar, 201
staff, 99
station amenities, 5, 112–13
station superintendent, 74
steam, 7, 8, 122–3, 127–31, 149–50, 209, 221, 231, 237
suburban services, 131
superfast trains, 47, 243–6

supplement, 47

taxis, 32
tea, 110
telegrams, 37
telephone, 37, 38
thieves, 106
ticketing 41–3
ticket doctor, 53
tier, 81
tiffin, 108, 158
Tiger Hill, 234
time, 32
timetables, 14, 118
tipping, 36, 251
Tiruchchirappalli, 130, 173–4
toilets, 89, 101
toiletries, 21
tourism, 1, 126
tourist, 2
tourist offices, 12
touts, 42, 251
track, 91
Trailfinders, 17
trains, 76, 91
Trains at a Glance, 14
trams, 164–5
Trivandrum, 18, 171–3
TTE, 100

Udagamandalam (*see also* Ooty), 219, 238
Udaipur, 140, 219, 229, 231
up trains, 95

vaccinations, 22
Varanasi, 216, 220–1
Vasco da Gama station, 221–2
Veraval, 231
vestibule, 93
Viceroy Special, 8
video, 30
Villupuram, 213
visa, 25–6, 197

water, 21, 23, 33–4, 112
Water Pipe station, 236
Wellington, 238
Western Railway, 128, 155
WEXAS, 17
wine, 34
women, 29, 80, 88
World War II, 123

yellow fever, 22
Yercaud, 216, 217